Tribal Land Question

Tribal Land Question

Case of Andhra Pradesh

PALLA TRINADHA RAO

RAWAT PUBLICATIONS

Jaipur • New Delhi • Bangalore • Guwahati • Kolkata

ISBN 978-81-316-0836-4

The publication of this book was financially supported by the ICSSR. The responsibility for the facts stated, opinions expressed, or conclusions reached, is entirely that of the author and that the ICSSR accepts no responsibility for them.

ICSSR Consultant: Professor Shashi Sahai, University of Rajasthan, Jaipur

Published by
Prem Rawat for **Rawat Publications**
Satyam Apts, Sector 3, Jawahar Nagar, Jaipur 302 004 (India)
Phone: 0141 265 1748 / 7006 Fax: 0141 265 1748
E-mail: info@rawatbooks.com
Website: www.rawatbooks.com

New Delhi Office
4858/24, Ansari Road, Daryaganj, New Delhi 110 002
Phone: 011 2326 3290

Also at *Bangalore, Guwahati* and *Kolkata*

Typeset by Rawat Computers, Jaipur
Printed at Nice Printing Press, New Delhi

Contents

Foreword

Tribal areas or rather the Fifth Schedule Areas in our country are among the most sacred geography of the subcontinent. However, this area is in deep turbulence. It has been so historically, whenever the outside powers and authorities tended to control and dominate them unimaginatively and without seeking the involvement, participation and cooperation of the communities who are the original inhabitants of this area. In spite of a plethora of ethnographic, anthropological and government sponsored reports, there are few area-specific studies which have captured the multidimensional and cross-disciplinary insights. This is especially true of the tribal areas of Andhra Pradesh.

Shri Trinadha Rao, by bringing out one such study of the tribal land question in Andhra Pradesh, especially focused on the Scheduled Areas in the East Godavari District has made a significant contribution. As a scholar and a practising advocate always championing the Scheduled Tribes, he has sought to combine the historical perspective, the trajectory of legal provisions, the socio-economic trends and the domination and deprivation suffered by these communities. The land question undoubtedly occupies a central position in the perpetuation of the historical injustice in these areas. The toxic combination of alienated and disaffected communities and individuals, bad politics, and lack of empowerment has reinforced their encounters with the state as unfair, oppressive and unjust. It would not be an exaggeration to say that the Adivasis in these areas are seeking revenge, retribution and recognition through their inherent or explicit struggles.

It is my sincere hope and trust that this study and similar area-specific studies would contribute towards appropriate socio-economic and political structures which alone can contain and control the disaffection in these areas and clear the path for their autonomous self-reliant and self-managed progress and development. Most states within which the Fifth Schedule lies have failed to implement rigorously, the five important and statutory rights in regard to land already existing vis-á-vis:

1. Effective measures to prevent alienation of tribal land and its restoration,
2. Implement the provisions of PESA conferring original jurisdiction and powers to the Gram Sabhas,
3. Re-examine and reopen the closed and rejected cases under Forest Rights Act, 2006,
4. Prevent displacement as far as possible and implement the provisions of Right to Fair Compensation and Transparency in Land Acquisition, Rehabilitation and Resettlement Act, 2013 (LARRA),
5. Determined policy and funding arrangements for universalization of basic minimum needs among all Scheduled Tribes and ensure that their institutions for elementary and secondary education, health care, public distribution system, drinking water and sanitation are all according to national and international standards.

It is my earnest hope that this contribution of Shri Trinadha Rao would generate a momentum in this direction. Only then, in the immediate future, can we hope to close the gap between promise and performance.

B.N. Yugandhar
IAS (Retd.)
Former Secretary and
Member of Planning
Commission of India

Preface

This book has evolved from two long-standing involvements. The first is my nearly three decades of active engagement with tribal land issues of Andhra Pradesh through the non-governmental organization, Laya, based in Visakhapatnam. I have taken up thousands of tribal land cases against non-tribals who have impinged upon tribal landholdings through dubious transactions. My involvement is both in the nature of legal advocacy and non-legal advocacy (extra court) interventions for the restoration of alienated tribal land. This has provided me with an opportunity to understand the complexities of tribal land issues. Land has been and continues to be the most significant asset for tribal communities and their sustenance is rooted in it. My other involvement is my doctoral research at the Centre for Economic and Social Studies (CESS), Hyderabad, on the various dimensions of tribal land alienation.

Both my academic study and understanding of tribal land rights issues through participation in grassroots movements led me to investigate various dimensions of social, political, administrative and legal aspects of the continued issue of tribal land alienation. It became clear that it is critical for tribals to secure their land rights to establish their de facto entity on land in the Fifth Schedule Areas of Andhra Pradesh. The nexus between the non-tribal entrants to tribal areas, political parties and the state has been contributory to marginalization of tribals in securing access to land. In the post-globalization era, the state itself has become a huge threat to tribal survival and access to landholdings in Scheduled Areas. The state has been displacing tribals from their living spaces and acquiring huge chunks of land for development projects.

There is substantial evidence to show that tribal land issues are not part of the agenda of mainstream political parties. There is a silent conspiracy at the higher level executive authorities regarding the tribal protective Land Transfer Regulation violations perpetrated by lower level staff including revenue authorities from the taluk to the district level. The number of working days noted at the level of the Enquiry Officer shows how inadequately the implementing machinery is functioning for the redemption of alienated tribal land to their rightful owners. The political parties which generally work to consolidate their vote banks in tribal areas, have been involved in pushing the progressive land legislations on one hand, and on the other, pulling back the executive forces to ensure non-implementation.

This study of tribal land issue in Andhra Pradesh examines the cause of tribal land alienation in general and the specific role of political and non-political bodies and the Tribal Advisory Council in protecting the land rights of tribal people in the Scheduled Areas of the state. It examines the historical evolution of the protective land laws and the forest laws in the light of the outcome of legal proceedings initiated against non-tribal occupants for restoration of lands, and the role of the judiciary in dispensation of justice. The case study of East Godavari District on the situation of tribal land corroborates the state's role in causing land alienation among tribals. This case study explores how some of the major changes in the relationship of people to land have affected land administrative systems and the role that land administration plays in tribal land alienation in the Scheduled Areas of East Godavari District.

This study notices that although Land Transfer Regulations 1 of 70 have been in force, its implementation has remained weak. The tribal land conflict resolution mechanisms have failed to restore alienated land to tribal people. The regulations are inadequate to address the land rights of tribal people in the Scheduled Areas and administrative and legislative changes are required for their effective implementation. The government is morally and politically obliged to rectify the legacy of land dispossession among tribals.

I first began exploring the issue of tribal land rights in 1986 as part of my intervention through voluntary organizations in the Scheduled Areas of East Godavari District. I started to understand the tribal protective land transfer laws applicable to Scheduled Areas of the state and taking up cases on behalf of tribals to argue for restoration of their land, now in possession of non-tribals. Laya provided me the opportunity to work on tribal land issues and understand the various legal dimensions of the problem. I am indebted to Laya for giving me an opportunity to associate with it and work for tribal land rights. I owe my special thanks to P. Rambabu, P. Murali Vasu, K. Pushparaju who helped me in obtaining the necessary information from the field and local offices.

The years that I devoted to research on tribal land issue at CESS, Hyderabad (2007–2012), were critical in the shaping and writing of this book. Prof. M. Gopinath Reddy of the Centre for Economic and Social Studies (CESS), Hyderabad, and my Supervisor, has generously given me his time to discuss and guide me in my research and thesis writing. I owe special thanks to Dr V.N.V.K. Sastry, former Director of the Tribal Culture and Training Research Institute (TCTRI), who acted as an observer during my presentations on the theme in seminars and giving valuable suggestions. Dr K. Balagopal, human rights activist, who passed away in 2009, initially inspired me to take up this research study. The library at CESS and other institutions in Hyderabad gave me access to a vast body of historical and contemporary material. The CESS facilitated several rounds of seminars invoking discussions on areas of my work with faculty members and experts on the subject. I am most grateful to the Director of CESS, Prof. S. Galab; Course Assistant Co-ordinator, Sri K. Venkatayya; and other faculty members. I thank the library staff of CESS for their warmth and help.

Comments from and discussions with many colleagues and friends provided me with essential feedback as the book progressed. It is not possible to name them all, but a few need particular mention. M. Bharath Bhushan, Prof. Nandini Sundar, Geetha Ramswamy, Shirish are among them. One person whose meticulous comments on several drafts of the book were invaluable is Sonal Baxi, who helped me to reshape my thesis as a book. I am especially grateful to my wife Annapurna, also an advocate, who has been my closest support during the writing of this book.

I am very thankful to Prof Shashi Sahai, Rajasthan University, Jaipur, Consultant of Indian Council of Social Science Research (ICSSR) who has evaluated my thesis work and recommended it for publication. This publication is financially supported by ICSSR, Ministry of Human Resources Development, Government of India, New Delhi.

Palla Trinadha Rao

Acronyms and Abbreviations

ADO	Agency Divisional Officer
Ac	Acres
APCCR	Andhra Pradesh Communist Committee of Revolutionary
Art	Article
AWD	Assessed Waste Dry
ALD	Andhra Legal Decisions
ALT	Andhra Law Times
AIR	All India Reporter
An. WR	Andhra Weekly Reporter
BC	Backward Communities
CMA	Civil Miscellaneous Appeal
CPI(M)	Communist Party of India (Marxist)
CPI(ML)	Communist Party of India(Marxist and Leninist)
CPI(ML) ND	Communist party of India (Marxist Leninist) New Democracy
CPR	Common Property Resources
DB Judgment	Division Bench Judgment
EC	Encumbrance Certificate
EG Dist	East Godavari District

EP	Execution Petition
EP	Election Petition
FB Judgment	Full Bench Judgment
FSO	Forest Settlement Officer
GO	Government Order
GoAP	Government of Andhra Pradesh
GoI	Government of India
GOMs No	Government Order Miscellaneous Number
Hec	Hectares
IAS	Indian Administrative Service
ILO	International Labour Organization
ITDA	Integrated Tribal Development Agency
Jn Asst	Junior Assistant
L&O	Law and Order
LTR	Land Transfer Regulations
LTRP	Land Transfer Regulation Petition
NA	Not Available
NGO	Non-Governmental Organization
NAC	National Advisory Council
OC	Other Castes (here refers to upper caste)
PO	Project Officer
PESA	Panchayats Extension to Scheduled Areas
PTG	Primitive Tribe Group
PWG	Peoples War Group
RDO	Revenue Divisional Officer
Ref No	Reference Number
Rev Dept	Revenue Department
RoFR	Recognition of Forest Rights

RoR	Record of Rights
RSR	Resettlement Survey Register
SC	Scheduled Caste
SC case	Supreme Court case
SW	Social Welfare
SDC	Special Deputy Collector
Spl DT	Special Deputy Tahsildar
Sr Asst	Senior Assistant
SLP	Special Leave Petition
TW	Tribal Welfare
TAC	Tribal Advisory Council
TGMS	Telugu Grameena Magani Samaradhana
TSP	Tribal Sub Plan
UDRI	Upper Divisional Revenue Inspector
VSS	Vana Samrakshana Samithi
WG Dist	West Godavari District
WP	Writ Petition

Glossary of Local and Legal Terms

Abkari tax	Excise tax.
Adangal	A revenue account which shows cultivation and pattadar details of land.
Adivasi	Original inhabitants/aboriginal, member of Scheduled Tribe.
Agency Areas	Areas are governed by Agent to Government. They refer to the areas governed by the Agents to the Government during the British period for administration of both civil and criminal justice. The revenue officials are designed as Agent, Asst. Agent and Agency Munsif. The Scheduled Areas are also popularly called as Agency Areas.
Agency Divisional Officer	An officer in charge of a revenue division.
Agency Munsif	An office in charge of a Taluk.
Agent to Government	Government official of the rank of District Collector is designated as Agent to Government, during the British period under A.P. Agency Rules 1924 for administration of civil justice in Agency Areas.
Amarakam accounts	Records show land given by the Zamindar/Mukhasadar to the cultivator

Assigned or D form patta lands	Lands which are assigned by the revenue officials to the landless eligible persons for enjoyment of government lands.
Asst. Agent to Government	A subordinate officer to the Agent to Government. The official rank of Revenue Divisional Officer/Sub-Collector are designated as Asst. Agent to Government for administration of civil justice.
Banjara lands	Government waste lands.
D form Patta	Land title issued by the government on assigned lands.
Deshmukh	District revenue official.
De hors	Outside or beyond the bounds of.
Diwan	Supervisory staff of a landlord's estate or jagir.
Encroachment	Encroachment means the unauthorized occupation of government land.
Fair Adangal	A settlement register.
Fasali	The revenue year commencing from the first of July to the end of June the following year.
Fifth Schedule	Fifth Schedule of the Constitution of India pertains to the governance of Scheduled Areas.
Fituris	Uprisings.
Gadappannu	House-wise tax.
Hill tribe	Anybody or class of persons resident in the Agency Tracts.
Illotom	Residence in the house of one's wife's father.
Ipso facto	By the fact itself.
Izara dar	A lease holder or farmer of land held at a defined rent or revenue.
Izara land	A lease or farm land held at a defined rent or revenue.
Karnam	Village level revenue official.
Kist	Payment of revenue on instalment basis.

Kowl	Kowl is the grant of land on certain terms such as free of assessment for specified periods.
Land tenure system	Arrangement made by the British administration to collect land revenue from the cultivators of the land.
Mahal	Unit of revenue assessment.
Mansabs	Feudal chieftain/a headman of village/watch and ward
Mukhasadar	Head of Mukhasa villages and tax collector, during the British period. He used to exercise the power on grant of Sanad.
Muchalika	A written obligation or agreement or cultivators of land agreeing to the rates of assessment imposed by the landlord or government.
Mukhasa	Mukhasa is a village or land assigned to an individual either rent-free or at a low rent, on condition of services.
Mutta	A village or group of villages held by a Muttadar.
Muttadar	A person who holds Mutta under a Sanad granted by the government, subject to payment of a fixed amount of land revenue and who assists the government in maintaining law and order in the Mutta.
Patta	Land entitlement deed.
Pattadar	The Ryotwari proprietor is usually termed as pattadar.
Pasupukunkuma	Gift of properties given by parents to their daughters on the occasion of marriage.
Peshkush:	Land revenue payable to the government.
Per se	Itself.
Plain area	Other than the Scheduled Area.
Podu	Shifting cultivation/Slash and burn cultivation.
Poromboke	Poromboke is a land belonging to government which is not prima facie available for assignment.

Proprietor	Landlord or landholder of villages held by Estate, Mutta, Mukhasa.
Rampa country	The Agency Area of Rampa notified as Rampa country in June 1879 under the Scheduled Districts Act 1874 in Madras Presidency.
Res judicata	No court shall try any suit in which the matter between the same parties, litigating under the same title, was already tried and decided by the competent court. The earlier judgement operates as res judicata in subsequent suit.
Revenue village	A local area which is designated as a village by the government in the revenue accounts for the purposes of revenue administration.
Ryot	Cultivators of land.
Sanad	An acknowledgement and documentary proof of rights conferred upon by the government.
Scheduled Areas	The Fifth Schedule under Art. 244(1) of the Constitution defines 'Scheduled Areas' as such areas as the President may, by order declare to be Scheduled Areas after consultation with Governor of that State.
Scheduled districts	Districts notified by the British under Scheduled Districts Act 1874.
Scheduled Tribe	Any tribe or tribal community or part of or group within any tribe or tribal community and specified as such in relation to the state of Andhra Pradesh (AP) notified by President of India under Article 342 of the Constitution of India.
SDC Court	Special Deputy Collector (Tribal Welfare) is a designated enquiry officer under Land Transfer Regulations to conduct enquires for restoration of lands from the possession of non-tribals in the Scheduled Areas. The court is manned by SDC.
Settled villages/Govern-ment villages/ Ryotwari	Villages which were surveyed and settled during the British period in the year 1902 –1905 and 1932–35. Ryotwari tenure means the lands which were not covered by Zamindari, Muttadari, Mukhasadari, etc.

Settlement Patta	Land title issued by the Settlement Officer under Survey and Settlement Regulations under 2 of 69; 2 of 70, etc.
Shikmidar	Shareholder of landed property.
Shivaijama occupation	Unauthorized occupation (encroachment) of government lands.
Status quo ante	State of affairs that existed previously.
Suo moto cases	Cases identified and taken by the government on its own initiative.
Survey	Includes all operations incidental to the determination, measurement and record of a boundary and includes re survey.
Survey Number	Land numbered by the Survey and Settlement Department of the Government.
Suo moto	On its own motion.
Taluk	Geographical revenue unit.
Tenant	A person who holds on lease, land belonging to another.
Tribal	Notified as Scheduled Tribes under the Constitution of India.
Unassessed wasteland	Unassessed wasteland is a land to which no classification and assessment have been assigned. It is one of the items of land that are prima facie available for assignment.
Zamindar	Landlord/landowner.
Zamindari	Estate owned by Zamindar.

CHAPTER 1

Tribal Identity and Land Alienation

Before looking into the broader context of the problem of tribal land alienation and related legislations, it is necessary to address the basic question of who are the Tribes and what constitutes their identity? It is estimated that there are about 190 million indigenous people in Asia of whom some 75 million live in India. According to the Minority Rights Group International, the Indian indigenous people broadly comprise of the population currently declared as Scheduled Tribes and Scheduled Castes as well as a section of those who lay claim to be part of these categories as Adivasis or Tribals, Dalits, Assamese, Manipuris, Jarowa tribes of Andaman Island, Naga natives of Nagaland and Tharus of India.[1]

Particular communities scheduled in the Constitution of India are known as Scheduled Tribes (STs) and they account for 8.2 per cent of India's population of the total population of 84.3 million as per the 2001 Census. They are distributed across all states and Union Territories (UTs), except for the states of Punjab, Haryana, Delhi and the Union Territories of Pondicherry (now Puducherry) and Chandigarh. They all belong to state-specific Scheduled Tribes as per constitutional provisions. However, there are several communities across the country who claim to be tribals or *adivasis* and who are not part of the 'Schedule of Tribes'. Difference in opinions regarding the status of various communities in relation to the Scheduled Tribes category is primarily related to the differences in context and kinds of definitions in which a Scheduled Tribe is defined or differentiated, as well as politico-legal implications of these.

Figure 1.1

State-wise Tribal Population Percentage in India

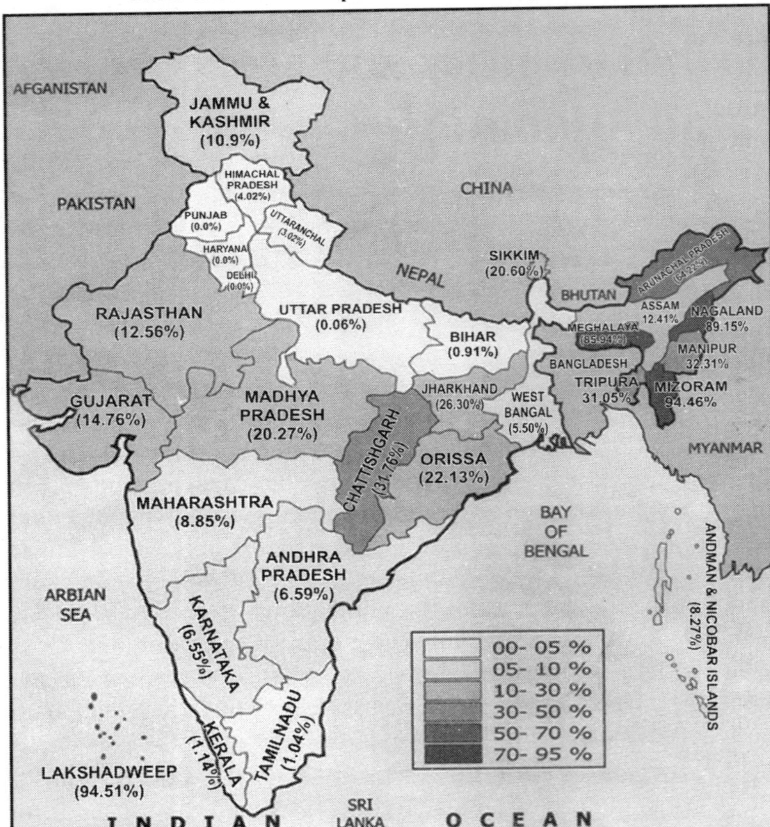

Source: Website of Ministry of Tribal Affairs, Government of India.

The identification of Scheduled Tribes in India is done on the basis of either any or all of the following characteristics: (i) primitive traits; (ii) distinctive culture; (iii) geographic isolation; (iv) shyness of contact with the community at large; and (v) backwardness.

However, it is observed that not all the tribal communities are at the same level of development. In fact, there are certain communities which are at a much lower level of development compared to the other Scheduled Tribe communities. It is also observed that in the matter of devolution of funds for the development of the

Scheduled Tribes, the major share is claimed by communities that are more assertive and in an advantageous position for demanding such benefits. As a consequence, the marginalized Scheduled Tribes are excluded from the process of development.

In order to ensure the development of the tribal communities, certain groups were identified for the first time in 1975–76, and again in 1993 as the poorest of poor amongst the Scheduled Tribes and were named Primitive Tribal Groups (PTGs). The criteria fixed for the identification of such Primitive Tribal Groups included: (i) pre-agricultural level of technology; (ii) very low level of literacy; and (iii) declining or stagnant population. The term Primitive Tribe Group was later redefined as Particularly Vulnerable Tribal Group (PVTG). Thus, there prevails internal land alienation problems among the developed tribal and under-developed tribal communities. Since the laws do not prohibit transfer of lands between tribals, the land transfers have generally been observed to take place between the more developed tribal communities and the PVTGs.

Scholars have specific views with regard to the definition of the term 'tribe'. Anthropologists, sociologists, economists and administrators differ in their definitional approach of the term and in addressing the problem of defining 'tribals'. The Tribe in India holds varied connotations for different sections of society. To the ordinary person the word suggests simple folk living in hills and forests; to the people who are a little better informed, it signifies colourful folk, known for their dance and song; to an administrator it means a group of citizens who are the special responsibility of the President of India; to an anthropologist it indicates a special field for study of social phenomenon.[2] According to the Oxford Dictionary, a tribe is 'a group of people in a primitive or barbarous stage of development acknowledging the authority of a chief and usually regarding themselves to having common ancestors'.

The term 'tribal' was at one time used by anthropologists and social scientists in general to refer to pre-state communities which progressed from bands to tribes, to states. 'Tribes' numbered usually in thousands, bands in hundreds, state societies in millions. The term thus refers to a 'backward' mode of production and is understood similarly.[3]

The tribe as a social category is distinct from the Hindus and Muslims. For this reason there is a legal bar on application of personnel laws of the Hindus and Muslims to the Scheduled Tribes. For the purpose of discussion on the issue of tribal land alienation, this study uses the term 'Scheduled Tribe' for its legal implications and analyses the impact on the increasing or decreasing access to land. The analysis also takes into consideration their historical, cultural and geographical locations.

The Supreme Court of India in *State of Kerala vs. Chandramohanan*, (SCC at P. 432, para 4) cited the definition of the word 'Tribe' given by Dr Jai Prakash Gupta in the Customary Laws of the Munda and the Oraon, as follows:

> (A) Tribe has been defined as a social group of a simple kind, the members of which speak common dialect, have a single Government and act together for such common purposes as warfare. Other typical characteristics include a common name, a contiguous territory, a relatively uniform culture or way of life and a tradition of common descent. Tribes are usually composed of a number of local communities, e.g. bands, villages or neighbourhoods and are often aggregated in clusters of a higher order called nations. The term is seldom applied to societies that have achieved a strictly territorial organization in large States but is usually confined to groups whose unity is based primarily upon a sense of extended kinship ties though it is no longer used for kin groups in the strict sense, such as clans.

Much of the present discourse on the tribal population and the understanding of tribals are largely entrenched in the way anthropologists have defined and explained tribal societies in the country. 'Tribe' in the Dictionary of Anthropology is defined as 'a social group, usually with a definite area, dialect, cultural homogeneity and unifying social organization. It may include several subgroups, such as *sibs* (kinfolks) or villages. A tribe ordinarily has a leader and may have a common ancestor, as well as patron deity. The families or small communities making up the tribe are linked through economic, social, religious, family or blood ties'.[4]

The lists of Scheduled Tribes in the Constitution of India had its origin during the British rule. The rationale for listing tribes as 'Scheduled' is based more on pragmatic considerations rather than any rigidly defined criteria. It is only since the 1931 Census conducted by J.H. Hutton that the distinction between 'tribe' and 'caste' gained significance, following which tribes gradually came to be viewed more in religious rather than in ecological terms. If a group could be shown to be clearly 'Hindu' in its religious beliefs and practice, it was a caste, if it was 'animist' it was to be considered to be a tribe. Thus, there is no satisfactory definition of the term. Even the Constitution of India has not defined the term clearly except by scheduling the tribes under Article 342, and stating that the Scheduled Tribes are 'such tribes or the tribal communities or parts or groups within such tribes or tribal communities'.[5] The Constitution further states that the Scheduled Tribes are to be notified by the President after consultation with the Governor, specifying the tribes or tribal communities or parts of the group within tribes or tribal communities in relation to that State or Union Territory, as the case may be.

In India, the term 'Adivasi' has gained immense popularity in the last few decades for referring to tribes. This term is more commonly brought to use by NGOs and activists. The term has gained currency amongst the tribes mainly belonging to central India. In Kerala too, the tribes of late have preferred to be identified as 'Adivasi'. In the Hindi language, the term 'Adivasi' means 'original settlers'.[6] As these communities form the oldest ethnological sector of the population, some refer to them by the term 'Adivasi' which means the original inhabitant of the land. Most controversial polemics are seen in regard to defining societies and communities as Adivasis or other similar groups that have reference to being the indigenous populations.

The term 'Adivasi' has a political underpinning. It has often been used to convey the position of exclusion of the tribes from constitutional provisions. The term 'Adivasi' has been even used to focus on tribal rights. Although there are difficulties with the concept of 'indigenousness' of certain groups of people in India, the term 'Adivasi' is a political construct rather than an empirical reality.

In India there is a continual debate on the appropriateness and the use of the term 'indigenous people' as it has been problematic to identify the indigenous people in the country. 'Adivasis' is an umbrella term used for a heterogeneous set of ethnic and tribal groups believed to be the original or indigenous population. It is necessary to state that though the Government of India does not recognize their indigenous status at present, historically they have been accepted as the first settlers of India.[7]

On the question of indigeneity, it would be pertinent to ask what is the basis of the indigeneity of Adivasi communities: class or ethnicity? In the late twentieth century there was an effort to assimilate and integrate the indigenous populations into homogenized modern nation states. This view was further encouraged by the International Labour Organization (ILO) and was supported under its Resolution of 1957. However, the Marxist approach was different, stating 'indigeneity' to be a 'false consciousness'; on the contrary it emphasizes class unity and revolution.[8]

According to the International Labour Organization (1994), indigenous people are not homogenous and are concentrated in remote and inaccessible areas, usually hills and forests. They differ from one another not just in terms of their ecology, cultural identity, economic organization, social and religious practices, but also in terms of the nature of their relationship to national political and economic systems.[9]

Owing to wide differences in the definitions and applications of different nomenclatures given to the tribal people, there is a growing emphasis on adopting the legal and constitutional perspective, because of its overriding importance in the functional sense of application of entitlements or safeguards of the communities known as tribes. That does not negate the continued struggle of certain communities to be treated as tribes or Adivasis or indigenous people. It is also important to appreciate how the notifications regarding the communities and definition of tribes affect the rights of Scheduled Tribes.

The first legislation enacted for protecting tribal land was the Andhra Pradesh Agency Tract and Land Transfer Act of 1917 (or 1 of 1917) in the Madras Presidency. The object of the Act was to regulate the rate of interest on amounts borrowed by tribals from non-tribals and the transfer of their lands in the Ganjam, Visakhapatnam and Godavari Agency Tracts. The British legislation defined 'Hill tribe' as any person or a class of persons residing in the Agency Tracts (not being a landholder as defined in the Andhra Pradesh (Andhra Area) Estates Land Act, 1908 (Act 1 of 1908) that may from time to time be notified as such for the purposes of the Act by the Government.

The definition of 'hill tribe' is ambiguous in this Act as any non-tribal who was a resident in the Agency Tracts could also acquire land from a member of a hill tribe with the prior consent of an agent of the Government or a prescribed officer under the 1917 Act. A large number of moneylenders and traders from the plains migrated to the Agency Tracts and settled there to take advantage of this Act. The original notification of the Government of Madras defining the hill tribes was issued on 25 January 1918. Subsequently, the list of hill tribes was amended on four occasions till the year 1932.

This definition was substituted by the Andhra Pradesh Scheduled Areas Land Transfer (Amendment) Regulation, 1978, which used the term 'Scheduled Tribe', meaning any tribe or tribal community or part of, or group within any tribe or tribal community and specified as such, in relation to the State of Andhra Pradesh by Public Notification by the President under clause (1) of Article 342 of the Constitution.

In designating a tribe as a Scheduled Tribe, the government would consider its traits, distinctive culture, geographical isolation, level of contact with communities beyond their own; social and educational development and religion is not a consideration[10] for defining a tribe.

Scheduled Tribe is an administrative term used for the purpose of 'administering' certain specific constitutional privileges, protection and benefits for a specific section of peoples, who are historically considered to be disadvantaged and 'backward'.[11] However, there are different perceptions and interpretations of the term. A 'Scheduled Tribe', in India, is also considered to be 'Adivasi', literally meaning 'indigenous people' or original inhabitants, though the term 'Scheduled Tribe' (ST) is not coterminous with the term 'Adivasi'.[12]

However, in the context of tribal land alienation, the law permits the availing of the benefit of protective land laws only if the land transferor belongs to a notified Scheduled Tribe. The members of the notified Scheduled Tribe alone can seek Constitutional benefits from the date of effect of notification, but not by virtue of their social or cultural or political labels/connotations as 'vanavasi', Adivasi, tribal, indigenous or subaltern. The social status of such a person in the pre-notified date would be non-tribal. Therefore, the date of the transaction of the land transfer between tribal and non-tribal is taken into consideration to decide the land cases.

For instance, the Andhra Pradesh High Court held that on the date of transaction, 20 October 1917, the present Koya – Scheduled Tribes were not a 'hill tribe' within the meaning of the said expression in Section 2 of the Agency Tracts Interests and Land Transfer Act 1917. The Act prohibits lands transfers only between hill tribes and non-hill tribes. By the time of the Act coming into force, Koya was not notified as a hill tribe. Thus, the transfer between Koyas to non-hill tribes was not prohibited nor was it invalid.[13] The Constitution of India does not clearly define a 'tribe'. The President of India is empowered by Article 342(i) to notify and specify any tribe or tribal community from any area as a 'Scheduled Tribe'. On such notification the tribe, so specified, is added to the List of Scheduled Tribes in the Fifth Schedule and is thus entitled to all Constitutional safeguards and protections. Thus, what seems to be indirectly defined is the concept of a Scheduled Tribe but not a 'tribe'. Article 366 specifies the meaning of Scheduled Tribes which means (Clause 25 of the Article), 'such tribes or tribal communities or parts or groups within such tribes or tribal communities as are deemed to be Scheduled Tribes for the purpose of this Constitution'.[14]

The purpose of defining a particular group or community as a tribe is rooted in the state's obligation to protect them from exploitation from the neighbouring non-tribal communities. The Supreme Court Bench observed that 'under the scheme of the Constitution, the Scheduled Tribes as a class require special protection against exploitation. The very existence of Scheduled Tribes as a distinctive class and the preservation of their culture and way of life based as it is upon agriculture which is inextricably linked with ownership of land, requires preventing an invasion upon their land ...'[15]

Classification of Tribal Population in India

Tribal society in India is generally classified on the basis of three characteristic features, viz. location, ethnicity and language.

Geographical Classification

Geographical or regional distribution forms the first criterion of classification. On this basis the tribes are distributed in the following five regions:

1. North-Eastern Region: This region consists of Assam, Arunachal Pradesh, Mizoram, Nagaland and Tripura. The major tribes in this region include the Garo, Kuki, Mizo, Khasi, Munda, Sema, Nagas, Riyang, Miri and Apa-Tani.

2. The Sub-Himalayan Region: This includes north and north-west India and Himachal Pradesh. The major tribes in these regions are the Gurjar, Gaddi, Theru and Jaunsari.
3. Central and East India: The region comprises West Bengal, Bihar, Orissa (Odisha), Madhya Pradesh and Uttar Pradesh. The tribes living here are the Baiga, Bondo, Juang, Kol, Khond, Santhal, Uraon, Ho, Munda, Lepcha, Korwa, Bhils and Pahadiya.
4. South India: This includes the states of Tamil Nadu, Kerala, Andhra Pradesh and Karnataka. The main tribes here are the Toda, Kol, Kadar, Chenchu, Koya, Gonds, Cholanaiken and Gadaba.
5. Western India: This includes the states of Rajasthan, Gujarat and Maharashtra. The tribes in this region include the Bhils, Garasia, Gonds, Kolams, Pardhans, Korku, Koli, Thakar, Katkari, Warli, Pawra, Munda, Kol, Khond and Dubla.

Linguistic Classification

Another classification of tribes is based on the languages spoken by the various tribes. Their linguistic classification are:

1. Austric Language Group: The tribes speaking languages from this group include the Kol, Munda, Khasi, Nikobari, Korku, Santhals and Gadaba.
2. Tibeto-Chinese Language Group: This includes the Naga, Khasi, Kuki, Miri, and Mizo people.
3. Dravidian Language Group: The tribes belonging to this group are the Gond, Toda, Kolam, Koya, Pardhan are Uraon.
4. Indo-European Language Group: The group includes the Bhils, Warlis, Thakurs and Koli.

Ethnicity

Another classification is based on the ethnic roots of the tribes. The more predominant are:

1. Mongoloid: The Nagas, Mizo, Sema, Jaunsari, Apa-Tanis, Tharu are of Mongoloid origin.
2. Proto-Austroloid: This group usually speaks the Kherwarian or Kaularian languages and includes the Munda, Ho, Bhil, Pahadia, Korku, Korwa, Baiga and Gond tribes.
3. The Negrito: We usually recognize the groups as being of Dravidian origin and include the Toda and Kota.

According to another view, the tribes from the South, as the Gonds, Kolam, Toda, Koya, are considered to be Dravidian in origin though they are a part of the Austroloid group.[16]

Land Alienation among Tribals

The question of land tenure has been a pivotal and sensitive political issue in the context of Scheduled Areas[17] of the Indian State. Agriculture continues to be the main source of livelihood for majority of the tribals. However, large tracts of tribal land are concentrated in the hands of predominantly elite non-tribal sections of society. Consequently, tribals are strategically marginalized and deprived of their traditional land rights. The alien systems of land tenure introduced during colonial times have had far-reaching adverse effects depriving tribals of their dignity and and their access to land justice.

Historically, tribals have had a rich cultural linkage with the natural resources. The cultural landed relationship, however, was altered or even eroded on the arrival of the non-tribal settlers from plain areas. The introduction of various land-related documents in tribal areas, and the imposition of unfamiliar modes of governance, began a cycle of incorporation of land occupations by non-tribals, legitimization of such legal occupations through land reforms, policy and law, and finally, dispossession of tribals from their control over land. Underlying these problems is a loss of identity and helplessness from having their values oppressed and their rights ignored. Tribals have restricted access to government waste land and legal entitlements. A large portion of the land which was given over to non-tribals under inalienable freehold title by proprietors of land tenures got legitimacy through subsequent state legal process of land claims during the land survey and settlement operations.

Literally, the term 'alienation' refers to 'separation' or 'detachment'. The separation of land from tribal communities can be understood in a more scientific and substantive manner with the help of the concept of alienation. The concept of alienation was introduced into Social Sciences by the German idealistic philosophy. Hegel used the concept of alienation at a metaphysical level, for assessment of material reality. Karl Marx later redefined this concept as a tool for sociological enquiry. For Marx, alienation meant that man did not experience himself as the acting agent in his grasp of the world, and that the world (nature, others and himself) remained alien to him. Hence, the world continues to stand above and against one as objects, even though it may be the object of one's own creation. The concept of 'alienation' itself has its origin in the Hegelian conceptual framework of the Absolute Idea. Marx derives this term from Hegel and redefines it to suit his own theoretical formulations. In essence, 'alienation' is basically a particular relation of property, involving involuntary surrender to antagonistic other.[18]

The alienation of humankind in a fundamental sense refers to the loss of control; its embodiment lies in an alien force which confronts the individual as a hostile and potentially destructive power. When Marx analysed 'alienation' in his Economic and Philosophic Manuscripts of 1844, he indicated four principal aspects: the alienation of human beings from nature, their own productive space, as a member of the human species and from each other.[19] Alienation, in the Marxist conception of man in the capitalist society, is the process that facilitates the exploitation of many by a few.[20]

Alienation as a philosophical concept is vividly discussed by Hegel and his interpretation is highly non-materialistic and idealistic with mystical overtones. To him, it is not real living people but the Absolute Idea that undergoes alienation. Marx criticizes Hegel's philosophy for it suffers from the double defect of reflecting at one and the same time, denoting 'uncritical positivism' and 'uncritical idealism'.[21] As Satyadeva has pointed out, alienation is inherent in exploitative relations of production and its nature varies with that of exploitation. Hence the manifestation of alienation differs among societies, based on slavery, serfdom and capitalism.[22]

Seen from the tribal point of view, tribals may be thought of as an alienated group. They suffer from several forms of alienation since, 'in a system of cumulative inequalities, privileges, property and power are combined in certain individuals, while the socially underprivileged are economically and politically deprived'.[23] Alienation of land itself, however, constitutes just a small component of this entire process of alienation, albeit an essential one. It is, therefore, imperative to view this single phenomenon within the holistic context of tribal existence and tribal cultural ethos.[24]

In the context of tribal regions, the alienation of tribals from their traditional habitat is caused due to the policies of the State. The process of induction of non-tribal population into these

Scheduled Areas was expected to bring progressive assimilation of the local tribals into the new socio-economic order of the immigrants, while raising their income, productivity and standard of living. 'However, often the outcome has been contrary to the above expectations, reducing the share of tribals in the gross regional product, substituting one institutional exploitation by another, uprooting them from their native land and reducing them to the status of aliens on their own soil'.[25]

For the purposes of this analysis it is necessary to understand the 'alienation of an individual from the product of his labour'. In the early years of the 20th century, many tribal communities lived by and large freely, in all pre-capitalistic socio-economic formations.[26] This is because the community ownership of land in India was not commoditized prior to the British rule. Tribals in their pre-capitalistic socio-economic formations had not regarded land as a commodity as it was freely available to them for the cause of cultivation. Thus, the concept of alienation with regard to the problem of land alienation in tribal areas can be understood in relation to the concept of private property relations, commoditization of the means of production as land, labour and capital, and the very process of penetration of the private sphere by the state capital. Hence, the historical and theoretical connotations of the concept of alienation as propounded by Marx hold relevant in the case of India as far as the tribal communities and their land problems are concerned.[27]

Tribal Identity and Land Rights

The nature of association between the tribals and their land is very crucial within the tribal context. Tribals share a symbiotic relationship with natural resources. Agronomic practices and their relationship with land are based on the nature-man-spirit complex and sustenance of the economy which is unique to tribal cultures in many parts of the country.[28] The interplay of nature and culture in their little traditions and the myriad ways in which they have adapted to nature, indicates that tribal lifestyle, economy and social organization 'are closely inter-related, inter-dependent and interacting' with nature and any interference resulting in disturbances evokes severe resistance from the Adivasis. In the post-Independence decades public and private enterprises have encroached upon the indigenous peoples' traditional domains, extracting minerals and timber and building dams and roads. Displaced in the name of progress, the indigenous people find their identities destroyed and their traditional livelihoods difficult to sustain.

Traditional communal land tenure systems continue to exist even where formal land tenure systems emphasize on individual property rights.[29] In the predominantly agricultural societies, the importance of land cannot be overemphasized. It is a symbol of security, the main source of income and wealth, as well as of social, political and economic power. 'The land tenure system reflects social class structure and class relations, as they represent an array of legal, contractual or customary arrangements whereby people engaged in cultivation gain access to productive opportunities linked with land and thereby income'.[30]

In recent decades the Adivasis have begun to promote their rights and privileges because their very survival has been at stake. They have been victims of exploitation and alienation at various levels. In the absence of a mechanism or power to safeguard their interests, a new form of identity or indigeneity is crystallizing among the tribes across India. The Adivasi communities now use the notion of indigenousness to identify and define themselves in differentiation from the non-tribal population. As Xaxa (1999) has observed 'the identity being expressed now by the term 'Adivasi' is indeed an expanded identity cutting across tribes bearing different names, speaking different languages or dialects. It also goes beyond groups and communities or sub-groups that are listed in the Constitution'.[31]

Tribal people in India have also been experiencing the impacts of globalization which encourages private ownership. Globalization reaches local communities largely through the market. New goods may be seen on the television or other media. It is through the market that the producers come to know what they can sell. In turn, the growth of the market has led to a process of privatization of former communal land and devolution of ownership from community or clan to the family.[32]

Tribal people suffer from physical displacement in several parts of the country due to development projects initiated by the government. Displacement among the tribals is on a massive scale and often with adverse implications on the communities, mainly due to laws that do not recognize the communal and customary rights of tribal people over their territories. Resettlement literature is replete with case studies on development projects that ignore the customary rights of the tribal people and treat them as illegal occupants of government land. Such an approach invariably leads to the impoverishment of once well settled communities; precisely the opposite of what development promises.[33]

The Panchasheel of Pandit Jawaharlal Nehru laid the foundation of the State policy aiming to recognize the customary rights of Adivasis over natural resources. The tribal, who lives on a subsistence economy, perceives land primarily as a source of survival. On the contrary, for the non-tribal, it is the primary source of power and control and is understood as 'the ability to do things to others which you do not expect they can do on to you'.[34] It is acknowledged by scholars that

> Indigenous people often have a special relationship with the land – for many it is still their source of livelihood and sustenance and the basis of their existence as communities. The right to own, occupy and use land collectively is inherent in the self-conception of indigenous people, and this right is generally vested not in the individual but in the local community, the tribe or the indigenous nation.[35]

The British legal concept of individual private property destroyed the tradition of joint ownership and sharpened tensions within the Adivasi society while eroding their relationship with nature. These same tendencies are visible today in various developmental policies that are being implemented in the country in the post-independence era.

It is because of these conflicting understandings of land – the colonial and indigenous – that there have been conflicts between the tribals and the larger non-tribal society. The Indian state modelled on the colonial state has been faithful to the colonial understanding of land and has followed the British legal and economic concept of land as a commercial commodity to be bought and sold. However, indigenous groups look at land as a source of identity, security, existence and life.

The entire world-view of Adivasis is situated around their land. They cannot imagine their physical existence apart from it[36] and therefore, eviction from their land or encroachments by outsiders has resulted in resistance and even armed struggles in Andhra Pradesh, ever since the British era. There have been and continue to be, several rebellions across the country. Prominent among them in Andhra Pradesh are Alluri Seetarama Rao's armed resistance in Vishakapatnam Agency and the Gond Rebellion[37] led by Komram Bheem in Adilabad Agency in Nizam state. The Rampa Rebellion (1922–23) from East Godavari to Vizianagaram under Alluri Seetarama Raju was in protest of the Madras Forest Act of 1882 which placed restrictions on the free movement of tribals in the forest areas and prevented them from engaging in their traditional practice of *podu* or slash and burn cultivation.

Post–independence, tribal unrest has been primarily on issues relating to restrictions on podu cultivation and encroachment of non-tribals in large numbers into Agency Areas (tribal areas), posing threat to the existence and identity of tribal society. Bharath Bhushan observes that 'land alienation issues in Agency Areas have significant direct consequences to the demographic, political, ethnic and gender aspects of tribal societies'.[38] Special laws to protect the tribals from land alienation have been violated and about forty-eight per cent of the land in Agency Areas is formally owned by non-tribals. Large scale manipulations during the Survey and Settlement period of 1970–76 led to grant of land entitlements of tribal land as settlement *pattas* in the name of non-tribals. According to the Koneru Ranga Rao Land Committee Report, 'Every year more and more land is passing into the hands of non-tribals and if not checked with a very strong executive force, very soon the tribals may not have any land at all.'[39]

The contradictory stances of the Government of India, on the one hand denying the existence of indigenous peoples in India and on the other hand, classifying them as Adivasis, stems from these very lopsided economic and political policies. The acceptance of the presence of indigenous peoples would mean the government's acceptance of the International Labour Organization Conventions 107 and 189, the first of which it has ratified. The International Labour Organization Convention 107 affirms 'the right of ownership, collective or individual, of the members of the populations concerned over the land, which these populations traditionally occupied, shall be recognized and respected.' This view does not support the policy of assimilating the Adivasis into the mainstream through the process of cultural transformation on the one hand, and depriving them of their natural resource base, on the other. However, given the diversity of its social composition, the ideological elements in the battle for subaltern identity are not uniform in quality and density. At times such diversities, as explained by Dhanagare,[40] lead to the pursuit of sectional interest, economic diversion, as well as splits that tend to undermine the horizontal alliance in the domain of the subaltern.

Fifth Schedule and Land Alienation

The future of land ownership and cultivation constitutes perhaps the most fundamental issue in national development. To a large extent the pattern of economic and social organization will depend upon the manner in which the land problem is resolved. (First Five-Year Plan Document, 1951)

A review of literature on the subject provides a clear indication of the issues involved in landlessness and the magnitude of the tribal land alienation problem. The land rights guaranteed under the various domestic and international legal instruments, protecting tribal interests, are not reaping the envisaged benefits. The loss of private holdings by tribals, despite a number of laws being passed by both the pre-colonial as well as post-colonial state to check land alienation, has been a cause of concern. These laws had many shortcomings and were unable to check the transfer of land from tribals to non-tribals.[41] Even where legislation is designed to protect tribal land interests, such as restricting alienation of tribal land or ensuring that tribals receive the benefit of land tenure reforms, the results have been disappointing.[42]

The International Labour Organization's Convention (1989) on 'Indigenous and Tribal Peoples' was ratified by India. The Convention includes right to protection of their land and refusal of displacement from their land. The Convention extended its support to the tribals to have control over their political, cultural and economic aspects of life. Article 8 of the Universal Declaration on the Rights of Indigenous Peoples says that 'States shall provide effective mechanisms for prevention of, and redress for any action which has the aim or effect of dispossessing the indigenous people of their land, territories or resources'. Article10 in the same Declaration reinforces this statement by asserting the same. However, these conventions have no statutory binding. The Constitution of India enjoins upon the States, the obligation to promote the interests of Scheduled Castes and Schedule Tribes and to protect them from social injustice and all forms of exploitation.

Land and land tenure are placed under the exclusive legislative and administrative jurisdiction of the States. However, the

Central Government has been taking on an advisory and coordinating role in the field of land reforms ever since the First Five-Year Plan. However, for the land matters concerned with the Fifth Scheduled Areas, special provisions were made under the Constitution of India.

Article 244 is the most significant article in the Constitution regarding Adivasi rights. Article 244, in the spirit of Nehru's five principles, states that the traditions and culture of Scheduled Tribe communities are to be respected and the Scheduled Areas should function autonomously. The Fifth Schedule allows the President of India to declare areas as scheduled and gives the Governor of a State the power by public notification to not apply acts of Parliament or to modify them in accordance with the needs of Scheduled Tribes. Crucially, the Fifth Schedule permits the Governor on the recommendation of the Tribal Advisory Council, to prohibit the transfer of land by or amongst Scheduled Tribes as well as to regulate the allotment of land to non-Scheduled Tribes and the working of moneylenders.[43]

In exercise of the powers conferred by paragraph 4(3) of the Fifth Schedule to the Constitution of India and in supersession of all the previous rules on the subject, the Governor of Andhra Pradesh outlined rules for the constitution of a Tribes Advisory Council in Andhra Pradesh. These rules are known as the Andhra Pradesh Tribes Advisory Council Rules 1958. These rules came into effect from 28 January 1958. The strength of the Council is to consist of twenty members of whom not less than fifteen should be representatives of the Scheduled Tribes in the Andhra Pradesh Legislative Assembly. If the member representatives of the Scheduled Tribes in the Andhra Pradesh Legislative Assembly is less than fifteen, the remaining seats would be filled by other members of these tribes.

The members shall be appointed by the Governor by Notification in the Andhra Pradesh Gazette. The term of the Council shall ordinarily be three years. The Minister in-charge of the Welfare of Scheduled Tribes shall be the ex-officio chairman of the Council. The council shall meet as often as may be necessary and, in any case, not less than twice every year. The objective of the Council is to advise the Governor in matters pertaining to welfare and advancement of Scheduled Tribes.

In many villages in the Fifth Scheduled Areas of the country, tribals slowly lost their land to the non-tribal moneylenders and landlords, reducing their status to that of tenants or labourers. In some places, the tribal chiefs were converted to Hinduism and they invited the non-tribal peasants to settle in tribal areas. The latter being experienced farmers, seized the land from the tribals and employed the natives as labourers'.[44] Several legislations have been passed since Independence but 'despite the legislation in force against alienation of land from tribals to non-tribals, a fair proportion of them have either been dispossessed of their land or have parted with their land due to some other reason'.[45]

The tribal practice of shifting cultivation made the land that they relied on, vulnerable to settlement by immigrant farmers.[46] In addition, various groups including colonial powers and governments, have exploited the tribal people at the cost of their land. In response, states enacted restrictions on the alienation of tribal land in order to protect the heritage and livelihood of some of the country's most marginalized people.[47] Unfortunately, despite most legislations being in place for more than forty years, restrictions on alienation have not been successful at protecting tribal land from alienation.[48] Various accusations fly back and forth. Some contend that the tribal land rights legislation is not restrictive enough, that it contains too many gaps and loopholes, and is not appropriately enforced.[49] Others argue that the legislation is too restrictive, does not adequately address the realities of tribal life and diversity of the tribal population, and has driven the non-qualifying mortgages and sales underground, where there are no protections.[50]

Land alienation can be defined both in a narrow and broad sense. In the narrow sense, it could mean the alienation of individual landholdings and means of livelihood. In the broader sense, alienation includes the loss of common property and rural commons.[51] Assetless SC and ST casual wage labour households are at a 'double disadvantage'; the Scheduled Tribe agricultural labour households form the poorest social group in India.[52] This is obvious from the fact that the percentage of tribal cultivators has decreased in India from 68.15 per cent in 1961 to 54.5 per cent in 1991. Conversely, the percentage of agricultural labourers has increased from 19.71 per cent in 1961 to 32.69 per cent in 1991.[53] As per the 2001 Census, cultivation is the main occupation of 44.7 per cent of the Scheduled Tribes while 36.7 per cent are engaged as agricultural labourers. Only 2.1 per cent of the tribals are employed as industrial workers. This makes 82 per cent of the Scheduled Tribes dependent on agriculture. Nearly 2 lakh Scheduled Tribes families in almost 5,000 forest villages did not have rights to the land which they had been cultivating for decades in India. The Scheduled Tribes started with an initial advantage of a higher population having land ownership. But unprecedented increase in landlessness has set in due to displacement by development projects and land alienation by numerous other methods. In states which have a high concentration of tribals, their landholding is also lower in comparison to other communities.[54]

The tribal communities all over India have been subjected to various forms of deprivation such as alienation from land and other forest resources since the British rule. The problem, however, did not cease with India gaining independence. On the contrary, it has only increased in magnitude and complexity.[55] The entire tribal life process was centred and built upon two major means of production: i.e. the forest and the land, which are described as the twin pillars of tribal economy. Their relationship with these, especially with the latter, is linked to their 'philosophy of life'.[56] Tribal rights to the land they occupy and cultivate outside the reach of forest laws have been similarly insecure. State and central governments have usurped large tracts of tribal land for public projects and industrial activities, and the land in many areas has been indiscriminately stripped of minerals and resources.[57]

The process of alienation of tribal land began with the stabilization of the British rule in India. This process was accelerated by the development of transport, establishment of individual rights over agricultural land, commercialization of agriculture and the spread of the English judicial system.[58] The White colonization of southern Africa, the Americas, Australia and New Zealand was based on the principle that one could occupy land ostensibly belonging to none. This principle was struck down as unconstitutional by the Australian judiciary[59] but it continues to be the basis of land laws in India as its eminent domain principle. Its first facet is that the natural resources such as forests as well as land with no individual title, belong to the State. Its second facet is that the State alone has the right to decide what constitutes the public purpose and in the process deprives individuals of their assets in its name. Development induced displacement and other forms of deprivation arise from this principle.[60]

The twenty-ninth report of the Commissioner of Scheduled Castes and Tribes (1990) says that even though tribal people form about 7.5 per cent of the population, over 40 per cent of the people displaced till 1990, belonged to these communities. A report of the Official Working Group on Development and Welfare of Scheduled Tribes during the Eighth Five-Year Plan (1990–1995) on the rehabilitation of tribal people, based on a comprehensive study of 110 projects, has concluded that of the 1.694 million people displaced by these projects, almost 50 per cent (8,14,000) were tribals.

While displacement caused due to development projects has resulted in confrontation between authorities and local tribals, there are other factors such as growing indebtedness, forcible eviction of tribals from their land by non-tribals, conversion of land from communal ownership to individual ownership, increasing urbanization, treating tribals as encroachers on traditionally occupied forest land and lack of substantive possession by tribals of government land allotted to them that have caused land alienation. In order to prevent further deterioration of the situation, there is an urgent need to look into the ownership of resources by tribals, especially the resources on which they depend for livelihood, such as land, forest and water.[61]

Another piece of legislation which speaks about the protection to tribal land and prevention of land alienation is the Panchayats (Extension to Scheduled Areas) Act, 1996 (PESA). The PESA provides for tribal self-rule on matters affecting tribal society and economy at the village level and enlarges the authority of local government to include various levels of control over local resources and programmes.[62] But implementation of the PESA and the realization of its goals have been spotty, in large measure, because the PESA granted local communities authority over resources, in conflict with the existing laws.[63]

Loss of land has led to loss of livelihood of tribal people. A major consequence is the growing number of agricultural labourers, an indication of the 'de-peasantization' process.[64] In addition, the precarious economic circumstances of many tribals have resulted in the chronic and continuing transmitting of tribal land to non-tribals.[65]

Literature on tribal land alienation with regard to various governance structures and their impact on land alienation among tribal communities covered under varied systems of land tenure is scanty. Several studies focused on the magnitude of land alienation in Agency Areas have drawn out the historical factors and political dimensions by documenting the struggles of tribal communities from pre-independence times to the promulgation of legislations and tribal development policies and administrative structures in the seventies. Most of these studies provide insights into the magnitude of the tribal land alienation and de-peasantization process, the outcome of legal measures in restoration of the alienated tribal land, and the movement behind the promulgation of Land Transfer Regulations 1 of 70 in general. Available literature has perceived the tribal land alienation situation in a general manner giving greater attention to the magnitude of land alienation in the Scheduled Areas of Andhra Pradesh without examining the role of specific land tenure systems. The land administration practices have had diverse consequences on the process of land alienation in Agency Areas. Further, there is little awareness about the specific reasons for failure in restoration of the alienated tribal land and setbacks in the state policies and laws in addressing the tribal land rights issue. These studies are of limited help in explaining the actual cauzation and resultant factors with reference to different land tenure systems. How the varied land tenure systems affect the process of land alienation or restoration of tribal land is largely ignored as most of the studies have assumed that the structure of land relations are uniform across the state.

The present study attempts to document the causes and consequences of tribal land alienation under different land tenure systems in the Scheduled Areas of East Godavari District of Andhra Pradesh and the impact of policies and law in addressing the problem of land alienation in the region.

Scheduled Areas in Andhra Pradesh

The total population of the Scheduled Tribes constitutes 3.9 per cent of the entire population of the East Godavari District. The tribal population in the district is mostly concentrated in the 664 habitations in 608 Revenue villages of 7 Scheduled Area Mandals and 4 Sub-plan Mandals as per the 2001 Census. There are 550 revenue villages in the Scheduled Areas of the District.

The total population in the Scheduled Area is 2.16 lakhs, while the Scheduled Tribe population is 1.46 lakh constituting 67 per cent of the total population, the population of the non-tribals is 70,534. The tribal households are 35,478, while the non-tribal households are 17,129 as per the 2001 Census. The Scheduled Mandals are Addateegala, Devipatnam, Gangavaram, Maredumilli, Rajavommangi, Rampachodavaram, and Y. Ramavaram. There are several tribal communities, the more dominant among them are Konda Reddis, Koya Dora, Konda Kammara, Valmiki, Mannedora and Konda Kapus. Among these the Konda Reddi are termed as Primitive Tribe Group (PTG) for administrative purposes.

Table 1.1

Demographic Details of Tribal Communities in the District

S. No.	*Tribal Sub-Caste*	*ST Population*	*ST Households*	*Per cent to Tribal Population*
1.	Kondareddi	65,001	15,718	40%
2.	Koyadora	56,876	13,753	35%
3.	Kondakammara	19,499	4,715	12%
4.	Kondakapu	6,499	1,572	4%
5.	Valmiki	8,126	1,964	5%
6.	Mannedora	3,249	786	2%
7.	Others	3,249	786	2%

Source: ITDA office, Rampachodavaram–2001.

The tribal villages in the area, by and large, lie in the remote and interior areas, with little access to transport. The villages are surrounded by hills and forests. The terrain is moderately elevated. Nearly 30 per cent of the area is covered by forests. The area is drained mostly by the Pamuleru, Yeleru and Sileru rivers in the upland area, and by the Godavari in the delta region. The river Pamuleru drains most of the Agency Areas of East Godavari and joins the Godavari at Kolluru village. The Seethapalli rivulet drains part of the Agency Area and joins the Godavari between Veeravaram and Pudipalli villages near Devipatnam.

The tribal communities in the area, predominantly depend upon land cultivation for their livelihood. The major problems in the area include food insecurity, land alienation, displacement, exploitation, erosion of tribal cultural values, lack of access to government programmes, inadequate enforcement of land policies and law and order.

The research area covers the Scheduled Area of East Godavari District, Andhra Pradesh. East Godavari District is the residual

Figure 1.2 *Andhra Pradesh and the Study District of East Godavari*

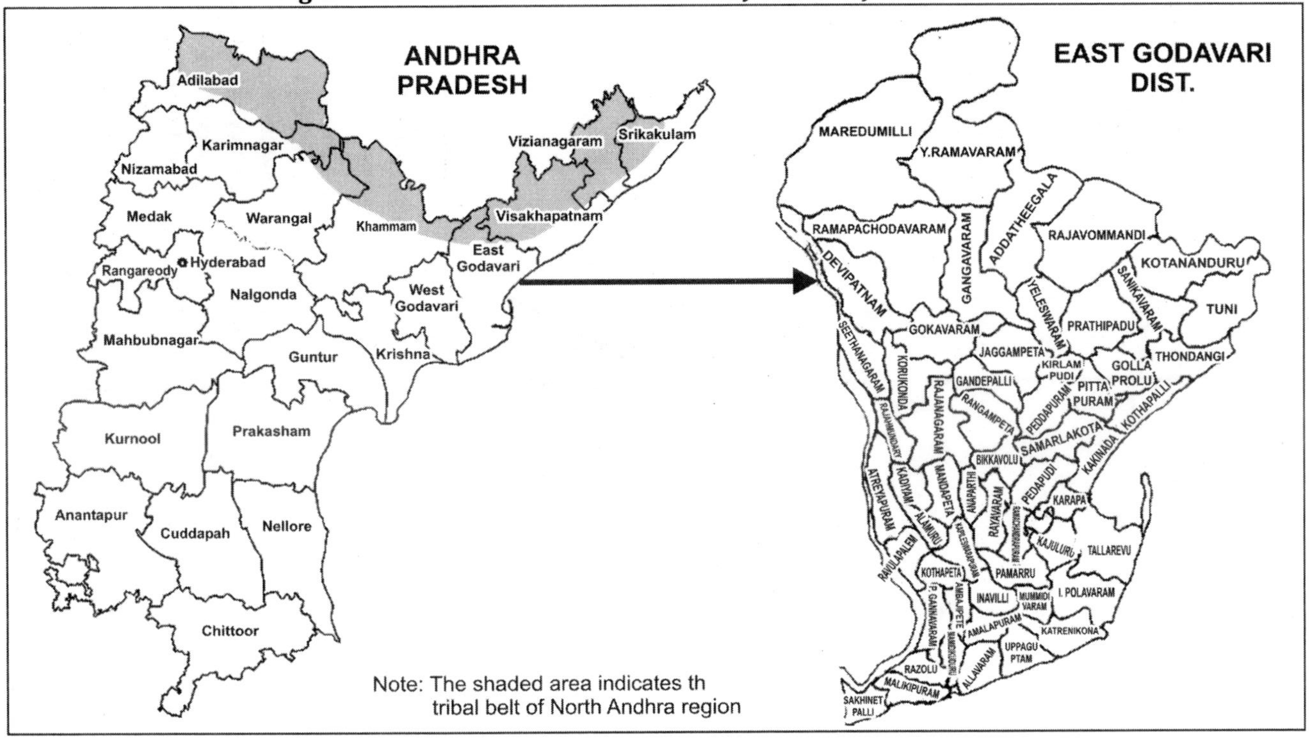

Note: The shaded area indicates th
tribal belt of North Andhra region

Figure 1.3

Sample Villages and Case Study Villages in the Scheduled Areas of East Godavari District

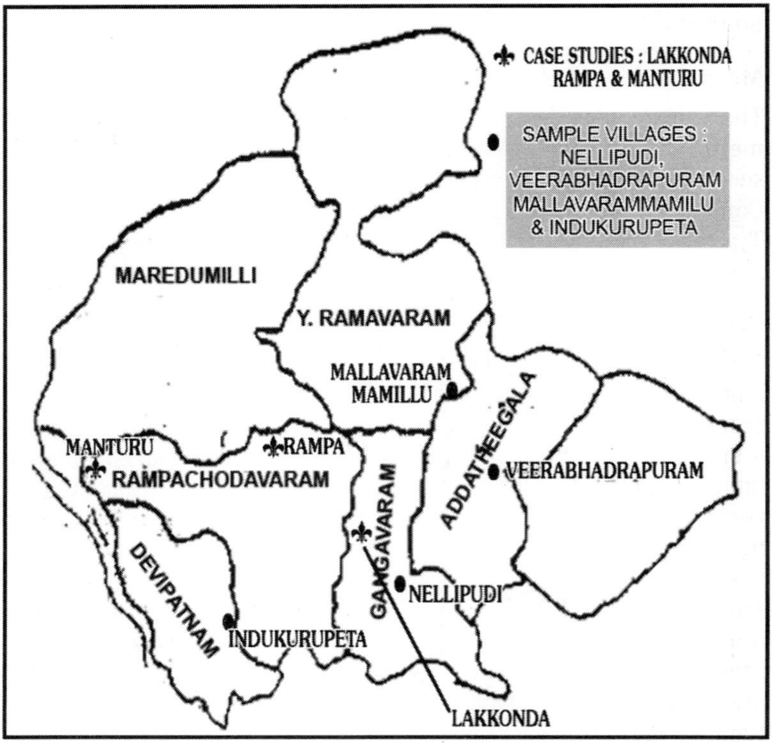

portion of the old Godavari Districts, after West Godavari was separated in 1925.

East Godavari District can be broadly classified into three natural divisions: the Delta, Upland and Agency or hill tracts. The general elevation of the district varies from a few metres near the sea to about 300 metres in the hills of the Agency. The Eastern Ghats rise by gradations from the level of the coast and spread throughout the erstwhile Agency taluks of Rampachodavaram and Yellavaram. The delta portion constituting the whole of Konaseema and portions of Kakinada, Ramachandrapuram and Rajahmundry erstwhile taluks, presents a vast expanse of rice-fields surrounded by plantain, betel, coconut gardens and palmyrahs. The erstwhile taluks of Tuni, Pithapuram, Peddapuram and portions of Kakinada,

Ramachandrapuram and Rajahmundry constitute the upland areas. The district shares its north eastern boundary with Visakhapatnam district and the northern boundary with Malkangiri region of Orissa (Odisha) State. The Godavari river forms its western and southern boundaries.

Methodology of the Study

The study has used a variety of triangulated data collection methods. These include both primary and secondary sources. The secondary sources include Governor Administration Reports from Commissionerate of Tribal Welfare and the Tribal Culture and Training Research Institute (TCTRI), Hyderabad CESS, and the State Archives at Andhra Pradesh and Madras (Tamil Nadu).

Problems and Limitations of the Study

The major difficulty encountered during the study was the access to land-related information from the government offices. The tribal respondents were unable to provide complete information in respect of the process of land alienation from the original tribal landowners as they were dead. In some cases the present tribal respondents were new entrants to the village. Therefore, the study had to rely on the information provided by the respondents. The respondents were unable to give accurate particulars of land held either by tribals or non-tribals, mostly due to illiteracy and non-familiarity with land records. The content analysis of the Judgements was done only by taking the cases from the court of lower level enquiry, i.e. 'Special Deputy Collectors' Court at Rampachodavaram. The final outcome of the legal process cannot be determined on the basis of this data alone. However, the data analysis helps to understand the outcome of the legal recourse for the restoration of alienated land at the lower courts and the loopholes in the existing land laws and administrative justice. The aspects of land alienation caused due to land occupation by non-tribals for housing, shops and other business establishments are not covered under this study. Similarly, land loss due to the establishments by state interventions in the Scheduled Areas of the district, is also an uncovered aspect.

Schedule Tribes in Andhra Pradesh

In Andhra Pradesh, 35 tribal communities are notified as Scheduled Tribes and their population is about 50.24 lakhs as per the 2001 Census reports. They constitute 6.59 per cent of the total population of the state. The Tribal Sub-plan area extending over 31,485.34 sq. km in the districts of Srikakulam, Vizayanagaram, Warangal, Visakhapatnam, East and West Godavari, Khammam, Adilabad and Mahaboobnagar Districts constitutes the traditional habitat of nearly 30 tribal groups. The tribal groups of Yerukula, Yanadi and Sugali or Lambada live mainly in the plain areas outside the Scheduled Areas.

On the basis of geo-ethnic characteristics, the tribal areas of Andhra Pradesh have been divided into the following five geographical zones:

1. The region of the Gonds which constitutes the tribals areas of Adilabad District in the extreme Gondwana region adjoining the districts of Maharashtra.

   The Gond community is subdivided into six tribes: (i) Raj Gond or Gond, (ii) Pradhan, (iii) Toli, (iv) Dadve, (v) Gowari, and (vi) Kolams. These communities are endogamous in nature.

2. The Koya-Konda Reddi region which included areas along the Godavari gorges, tribal areas of Karimnagar, Warangal, Khammam, West Godavari and East Godavari Districts.

   The Koyas are found along the Godavari river from Karimnagar to the East and West Godavari Districts. The Konda Reddis inhabit either side of the Godavari banks from Bhadrachalam area of Khammam District to Devipatnam and Polavaram areas of East and West Godavari respectively. Although they are spread over a large area, a majority of the population is concentrated in Maredumilli and Addatigala region of the East Godavari District.

3. The Khond-Savara region constitutes those tribal areas which are part of the Eastern Ghats, spreading across the forest and hill tracts of Srikakulam to Vizianagaram and Visakhapatnam Districts.

   The origin of Savaras is traced to the ancient Sabars who are migrants from the lower reaches of the Ganges. The Savaras consists of two classes: Kapu Savaras who dwell in the plains and Hill Savaras or Jati Savaras who consider themselves to be superior to their counterparts. The origin of the Khonds, however, is unclear. In the Visakhapatnam District Manual of 1869, they are recorded as owners and cultivators of the soil. They are divided into two groups namely, the Dondgria Khonds and the Desys Khonds.

4. The Chenchu region comprises of the tribal areas of Mahaboobnagar, Nalgonda, Kurnool, Prakasam and Guntur Districts. The traditional habitat of the Chenchus is found in the contiguous forest tracts of Nallamalai Hills. Most Chenchus of this area are more or less at the food gathering state of economy and they largely subsist on hunting and collection of roots, timber and honey. It is important to note, however, that although in the Census of 1971 more than 18,000 Chenchus were enumerated, only a few hundred still pursue their traditional lifestyle as semi-nomadic forest dwellers.
5. The plains areas comprise the Yanadis, Yerukulas and Lambadas. These three groups have been recognized as Scheduled Tribes in the Andhra region from 1956 and in Telengana from, as late as, 1976. The Yanadis are concentrated in the Andhra region, the Yerukulas throughout the state and the Lambadas, mainly in the Telengana region.

About two-thirds of the tribals of Andhra Pradesh live in the hilly and Scheduled Areas of Srikakulam, Vizianagaram, Visakhapatnam, East Godavari, West Godavari, Khammam, Warangal and Adilabad Districts. After the Constitution of India came into force, these regions came to be known as the Scheduled Areas under a special order in 1953.[66]

Table 1.2

Location of Tribes in the Scheduled Areas of Andhra Pradesh

S. No.	*Name of the District*	*Scheduled Tribes*
1.	Srikakulam	Savara, Jatapu, Gadaba, Konda Dora.
2.	Vizianagaram	-do-
3.	Visakhapatnam	Bagata, Gadaba, Kammara, Konda Dora, Kotia, Khond, Mali, Manne Dora, Mukha Dora, Reddi Dora, Porja Valmiki, Gond, Kulia.
4.	East Godavari	Koya, Konda Reddi, Kammara, Koya Dora, Valmikis, Konda Kapus.
5.	West Godavari	Koya, Konda Reddi, Yerukula, Yanadi.
6.	Khammam	Koya, Konda Reddi.
7.	Warangal	Koya, Lambada.
8.	Adilabad	Gond, Kolam, Pradhan, Thoti, Lambada, Naikpod, Andh.
9.	Mahaboobnagar	Lambada, Chenchu.

Sources:[67]

Figure 1.4 *Scheduled Areas of Andhra Pradesh*

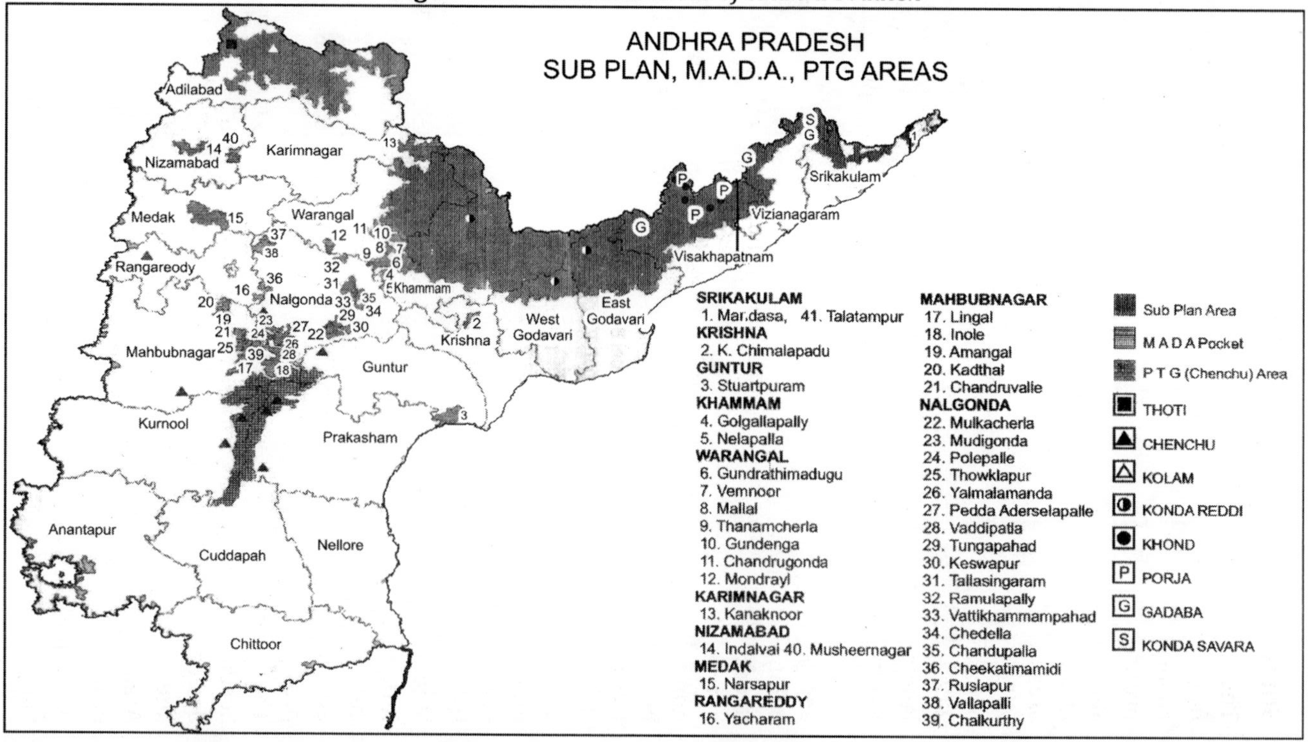

Source: Basic Statistics on Scheduled Tribes of Andhra Pradesh (2008), TCTRI, Hyderabad.

Study Site and Sample Frame

The study broadly categorizes the land tenure into customary and freehold land tenure systems. The freehold land tenure system is governed by explicit conditions imposed by either the land tenure proprietor or the state. The unwritten customary obligations were snapped by the imposition of the land tenure systems and resulted in the causation of tribal land alienation. The study covers all the areas of land tenure systems taking one purposive sample Revenue village from each kind of land tenure system in the Scheduled Area of East Godavari District. The total sample of the study covers all the 212 tribal households from the sample villages. The typology of land tenure systems of sample villages included are the Muttadari, Ryotwari (Government), Mukhasa and Zamindari (Estate).

The study is conducted within the purview of the historical and legal perspective that the land in the Scheduled Areas once belonged to tribals, unless and until contrary is proved that the land in occupation of non-tribals shall be deemed to have come through a transfer from tribals. So, the burden of proof lies on the non-tribals to legally prove that the land in their possession had been with them even prior to the Andhra Pradesh Agency Tracts Land Transfer Act of 1917, which restricts land transfer between the tribals and the non-tribals. The tribals have customary boundaries to the village and land is a community asset, rather an individualized economic asset. Their traditional customary practices and cultural life is rooted to the land. The separation of tribals from intertwined relationship of land is viewed as loss of land to others. The object of the Fifth Schedule of the Indian Constitution and the Land Transfer Regulations is to preserve tribal autonomy and their culture, to help in their economic empowerment, to ensure social, economic and political justice for preservation of peace, and good governance in the Scheduled Areas. The word 'regulate' in the allotment of land to members of Scheduled Tribes in the Scheduled Area in the Fifth Schedule must be read as an endeavour to ensure regulation of the land only for and among the members of the Scheduled Tribes in the Scheduled Area.[68] It is from this perspective that it is necessary to consider the issue of land alienation in the Scheduled Areas.

Three major sources were used to understand the process of land alienation: government land records; tribals alienated from their land; and Court judgments in cases of land dispossession. The first major source of data to understand the control of land by non-tribals was analysis of Adangal records and Survey and Settlement records available at the Taluk offices and Sub-Collector's office at Rampachodavaram, a Scheduled Area of the East Godavari District. The perception of the tribals about their land dispossession formed the primary source of data. The third major source of data was the judgments given by Special Deputy Collector's Court at the Integrated Tribal Development Agency (ITDA) level of the District. The data gathered through these three sources was supplemented with the information obtained through focus group discussions and interviews with experts, observation and case studies. The author is associated with Resource for Legal Action, a unit under Laya, a non-governmental organization and has been involved as a participant observer for the past twenty-six years in the documenting process and dynamics related to land dispossession and has lived for twelve years (1986–1998) in Rampachodavaram.

The villages were selected on the basis of the number of tribal land alienation cases that came from those villages and also a large extent involved in it to the Special Deputy Collector's court at Rampachodavaram during the study period 2005–2010. The cases in respect of land transfers between the parties for house sites is excluded from the analysis. The sample villages were selected from among the villages of the Scheduled Area of the East Godavari District on the basis of higher or lesser number of cases with more extent of land involved reported during five years period (2005–2010) before Special Deputy Collector's Court, Rampachodavaram, excluding the house site cases from the sample frame. Another equally important criteria that was followed for choosing sample villages from each category of land tenure of the Scheduled Area of the district was inclusion of all the historical land tenure systems. The study includes predominantly the tribal village Mallavarammamillu, a Mutta village. This village lies more in the interior than the other study villages. A few non-tribal families hold a large chunk of land in the village. Another village, Veerabhadrapuram, is a government village and a pre-independent period settlement village characterized by the presence of non-tribals over a long time. The village is situated between the border of Addateegala and Rajavommangi Mandal villages. All government villages share the same kind of land administration.

The other village Nellipudi, a Mukhasa village headed by a non-tribal Mukhasadar, prior to its abolition paved the way for non-tribals and reduced tribals to a minority over a period of time. The other Mukhasa villages are entirely tribal villages. The village Indukurupeta is an Estate village, whose proprietor was a non-tribal; numerically, the non-tribals form a majority here. It has one hamlet village namely, Pothukonda. But it consists of only 3 non-tribal families and 57 tribal families. Therefore, it is excluded from the sample . There are 9 estate land tenure systems. All the estate proprietors are non-tribals. The study village is on the border of the plains area. The villages represent the increasing tribal landlessness situation.

An empirical investigation was undertaken in these four villages covering all the Scheduled Tribe households of the villages to analyse the implementation of the land transfer regulations intended for the restoration of the tribal land from the non-tribals. The present and past land records of the study villages were collected to analyse the change in land ownership.

The historical understanding of the land alienation process in Andhra Pradesh reveals specific patterns emerging in the process of land alienation.

Non-tribals and the State in Scheduled Areas

Land is the key resource that the tribal communities depend on for their survival. Land of the tribal communities in this region has been taken away by the non-tribals who have penetrated the region for economic gains. The penetration of non-tribals was aimed at gaining access to forest economy and land. The non-tribals started penetrating the forest and hill areas to exploit the economic resources, thereby undermining the traditional economy and society of the tribals.[69] This penetration of the non-tribals into the tribal areas was engineered by the British to serve their own colonial interest. Otherwise, there was no reason as to why a mass of non-tribal people, should suddenly begin encroaching upon tribal land, something they had not done in the past. The newly imposed British land system was radically different from that prevalent among many tribal groups.[70]

The colonial period witnessed a progressive and aggressive monetization of the economy of the tribal region for revenue generation, making dependence on the forest ever more precarious and thus destroying tribal self-reliance. Moreover, as the forests were taken over by government agencies and commercial interests, the tribals were forced more and more to live by farming the land, where they were progressively pushed into bonded labour by exploitative landlords, moneylenders, government officials and other outsiders. The creation of private property rights over land was an equally disastrous break with tribal tradition in which land was always held by the community even when it was assigned to private use.[71]

The first phase of migration of non-tribal peasants from the plains occurred around 1820 when a number of zamindaris, either whole or in part, came into the auction market and the highest bidder got the rights of ownership. This auction process was initiated to raise revenue. But it paved the way for the non-tribals to infiltrate tribal areas. The administration made further steady inroads into the control of the productive resources of the tribals by passing forest laws in 1882 and *abkari* (excise) laws in 1864. These laws were meant to regulate the forest usage and consumption of toddy or alcohol.[72]

However, the commercial penetration did not wait for the road building in the 1880s. Even before the Rampa Rebellion of 1879–80 took place in the Agency Area of East Godavari District, traders and moneylenders were pushing into the hills and beginning to undermine the traditional economy. Malas, a caste of untouchables, who in the lowland areas were among the most despised of Hindus, were quick to see the economic opportunities created by the more stable conditions of the 1850s and 1860s, and by the gradual extension of British control after 1848. Operating at first as petty traders and spending months on trading expeditions into the hills, they acquired the capital and expertise to develop into flourishing traders. They extended their activities to moneylending to cultivators and Muttadars (hereditary local chiefs), and took over the hill villages as their own settlements. In the Malas' wake came the Komatis, the affluent and powerful trading caste that dominated commerce, especially the grain trade, in the plains. Unlike the Malas, the Komatis rarely lived in the hills, nor did they take trouble with petty trade. They sought the larger profits to be made from timber, opium and drink or from the mortgaging of Muttadars' estates in the Agency Areas of Madras Presidency.[73] Moreover, the Godavari river facilitated the movement of the non-tribals from the widely populated plain areas of East and West Godavari to the sparsely populated tribal areas, by country craft, mechanized boats and launches.[74]

As the Godavari river facilitated transport, towards the end of the nineteenth century the British began leasing out the rights to extract bamboo timber from the forests on both sides of the river to the non-tribal merchants of Rajahmundry. Since then, the Reddis of the riverside have been in contact with the plains people. When the motor boats were introduced in the second decade of 20th century, a larger number of merchants and their agents moved into these settlements.[75]

With the attainment of Independence, the zamindaris were abolished by the Estates Abolition Act XXV of 1948. Following this in the 1950s, land in the Agency Areas came into the open market in the form of thousands of acres. The non-tribals owning land in vast stretches, began to sell it in anticipation of the forthcoming land ceiling legislation. The stream of migration of the Kammas in the 1950s was of a different kind from the earlier migration stream of other peasant castes before Independence. While the latter was for subsistence, the former was for development.

As an illustration of Kamma colonization in the 1950s, we may see the process in Kanakapalli, a village located in the heart of the tribal area in the Buttayagudam block of Polavaram taluk. It is seen that the Koyas own and cultivate only 17.4 per cent of the cultivable area of 2,910 acres, the rest being owned and cultivated by the non-tribals. The Kamma migrants form the single largest group owning nearly 40 per cent of the total cultivable land. The village was first settled in 1899 for revenue. The Koyas and the Koya Nayaks owned most of the land at the time of settlement. In 1920, a rich zamindar from the delta area of West Godavari bought about 1,000 acres of semi-forest land of Kanakapalli in order to graze his large herd of cattle. Every year, a team of cowherds drove the herd over a distance of forty miles during July–November when every inch of land in the delta area was covered with paddy. The herd came back after the harvest when dry fodder became available.

The entry of commercial crop, tobacco replacing the traditional crops in the tribal areas witnessed a change in the tribal regions. The tobacco rush resulted in both extension of commercialized agriculture by the farmers who had already migrated, and also a fresh wave of migration of non-tribal farmers either as transients (for the tobacco season) or as domiciles. However, for the tribals, it meant further loss of land and control in the face of the exploitation of the vast benefits from commercialized agriculture. Although the non-tribal farmers were 'tenants' from the point of view of their tenurial position, they were the real exploiters in terms of production relations, reaping vast profits and the tribals, who were the landowners, became the exploited.[76] The penetration of the non-tribals into the tribal areas with their capital and other instruments of exploitation including exchange of goods or giving money for exchange of goods not only destabilized the tribals mode of life but it also affected their communal way of living.[77]

Besides acquisition of land, the huge influx of outsiders facilitated by the opening up of tribal areas, intensified the demand for land for diverse purposes – housing, infrastructure, business and social utilities which led to the dispossession of the tribals from their land through numerous processes of alienation. There is little doubt that tribal people are being consistently pushed off their own land in most parts of India. A practical way to get an idea of this is to travel by road through a long stretch of tribal country, such as from Bhadrachalam in the Khammam District of Andhra Pradesh to Raipur in Chhattisgarh, a distance of about 550 km and almost entirely a Fifth Schedule region, where tribal land may not be sold or passed on to the non-tribal people. Yet, it is easily noticeable that most of the shops and land along the roadside are owned or occupied by non-tribal people, blatant encroachers upon tribal land, but this is overlooked by a largely non-tribal government that accepts tribal people's displacement as a condition for development.[78]

The processes of globalization have increased manifold the pressure on land in the tribal areas. Earlier, the pace of penetration was limited by the availability of resources and within the framework of development pattern of the State. With economic liberalization, efforts are being made to attract direct foreign private investment; therefore, the pace has grown faster and the ambit of industrial and mining expansion has become more extensive.

Political Contestation over Tribal Land Rights

Political discourse on tribal land rights and land struggles is in a complex circumstance covering land administration, or the employment of laws affecting tribal interests, and mobilization of tribal communities in struggles by political parties as well as non-governmental agencies.

The political role of the Tribal Advisory Council too can be viewed based on the decisions taken by it. The analysis of this aspect would show that several decisions taken by the Tribal Advisory Council are at the instance of political pressures from both ruling and non-ruling political parties, in order to maintain their non-tribals vote bank in the Fifth Scheduled Areas of the State.

The role of the Tribal Advisory Council is crucial in the governance of Scheduled Areas and ensuring land justice to the tribals. The Tribal Advisory Council (TAC), a constitutional body under the Fifth Schedule of the Constitution, was created to advise the government in respect of matters pertaining to the advancement of the Scheduled Tribes. The Tribal Advisory Council consists of nominated tribal members of the Legislative Assembly and officials from the Tribal Welfare Department of the State.

It is noticed that some non-tribals are taking tribal women as kept mistresses to grab land in their name. In this context the Tribal Advisory Council passed a resolution stating that it 'resolved to request the Government (i) not to recognize the second marriage of a non-tribal with a tribal lady and to see that the land of tribals are not enjoyed by the non-tribals through such a marriage'.[79] However, this resolution has remained unimplemented.

It was further resolved that the Andhra Pradesh Scheduled Areas Land Transfer Regulation, 1959, should be amended to declare the land purchased in the name of tribal women, married or kept as concubine by non-tribal men, as null and void. There is a similar provision in the Orissa Scheduled Areas Transfer of Immovable Property (by Scheduled Tribes) Regulations, 1956.[80] But no amendment is made to the existing Land Transfer Regulations 1 of 70 laws to give effect to the recommendation of the Tribal Advisory Council.

The developed tribals from plain areas are infiltrating to Scheduled Areas and exploiting the land belonging to forest dwelling Scheduled Tribes as there is no prohibition of land transfer among the Scheduled Tribes. In the light of internal tribal land conflicts, the Tribal Advisory Council accepted the proposal to provide identity cards to the local tribals as there are a large number of cases of immigration of non-locals into Andhra Pradesh, to corner the benefits extended to the local Scheduled Tribes. This decision was made on the proposal of the Commissioner, Tribal Welfare, for banning alienation of land of Chenchus through an ordinance, in view of their backwardness and presence of a large number of young widows in Chenchu Project area, as their spouses have probably died due to Tuberculosis or Cirrhosis.[81] In fact, no such mechanism is put in place to check the infiltration of non-locals.

The successful tribal parties in land cases are unable to access the land due to delay in execution of the orders issued in their favour by the Special Deputy Collector Court. Although instructions were given by the Government to the authorities for the effective implementation of court orders through a circular No. 15857/79-C, 2 Revenue, Andhra Pradesh Hyderabad, followed by a subsequent circular Rc. No. JI/4206/79, dated 17 October 1979.[82] However, these circulars were never implemented. The data in other chapters establishes the same.

The term 'transfer' under Land Transfer Regulations which prohibits tribal land alienation, does not include testamentary disposition which means disposal of property through execution of a 'will'. This gives scope for further tribal land alienation. In this backdrop, the Tribal Advisory Council unanimously resolved to remove the term tesmentary disposition of property by bringing in an amendment to the provision of Section 2 clause (g) with the word 'transfer' under Land Transfer Regulations.[83] However, this decision has not been translated into action.

The Tribal Advisory Council resolved to approve amendment to the Regulations with retrospective effect, stating that as 'in view of the legal complication in implementing the Land Transfer Regulation in Scheduled Areas of Andhra Pradesh, it is desirable that the Andhra Pradesh Land Transfer Regulation 1959 which extended to Scheduled Areas of Telangana from 1 December 1963, may be amended so as to give retrospective effect from 31st October 1949', the date on which the Notified Tribal Areas Regulation came into force.[84] But except for issuing a statement, no efforts were made to bring the legislation into effect from the specified date of 31st October 1949. No amendment to the law was made giving a retrospective effect to the law.

Regarding rehabilitation of podu cultivators, members of the Tribal Advisory Council requested the concerned Ministry of Forests, Government of India for early clearance of the de-reservation of an adequate extension of forest land for rehabilitating the Podu cultivators.[85] No such steps were taken to de-reserve the land. Instead, tribals were evicted from the podu land in the Scheduled Areas of Visakhapatnam District as per the Rehabilitation and Resettlement Action Plan (2002) of the Government of Andhra Pradesh.

As part of discussions on implementation of Land Transfer Regulations, all the members of the Tribal Advisory Council unanimously approved the proposal in the year 1988 and recommended the government to amend all the regulations and other laws in the Scheduled Areas to restrict the power of stay of the Courts including the High Court, and to specifically declare that no stay should be granted against the tribals without hearing both the parties.[86] In fact, non-tribals continue obtaining land possession with the support of stay orders obtained from the High Court, stalling the implementation of the eviction order issued against them.

An attempt to water down the Land Transfer Regulations of 1970 was made in 1988. The government came to a firm decision to amend the regulation so as to permit the non-tribals to transfer their land in the Scheduled Areas to other non-tribals by sale. The then Chief Minister directed the Tribal Welfare Minister to steer the meeting of the Tribal Advisory Council and get its endorsement for the amendment. Between December 1987 and March 1988, the Tribal Advisory Council convened four times for this purpose (usually it meets once in a year). In order to secure the ratification of the Tribal Advisory Council, which is mandatory under the Fifth Schedule of the Constitution to proceed further in tribal affairs, the government brought in a strong pressure on the Council in the form of a consensus resolution passed by the floor leaders of all political parties convened by the Chief Minister on 9 April 1988.[87]

Subsequently, the Tribal Advisory Council was convened on 10 May 2000, to endorse the proposal to lease the land in the Scheduled Area for mining, but its concurrence could not be obtained. The Chief Minister then summoned the Minister for Tribal Welfare and some other members of the Council, and persuaded them on the benefits of leasing the land in the Scheduled Areas to a Dubai-based corporation, which would lead to the setting up of an aluminium factory. Then a second meeting of the Tribal Advisory Council was convened on 24 May 2000, where majority of the members were finally bamboozled into toeing the government directive. Somehow, the government decision was impeded by representations to the Governor and threats of legal action by human rights organizations, pro-tribal non government organizations and tribal groups.[88]

The giving over of Possession Certificates to non-tribals has been an issue before the Tribal Advisory Council. The Tribal Advisory Council decided on 12 July 1999 on the resolution already passed on 9 May 1998, approving non-tribals to construct houses in the Scheduled Areas.[89] This paved the way for issuing of a government order. The orders issued by the government vide G.O.MS. No. 2 S.W. (LTR) Department dated 1 July 2000, approving the Andhra Pradesh State Housing Corporation Ltd. as a financial institution, for the purpose of advancing loans to eligible non-tribals in Scheduled Areas on mortgage of superstructure as security towards loans.[90] However, this decision was challenged by a tribal, Tellam Venkata Rao and others before the High Court of Andhra Pradesh as it is against the provisions of LTR 1 of 70 in WP No. 3373/2000. The High Court struck down the contentious substance of the G.O. Ms. No. 2. However, the unsuccessful non-tribals filed SLP No. 28,423 of 2011 in the Supreme Court of India, which was dismissed.

A majority of the members, 10 of the 12 members of the Tribal Advisory Council supported the amendment to Land Transfer Regulation 1 of 70, enabling the State Government to acquire or grant any interest in the land including subsoil rights for Reconnaissance permit or Prospecting License or Mining Lease for major minerals, to any person or organization, whether or not under the control of State or Central Government suggested by the Advocate General of India.[91] However, the government could not bring the amendment due to strong opposition from the tribal groups.

Thus, the role of the Tribal Advisory Council is in tune with the State ruling class and the government. Although, some positive action has been taken by the Tribal Advisory Council for the economic empowerment of the tribals, it has never paid sufficient interest in the implementation of its decisions.

Tribal Land Dispossession in Andhra Pradesh

The cause of land dispossession is multifold. The tribal areas being rich in natural resources have attracted considerable investment in mines, industries, hydropower and irrigation projects, which has led to both direct and indirect eviction of the tribal communities.[92]

The decline in the percentage of cultivators among the Scheduled Tribes households from 45 per cent to 35.4 per cent during the period 1994–2005 indicates the loss of land resources and their increasing dependency on agricultural labour which increased from 37 per cent to 43.7 per cent during the period 1994–2005. It is to be noted that the percentage of population depending on agricultural labour increased only in the case of Scheduled Tribes, while it has declined for the Scheduled Caste.[93]

The problem of tribal land alienation has gained significance in the context of tribal economy because the forces of marginalization are very strong. With the depletion of forest resources, diversion of water resources to the plains and scarce land resources, the tribals are being alienated from their very sources of survival. Even the existing landholding of the marginalized have been alienated, in spite of score of laws in force for maintaining the land rights of the marginalized, especially the Adivasis.[94]

It is generally observed that the tribal areas are rich, whereas the tribals live in poor condition. Had history been more favourable, nearly 5 lakh tribal families living in the Scheduled villages of the state of Andhra Pradesh would have presently together been the proud owners of 18,48,209.30 acres of land with an average household landholding of 3.69 acres. But presently, more than 48 per cent of this land is cultivated by the non-tribals. In some Districts as Warangal, Khammam and Adilabad, more than 50 per cent of the land in the Scheduled villages is held by the non-tribals. It is an established fact that the pernicious poverty of the tribals has led them to become victims of schemes of non-tribal moneylenders, thus resulting in indebtedness and consequent alienation of land. To check the land alienation, several Land Transfer Regulations including 1 of 59 as amended by 1 of 70, were created prohibiting the transfer of land between tribals and non-tribals, and among the non-tribals since 1917. In spite of these restrictions on the transfer of land assets, land alienation is still prevalent[95] amongst the Adivasis.

The non-tribal population which constitutes 57.2 per cent in the Scheduled Areas of Andhra Pradesh, demonstrates the inexorable influx of non-tribals since the pre-independence era. The gravity of the tribal land alienation issues may be gauged from the fact that today, non-tribals own more than half of the land in Andhra Pradesh. The cultivable holdings of non-tribals are 52 per cent in Khammam, 60 per cent in Adilabad and 71 per cent in

Warangal Districts, despite the protective Land Transfer Regulations 1 of 70 that have been in force. These are official figures based on land records, and do not include other transactions as *benami* (fictitious) holdings.

Table 1.3

Extent of Land Under the Occupation of Non-Tribals in Scheduled Areas

S. No.	*Name of the District*	*Total Land in Scheduled Area in Acres*	*Land Under the Occupation of Non-tribals in Acres*	*Percentage*
1.	Srikakulam	14,949.17	359.20	2.20
2.	Vizianagaram	42,333.00	91.00	0.21
3.	Visakhapatnam	2,88,107.00	NA	NA
4.	East Godavari	1,73,417.49	33,739.89	19.46
5.	West Godavari	75,702.42	27,979.16	36.96
6.	Khammam	7,71,604.93	4,07,368.33	52.79
7.	Warangal	1,42,533.00	1,02,104.50	71.64
8.	Adilabad	2,97,170.95	1,80,349.40	60.69
9.	Mahaboobnagar	42,391.60	1,444.18	3.41
	Total	18,48,209.56	7,53,435.66	48.29 (excluding Visakhapatnam)

Source: Report of Tribal Welfare Department, Government of Andhra Pradesh, 1995.

What is more significant is the fact that tribals have lost possession over the most productive land, leaving them to cultivate poor quality land. Revenue records show that in West Godavari District, tribals have just 13,358 hectares of land while non-tribals own 28,567 hectares of land. In Jelugumilli Mandal of West Godavari District, which has been a major conflict site, non-tribals are reported to be controlling as much as 71 per cent of the land. In Khammam, non-tribals are stated to own as much as 29,000 hectares of land.[96]

A survey conducted by the Human Rights Centre of Resource for Legal Action, on land leased out by the tribals to outsiders, in the tribal Mandal of Rampachodavaram in East Godavari District, provides information on unrecorded land alienation. A survey in 93 villages indicated that 355 tribal parties gave away the land of

1,797.50 acres on lease to the non-tribals to tide over economic crisis in their families.

In 1917, soon after a two-year long hit-and-run tribal insurgency in the Godavari Agency, the British enacted the first Agency Tract Interest and Land Transfer Act, to prohibit land transfers between hill tribes and non-tribals without prior permission from the District Collector. Subsequently, several tribal protective Land Transfer Regulations 1 of 59, as amended by 1 of 70, were made. Despite these enactments which have been long in force, 56 per cent of the cultivable land in the Scheduled Areas (about 8.7 lakh acres) is owned by the non-tribals, while the extent of land restored to tribals under these enactments is only 9 per cent of this area (about 80,000 acres). And, if anybody can ever manage to estimate the extent of agricultural land that is supposedly owned by tribals, but in reality is being held and cultivated by the non-tribals, then these statistics would reveal an even more unequal state of affairs.[97] The Land Transfer Regulations 1 of 70 clearly states that the land in the Fifth Scheduled Areas of Andhra Pradesh once belonged to the tribals. In this connection, it is important to see the extent of alienated land that was restored to tribals and the effective enforcement of law.

Notwithstanding the protective regulations which adorned the statute book for several decades, land in the Scheduled Areas has continued to pass into the hands of the non-tribal exploiters. The greater part of land alienation occurred after the 1940s. The glaring fact that strikes one is that according to the official records, 55 per cent of cultivable area in the Scheduled Areas of Andhra Pradesh is now in the hands of the non-tribals.[98] There are several loopholes in the existing Land Transfer Regulations 1 of 70 applicable to Scheduled Areas of Andhra Pradesh. For instance, the law does not act retrospectively and thus cannot be applied to land transfer deals put in place between the tribals and the non-tribals prior to the enforcement of the Act. Therefore, the exploitive relations in Agency Areas still dominate the social structure, and the socio–economic formation of the tribal systems cannot be modified without disturbing the unequal land ownership. Hence, the problem of land alienation becomes part of the bigger problem of the existence of unequal class relations between the tribals and the non-tribals in the present-day society.[99]

There were restrictions on the tribals on tapping toddy from any palm tree, and on the migration of distillery castes who had bought the licence to tap, distill and sell liquor. The distillers easily had the tribals indebted to them, as the latter loved toddy and developed a taste for other kinds, including taking of land in lieu of their petty debts. This was similar to the practice of the merchants and moneylenders, who had acquired tribal land. Therefore, the tribals only lost more of their land to the non-tribals in this process.[100]

Yet another form of land alienation takes place when the States promote development projects such as hydroelectric power stations, mining and industries. These developmental activities do not confer any benefit on the tribals directly and render them landless.[101] The construction of irrigation dams and industrialization are the major reasons for massive and irreversible deforestation and subsequent land loss of the tribal communities. In the last sixty years, in the new era of development, tribal communities have been displaced on a large scale. Displacement has taken place as an offshoot of the economic development by the State itself and, in particular, its industrialization and irrigation policy.[102]

Added to resource displacement, is project displacement where development projects have threatened the livelihood needs of the tribal communities. For instance, there are 18 major dams in Andhra Pradesh and six of the large ones alone have been responsible in displacing about half a million people. The proposed Indira Sagar Project (Polavaram) threatens involuntary displacement of 2.37 lakh people from 276 villages in the Scheduled Areas of Andhra Pradesh, 55 per cent of them being tribals. The proposed Polavaram project will result in the submergence of 94,357 acres of land situated in the Scheduled Areas, of which 29,852 acres are *poramboke* (belongs to the government). In addition to this, the Polavaram Project will submerge 3,223 hectares of forest resources.[103]

The Revenue Divisional Officer, Ch Narsinga Rao of Rampachodavaram Revenue Division in East Godavari District (against whom there are numerous reports of corrupt practices appearing in local editions of prominent Telugu newspapers) incidentally,

> purchased total land of 572.91 acres situated in the Scheduled Areas of Addateegala, Gangavaram, Devipatnam Mandal in the East Godavari District from non-tribals in the name of Polavaram project rehabilitation through 49 land transactions and paying

more than ₹ 2 crore in violation of the present laws, particularly the tribal protective Land Transfer Regulation 1 of 70 and the Panchayat Extension to the Schedule Areas (PESA) Act 40/1996 and Act 7/1998. The acquisition of land from non-tribals without even verifying physical possession of land or proper enquiry under tribal protective Land Transfer Regulations has caused hardship to tribal communities in Agency Areas of the East Godavari District.[104]

The 1997 case of Samatha, a non-governmental organization, against the State of Andhra Pradesh in relation to permitting a private company for mining in the Scheduled Areas of Andhra Pradesh, is a classic example of the State violating its own Constitutional duty in the Fifth Schedule Areas. In an effort to promote economic development through industrialization, the state has been allotting tribal land to private industries and developmental projects as mining, hydroelectric projects, industries and tourism. Thus, the intervention of the State and individual non-tribals are responsible for causation of tribal land alienation problem in the Scheduled Areas.

Notes

1. Bengwayan, Michael A. (2003) *Intellectual and Cultural Property Rights of Indigenous and Tribal Peoples in Asia,* Minority Rights Group International, London.
2. Government of India (1960–61) *Report of the Scheduled Areas of Scheduled Tribes Commission,* Vol. I, Govt. of India Press, Rastrapati Bhavan, New Delhi, p. 1.
3. Omvedt, Gail (2005) 'Capitalism and Globalisation, Dalits and Adivasis', *Economic and Political Weekly,* Vol. 40, No. 47, November 19.
4. Bhowmik, K.L. (2004) *Tribal India: A Profile in Indian Ethnology* cited in Supreme Court Case 2004 (3 SCC 429; 2004 SCC CRI 818).
5. Mohapatro, Prafullo Chandro (1987) *Dynamics of Tribal and Non-Tribal Interactions in Economic Development of Tribal India,* Ashish Publishing House, New Delhi.
6. Roy Burman, J.J. (2009) 'Adivasi: A Contentious Term to Denote Tribes as Indigenous Peoples of India', *Mainstream,* Vol. XLVII, No. 32, July 25.
7. Upadhyay, S. and Upadhyay, V. (2002) *Handbook on Environmental Law, Volume I: Forest Laws, Wildlife Laws and the Environment,* LexisNexis Butterworths, New Delhi.

8. Baviskar, A. (2006) 'The Politics of Being "Indigenous"', in Bengt G. Karlsson and Tanka B. Subba (eds), *Indigeneity in India*, Kegan Paul, London.
9. ILO (1994) *Indigenous and Tribal Peoples and the ILO*, Geneva.
10. Hooja, Meenakshi (2004) *Policies and Strategies for Tribal Development: Focus on the Central Tribal Belt*, Rawat Publications, Jaipur.
11. Bijoy, C.R. and Raman, K.R. (2003) 'The Real Story: Adivasi Movements to Recover Land', *Economic and Political Weekly*, Vol. 38, Issue No. 20, May 17–23.
12. Ray, N. (1972) 'Introductory Address', in K.S. Singh (ed.), *Tribal Situation in India*, IIAS, Shimla.
13. Andhra Law Times (1979)(1)(HC).
14. Deogaonkar, S.G. (1994) *Tribal Administration and Development*, Concept Publishing Company, New Delhi.
15. All India Reporter (AIR) March 1985, Supreme Court (SC) AIR Publication, Nagpur, pp. 389–404.
16. Deogaonkar, S.G. (1994) *Tribal Administration and Development*, Concept Publishing Company, New Delhi.
17. Areas of Srikakulam,Vijayanagaram,Visakhpatnam, East and West Godavari, Kammam, Warangal and Adilabad Districts notified by the President of India under Fifth Schedule to the Constitution of India.
18. See Manohar, K. Murali (ed.) (1985) *Political Economy of Tribal Development*, Indian Institute of Public Administration, Warangal, pp. 63–94 and Rao, B. Janardhana (1987) *Land Alienation in Tribal Areas*, Kakatiya School of Public Administration of India, Warangal.
19. Meszaros, Istvan (2006) *Marx's Theory of Alienation*, Aakar Books, New Delhi.
20. Sharma, T.R. (1979) 'Karl Marx: From Alienation to Exploitation', *Indian Journal of Political Science*, Vol. 40, No. 3, September.
21. Colletti, Lucio (1975) *Early Writings: Karl Marx*, Penguin Books, London, p. 20.
22. Deva, Satya (1981) 'Alienation and Administration in Developing Countries', *Mainstream*, July quoted in Rupavath, Ramdas (2009) *Tribal Land Alienation and Political Movements: Socio-Economic Patters from South India*, Cambridge Scholars, UK, pp. 126–27.
23. Beteille, Andre (1974) *Studies in Agrarian Social Structure*, Oxford University Press, Oxford.
24. Viegas, Philip (1991) *Encroached and Enslaved*, Indian Social Institute, Delhi, p. 32.
25. For details see, Patnaik, S.C. and Patel, S. (1982) 'Impact of Modernisation on Tribals: Economic Dualism and Path of Change (A Case Study of Malkangiri Sub-division in Koraput District)', paper

presented at the Seminar on 'Prospectus of Economic Development of Tribals of Koraput District' held in October (Miemo), pp. 2–14.

26. Satyanarayana, K. (1975) *A Study of History and Culture of the Andhras*, People's Publishing House, New Delhi, p. 44.
27. Manohar, K. Murali and Rao, B. Janardhan (1985) 'Land Alienation in Tribal Areas', in Murali Manohar, P. Ramaiah and C. Sivakrishna Rao (eds), *Political Economy of Tribal India*, IIPA, Warangal, pp. 63–94.
28. See pioneering study of Vidyarthi, L.P. (1963) *The Maler: The Nature-Man-Spirit Complex in Hill Tribe of Bihar*, introducing the concept of 'nature-man-spirit' in anthropology and Bharath M. Bhushan and P.V. Satyamohan (1990) study of the tribal scenario in Andhra Pradesh *The Koyas: A Study of Nature Man-Spirit-Complex among the Koyas of Bhadrachalam* (mimeograph), explaining the inseparable link of land with tribal life. The ethnographic film *In Search of Ethnic Dimension: The Koyas* made for the UGC deals with the nature-man interaction and the associated belief system. It examines the features of the environment in relation to the Koya economic system. Also see http://video.google.com/videoplay?docid=1204160986501454199&hl=en#
29. Roy-Burman, B.K. (1986) *Communal Land System of the Tribals and Problems of Institutional Finance in Manipur and Tripura*, Council for Social Development, Delhi.
30. Mohan Lal, Morley (1988) *Poverty Alleviation: The Indian Experience*, Himalaya Publishing House, Delhi, p. 386.
31. Xaxa, Virginius (1999) 'Tribes as Indigenous People of India', *Economic and Political Weekly*, Vol. XXXIV, No. 51, December 18, pp. 3589–95.
32. Nathan, D. and Kekar, G. (2004) 'Civilizational Change: Markets and Privatization among Indigenous Peoples', in D. Nathan, G. Kekar and P. Walter (eds), *Globalization and Indigenous Peoples in Asia: Changing the Local-Global Interface*, Sage Publications, Delhi.
33. Nath, N. and Behera, D.K. (2006) 'The So-called Development, Displacement and Dispossession: An Analysis on Land and Forest Rights of the Project Affected People', in R.M. Sarkar (ed.), *Land and Forest Rights of the Tribals Today*, Serials Publications, Delhi.
34. Desai, M., Rudolph, S.M. and Rudra, Ashok (eds) (1984) *Agrarian Power and Agricultural Productivity in South Asia*, Oxford University Press, Delhi.
35. UNDP, Human Development Report (2004) *Cultural Liberty in Today's Diverse World*, Oxford University Press, New York.
36. Pinto, Ambrose (1988) 'Fillip to Land Transfers Land Acquisition Bill', *Economic and Political Weekly*, Vol. 33, Issue No. 49, December 5.
37. Sastry, V.N.V.K. (1989) *Between Gonds Rebellion*, Udyama Publications, Hyderabad.

38. Bhushan, Bharath M. (2011) *Land Rights of Women in Andhra Pradesh: A Status Paper* (mimeograph), Rural Development Institute, Hyderabad.
39. Ranga Rao, Koneru (2006) *The Land Committee Report 2006*, GoAP, Hyderabad, p. 57.
40. Dhanagare, D.M. (1988) 'Subaltern Consciousness and Populism: Two Approaches in the Study of Social Movements in India', *Social Scientist*, Vol. 16, No. 11, November, p. 20.
41. Ambagudia, Jagannath (2010) 'Tribal Rights, Dispossession and the State in Orissa', *Economic and Political Weekly*, Vol. 45, No. 33, August 14.
42. Trivedi, H. (1993) *Tribal Land Systems: Land Reform Measures and Development of Tribals*, Concept Publications, New Delhi.
43. Bijoy, C.R. (2000) 'Adivasi Rights and Struggles of Autonomy: A Review of the Indian Experience', in K. Krishnan (ed.), *Adivasi Groups in 2000* (mimeo).
44. Shah, G. (1990) *Social Movements in India: A Review of Literature*, Sage Publications, New Delhi.
45. Report of Commissioner for SC and ST, Fifth Report (1982–83), Ministry of Tribal Affairs, GoI, Delhi.
46. Bijoy, C.R. and Raman, K. Ravi (2003) 'Muthanga: The Real Story', *Economic and Political Weekly*, Vol. XXIV, No. 20, May 17, pp. 1975–80.
47. Karuppaiyan, E. (2000) 'Alienation of Tribal Land in Tamil Nadu', *Economic and Political Weekly*, September 9, pp. 3333–34; see also e.g., Singh, Nandita (1997) 'Emerging Problems of Ownership and Exploitation of Communal Land in Tribal Society', *Man in India*, Vol. 77, pp. 233–34; Gupta, Smita (1991) 'Tribal Land Alienation in Kanke Anchal', *The Administrator*, Vol. 36, No. 2, p. 873.
48. Reddy, T. Prabhakar (1989) 'Tribal Land Alienation in Andhra Pradesh', *Economic and Political Weekly*, Vol. 24, No. 28, p. 1573; Karuppaiyan, E. (2000) 'Alienation of Tribal Land in Tamil Nadu', *Economic and Political Weekly*, September 9, p. 3350.
49. Saxena, K.B. (1991) 'Tribal Land Alienation and Need for Policy Intervention', *The Administrator*, Vol. 34, pp. 89–98; Mohanty, P.K. (2000) 'Development of Scheduled Castes and Scheduled Tribes in Independent India: Leads and Lags', *Journal of Rural Development*, Vol. 19, No. 4, p. 551.
50. Vyas, N.N. (1975) 'Tribal Land Alienation: Recent Changes and New Dimensions', *Tribe*, Vol. 9, No. 3, p. 8; Roy Burman, B.K. (1982) 'Transfer and Alienation of Tribal Land', in B. Chaudhury (ed.), *Tribal Development in India*, Inter-India Publications, New Delhi, p. 77.

51. Sharan, Ramesh (2005) 'Alienation and Restoration of Tribal Land in Jharkhand: Current Issues and Possible Strategies', *Economic and Political Weekly*, Vol. 40, No. 41, October 8.
52. Sundaram, K. and Tendulkar, Suresh (2003) 'Poverty among Social and Economic Groups in India in 1990s', *Economic and Political Weekly*, Vol. 38, No. 50, December 13.
53. Report of the Steering Committee on Empowering the Scheduled Tribes, Planning Commission (2001) Report 91, New Delhi.
54. Radhakrishna, R. and Ray, Shovan (2006) *Handbook of Poverty in India: Perspectives, Policies, and Programmes*, Oxford University Press, New Delhi.
55. Rao, M.S.A. (1983) 'Non-tribal Colonisation and Tribal Deprivation in Andhra', *Social Action*, Vol. 33, July-September, ISI, New Delhi.
56. Rao, B. Janardhan (1987) *Land Alienation in Tribal Areas of Andhra Pradesh*, Kakatiya University, Warangal.
57. Singh, N. (1997) 'Emerging Problems of Ownership and Exploitation of Communal Land in Tribal Society', *Man in India*, Vol. 77.
58. Kulkarni, Sharad (1985) 'Maharashtra: Adivasi, Law and Social Justice', *Economic and Political Weekly*, Vol. 20, No. 28, pp. 1171–74.
59. Brennan, F. (1995) 'Parliamentary Responses to the Mabo Decision', in M.A. Stephenson (ed.), *Mabo: The Native Title Legislation: A Legislative Response to the High Court Decision*, Queensland University Press, St Lucia, pp. 1–25.
60. Ramanathan, U. (1999) 'Public Purpose: Points for Discussion', in W. Fernandes (ed.), *The Land Acquisition (Amendment) Bill 1998*, Indian Social Institute, New Delhi, pp. 19–24.
61. Planning Commission Report (2006) Government of India, New Delhi.
62. Mahipal (2000) 'Panchayats in Fifth Scheduled Areas', *Economic and Political Weekly*, May 6.
63. Ramanathan, U. (2002) 'Common Land and Common Property Resources in Land Reforms in India', in Praveen K. Jha (ed.) *Issues of Enquiry in Rural Madhya Pradesh*, Vol. 7, Sage Publications, New Delhi, p. 204.
64. Manohar, K. Murali and Rao, Janardhan B. (1992) 'Tribal Agricultural Labour: An Enquiry into the Depeasantisation Process', in Buddhadev Chaudhari (ed.), *Tribal Transformation in India*, Vol. I, Inter-India Publications, New Delhi.
65. Baviskar, A. (1994) 'The Fate of the Forest: Conservation and Tribal Rights', *Economic and Political Weekly*, Vol. 29, No. 38, September 17.
66. Ashokvardhan, C. (2006) *Tribal Land Rights in India*, Centre for Rural Studies, Lal Bahadur Shastri National Academy of Administration, Mussoorie.

67. Ibid.
68. Samata Vs. State of Andhra Pradesh AIR 1997, p. 3301.
69. Arnold, David (1982) 'Rebellious Hillmen: The Gudem-Rampa Risings 1839–1924', in Ranajit Guha (ed.), *Subaltern Studies I*, Oxford University Press, Delhi.
70. Shah, G. (1990) *Social Movements in India: A Review of Literature*, Sage Publications, New Delhi.
71. Heredia, Rudolf C. (2000) 'Tribal History, Living Word or Dead Letter', *Economic and Political Weekly*, Vol. 35, No. 18, April 29.
72. *Godavari District Gazetteer* (1907) Government Press, Madras, p. 101.
73. Arnold, David (1986) 'Rebellious Hillmen: The Gudem-Rampa Risings 1839–1924', in Ranajit Guha (ed.), *Subaltern Studies III*, Oxford University Press, Delhi.
74. Ashokvardhan, C. (2006) *Tribal Land Rights in India*, Centre for Rural Studies, LBS National Academy of Administration, Mussoorie.
75. Jayaprakash Rao, P. (1985) 'The Struggle for Land: Tribal Revolts in Two Villages', in K. Murali Manohar, P. Ramaiah and C. Sivaramakrishna Rao (eds), *Political Economy of Tribal Development*, Indian Institute of Public Administration, Warangal.
76. Rao, M.S.A. (1983) 'Non-tribal Colonisation and Tribal Deprivation in Andhra', *Social Action*, Vol. 33, July-September.
77. Manohar, K. Murali (1985) 'Political Economy of Tribal Development: A Theme Paper', in K. Murali Manohar, P. Ramaiah and C. Sivaramakrishna Rao (eds), *Political Economy of Tribal Development*, Indian Institute of Public Administration, Warangal.
78. Ramnath, Madhu (2008) 'Surviving the Forest Rights Act: Between Scylla and Charybdis', *Economic and Political Weekly*, Vol. 43, No. 9, March 1.
79. Minutes of the Andhra Pradesh Tribes Advisory Council 37th Meeting held on 5 February 1977 in Hyderabad.
80. Minutes of the APTAC Meeting held on 17 November 1995 in Hyderabad.
81. Minutes of the APTAC Meeting held on 14 February 1994 at 11.00 a.m. at Telugu Samkshema Bhavanam, Andhra Pradesh, Hyderabad.
82. Review of action taken on the minutes of the meetings of the APTAC (1979–80) in Hyderabad.
83. Minutes of TAC 102nd Meeting held on 18 March 2010 in Hyderabad.
84. Minutes of APTAC 46th Meeting held on 30 April 1982 in Hyderabad.
85. Minutes of the APTAC 52nd Meeting held on 28 November 1986 in Hyderabad.
86. Minutes of the APTAC Meeting held on 23 December 1988 in Hyderabad.

87. Reddy, N. Subba (1988) 'Depriving Tribals of Land: Andhra Move to Amend Land Transfer Laws', *Economic and Political Weekly*, Vol. 23, No. 29, July 16, pp. 1458–61.
88. Reddy, N. Subba (2006) 'Development through Dismemberment of the Weak: Threat of Polavaram Project', *Economic and Political Weekly*, Vol. 41, No. 15, April 15, pp. 1430–31.
89. Minutes of the Andhra Pradesh Tribes Advisory Council Meeting held on 26 June 1999 in Hyderabad.
90. Minutes of the APTAC Meeting held on 12 April 2000 in Hyderabad.
91. Minutes of the Meeting of the TAC held on 24 May 2000 in Hyderabad.
92. Report of the Ministry of Rural Development Department of Land Resources (2000) Government of India, Delhi.
93. CESS (2007) Report on Human Development, Begampet, Hyderabad.
94. Trinadha Rao, P. (2004) *Tribal Development in Question*, Laya Publications, Visakhapatnam.
95. Report of the Tribal Welfare Department (1995) Land Reforms and Land Transfers, Government of Andhra Pradesh, Hyderabad.
96. D.V.L.N. Murthy Committee (2005) Report on Tribal Land Issues, Ministry of Rural Development, Government of Andhra Pradesh, Hyderabad.
97. Balagopal, K. (1989) 'Pitting the Tribals against the Non-tribal Poor', *Economic and Political Weekly*, Vol. 24, No. 21, May 27, p. 1151.
98. Reddy, N. Subba (1989) 'Sword of Damocles Over Tribal People of Andhra Pradesh', *Economic and Political Weekly*, Vol. 24, No. 26, July 1, pp. 1442–43.
99. Rao, B. Janardhana (1987) *Land Alienation in Tribal Areas of Andhra Pradesh*, Kakatiya University, Warangal.
100. Rao, M.S.A. (1983) 'Non-tribal Colonisation and Tribal Deprivation in Andhra', *Social Action*, Vol. 33, July-September, Indian Social Institute, New Delhi.
101. Draft National Policy on Tribals (2004) Ministry of Tribal Affairs, Government of India, New Delhi.
102. Rao, B. Janardhana (2000) *Adivasis in India: Characterization of Transition and Development*, Adhyayana Publications, Warangal.
103. Trinadha Rao, P. (2006) 'Nature of Opposition to the Polavaram Project', *Economic and Political Weekly*, Vol, 41, No. 5, April 15, pp. 1437–39.
104. Uma Maheshwari, R. (2007) 'Polavaram Rehabilitation via Forced Consensus', *Economic and Political Weekly*, Vol. 42, No. 25, June 23.

CHAPTER 2

Land Alienation under Different Tenurial Systems

Administrative and Legal Dimensions

Land is the most important natural asset from which the tribals derive their security and social status. The nature of tribal relationship with land is distinct from the economic relationship that the non-tribal society has with land. In the context of tribal life the relationship is not merely economic in nature but occupies a spiritual and emotional space in tribal life.

The alienation and restoration of Adivasi land and land rights has been one of the most complex and sensitive issues in Andhra Pradesh, despite the tribal protective Land Transfer Regulations that have been in force. The phenomenon of land dispossession is complex and varied. Over the years, the Adivasis have witnessed continued dispossession of both individual and community control over their resources. The continued alienation has not only aggravated their poverty but has also seriously threatened their identity in their own homeland. In spite of protective legislations which have been implemented since the British period, the process of alienation of land belonging to the tribals continues unabated.

Land Tenure Systems in Andhra Pradesh

We use the terms 'land revenue systems' or 'land tenure systems' to refer to the arrangements made by the British administration to collect land revenue from the cultivators of the land. All cultivable land in British India fell under one of the three alternative systems: landlord-based systems (also known as *zamindari* or *malguzari*), individual cultivator-based systems (*raiyatwari*) and village-based systems (*mahalwari*).

The land tenure systems varied during the different historical periods as the form of institutions changed over time as Muttadari, Mukhasa, Zamindari, Ryotwari, etc. The land tenure systems also differed from region to region. The state largely depended on land revenues for administrative, military and other necessary expenditure. The land tenure systems involved much more than economics and cannot be treated in policy terms that consider only material dimensions. The land tenure systems also have anthropological, political and social dimensions that influence the non-material aspects of life in significant ways. Land tenure rules set the platform for social and political institutions.[2]

There are two important differences between the formal land tenure law and the customary land tenure law. The formal land tenure law involves the issue of land alienability or transferability of land. Most formal land tenure law systems allow for relatively unrestricted alienation of land rights, or at least do not normally distinguish between alienability within or outside a given social group. The customary land tenure law systems often prohibit the alienation of land rights to outsiders but allow alienation within the group.

The second difference is the degree to which the land possessor may exclude others. The formal land tenure systems typically emphasize the right of right-holders to exclude others, whereas customary land tenure law more, typically, emphasizes inclusivity and the right not to be excluded.[3]

The tribals are a marginalized group that requires special attention in an effort to strengthen tenure security. Those efforts have the potential to both harm and to benefit the tribals. Past titling efforts in many parts of the world have provided governments with the political cover to dispossess tribals of land they have traditionally possessed and used.[4]

The concept of private property and a governance system to back it was introduced with permanent settlement in 1793, which converted independent tribal landowners into tenants of *zamindars*. This exposed them to a multifaceted exploitation which was beyond their capacity to handle.[5] Before the alien system of landownership was introduced, commune or the common landholding, was the typical agrarian structure. The members of the community who were agnate, distributed the land among themselves according to individual needs and cultivated the allotted land on a co-operative basis. There was no system of measuring land for the sake of revenue collection, and there was no authority to which any share crop was paid as tribute, tax or revenue. In course of time, this was replaced by individual land tenure under the overlordship of feudal chiefs. During this period, there were no intermediaries between the cultivator and the ruling chief because of the limited dimension of the kingdoms and direct contact of the chief with the peasantry.[6]

Therefore, the British presence in India changed the Adivasis' relationship with the land, introducing the notions of individual property rights where there had been communal and occupancy rights and exploitation for profit, and where there had been a sustainable lifestyle. From the beginning of their presence in India, the British established links with local elites representing landholders, accountants, registrars and watchmen to consolidate their power. By doing so, they reinforced the semi-feudal agrarian system in place at the time, and imposed a system of landlord and tenant where there was none. Towards the end of the eighteenth century, settlements were established to capitalize on the land, and a revenue system that ignored the tribal tradition and customs was imposed.[7]

Land Tenure Systems in Tribal Areas

Zamindari System

It may be noted that the East India Company received the Northern circars (formerly a province of Hindustan) of southern Orissa (present Koraput, Ganjam and Phulbani Districts) in 1766 as a gift from the successor of Salahar Jang, the Nizam Ali of Hyderabad. The Nizam asked the Zamindar of southern Orissa (now Odisha) that they should regard the English Company as their sovereign in future, and to pay their rents and obedience to the said company or deputies without raising any trouble or disturbance. however, there were a number of zamindars who opposed the company government and incited resistance. much of the time and energy of the government had to be devoted to restore order. after nearly four decades of British rule, the madras permanent settlement regulation was enacted in 1802.

In the early years, the British put in place a landlord-based system in most areas to a substantial extent as relying on landlords to do all the revenue collection work spared them the effort and expense of setting up a large administrative machinery. In these areas, the revenue liability for a village or a group of villages lay with a single landlord who was free to set the revenue terms for the peasants under his jurisdiction and to dispossess any peasants who did not pay the landlord what they owed him.[11]

During the oppressive ruling, the ryots (cultivators) were compelled to pay to the government all their paddy and had to themselves subsist on coarse grains. They also suffered from constant ejectment from their holdings and frequently resorted to borrowing from moneylenders, to pay their *kistu (*payment of revenue on instalment basis), which fell due before the crop was ready.[12]

The drawbacks arising from these fluctuating and temporary arrangements came to an end with the introduction of Permanent Settlement in 1802. It provided that the existing zamindars should be considered as proprietors of their estates upon a permanent *peshkash* (a fine) per annum. Commenting on the merit of the settlement, Mr Peter Cherry, the then Collector of Ganjam District in Orissa (now Odisha), remarked, 'I consider the introduction of permanent settlement as offering the only prospect of permanent peace and well-being to the tribals of Ganjam'.[13] However, it has also been observed that the permanent settlement satisfied neither the ryots nor the zamindars and chronic disturbances broke out in Koraput as well as in Ganjam District.[14]

In 1832, the disturbances in the district and in the Parlakhemundi Zamindari of Ganjam rose to such a height that the government was compelled to appoint Mr Russel as Special Commissioner, arming him with extraordinary powers and a large military force to suppress the revolt.[15] In 1939, on his advice, the Act XXVI was passed. According to this Act, 7/8th of the district was removed from the operation of much of the ordinary law and administered directly by the Collector with special powers. Thus, the British Government deferred the operation of the permanent settlement among the hill-chiefs.

Ryotwari System

The first major shift away from landlord-based systems was in the Madras Presidency, where the administrators Captain Alexander

Read and Sir Thomas Munro began advocating for the establishment of an individual cultivator system in the late 1890s. Under this *royatwari* system, the revenue settlement would be made directly with the individual *royat* or cultivator.

With the failure of the Permanent Settlement Act of 1802–1803, the old zamindaris were parcelled into small blocks and sold for arrears. In the absence of bidders, the government took possession of them and made a survey of land and settled them. Thus, the first ryotwari settlement was carried out in 1809 and a resettlement was done in 1933. The government villages were called *izara* villages and the revenue was collected directly through the village *munsif*, who was assisted by the village accountant known as *karnam* and servants known as *talaris*. Thus, in the Polavaram taluk, different kinds of tenure villages co-existed: there were the zamindari villages, *inam* villages and land, *agraharam* villages (villages granted to Brahmins) and izara villages. The cultivators, merchants and others who had influence with the administration could move into the Agency Area and 'buy' land with permission from the administration. Rich zamindars from the delta area bought large chunks of land in the semi-forest area, in order to graze their cattle. Thus, the izara and zamindari villages received more migrants consisting of peasants and labourers from the plains.[16]

Muttadari System

Mutta means a village or group of villages held by a Muttadar. Muttadar means a person who holds a Mutta under a *sanad* granted by the government, subject to the payment of a fixed amount of land revenue to the government. The Muttadar assists the government in maintaining law and order in the *Mutta* and includes his succession in interest. This means the rights and control over the Mutta devolves through succession to his successors.

The *Muttadari* system provided an institutional structure that formally united the various hill communities. Its origins cannot be stated with any certainty. According to Furer-Haimendorf, it was introduced into Rampa by the Reddi kings of Rajahmundry during the fourteenth century. Though, as the term is Persian and Urdu, it might have been applied to an already established arrangement during the period of Muslim rule overlordship from Golconda (1571–1686).[17]

The Muttadari land tenure system continued during the British times. In deciding to restore Rampa to the *mansabdari* family, the Board of Revenue of Madras Government observed in 1848, that 'tracts such as that under consideration – wild and unproductive – and which from the character of the country and climate must be difficult of management by the officers of Government, are always best confined to the administration of their native chiefs'.[18] Thus, the difficulties of external control over the hills forced the Madras government to follow the earlier expedient of indirect control through the *Muttadari* system.

The *Muttadari* system was needed by the pre-colonial and colonial states at a time when land revenue and related taxes were a major source of income for the ruling classes. The tribals hated it both for the plunder it entailed and the oppressive practices the *Muttadars* developed using their power.[19]

A study was conducted in Adilabad, Cuddapah and East Godavari Districts of Andhra Pradesh where 430, 370 and 248 persons belonging to tribals respectively were interviewed. The survey revealed that indebtedness of tribals was mainly responsible for the existence of the Muttadari system.[20]

Recommending the abolition of the *Muttadari* system in 1951, the team of experts headed by R.S. Malayappan, Special Agency Development Officer, said that the 'The Muttadars, at least, some of them are still enforcing 'vetti' or forced labour and appropriating to themselves the best lands in every village of Mutta. So long as they exist, they will not allow the hillmen to come up'.[21]

The system is one of the main causes of land alienation. Under the *Muttadari* system, the tribes used to pay *mamool* or rent to the *muttah-heads* who in turn, paid *kattubadi* (payments made as land revenue for the land held) to the *Muttadars*, who then paid a fixed annual tribute known as *peshkash* to the British Government. The rate and type of *mamools* were arbitrarily fixed. They were out of proportion to the legitimate rise in proceeds and extension of cultivation. The attitude of the tribals towards the excessive demand by the *Muttah-head* was one of complacence and mute submission.

Under this land system, the *Muttadars* and *Mutta-heads* had no power to eject the ryots and enhance 'mamools' or rents, for neither had the rights of transferring a piece of land in the Agency Areas from the tribals to the non-tribals. But these principles were frequently violated in practice. The non-tribals who were employed in the offices of *Muttadars* and *Mutta-heads,* were given land grants for the services they rendered, and all the land belonged to the tribals. During the period, the area was sparsely populated and land was available in plenty. The dispossession of the tribals from their land did not pose any serious problems to the tribals. A dispossessed tribal could readily shift to a new area, bringing it under cultivation and cultivated it in his possession until he was again evicted by a *Muttadar* or *Mutta-head.*[22]

Mukhasa System

The definition given to *Mutta* has been extended to the *Mukhasa* system. This system was abolished in 1989 and the provisions of *Muttadari* system for survey and settlements were extended in the Fifth Scheduled Areas.

Mahals System

The Mahals system is another kind of land tenure system. The Mahaldar is head of the Mahal which is a constituent of a few notified estates. However, the Mahals system was abolished by the Government of Andhra Pradesh and the Mahals Regulations 1 of 1969 were introduced for determination of land rights of cultivators. For the purpose of these Regulations, *Mahal* refers to the Nugur, Albaka and Cherla estates and includes the area comprised in each of the villages of Subbannapeta, Dandupeta and Sarangapani, but does not include a survey number as per the definition given under Section 2(d) of the Andhra Pradesh Mahals (Abolition and Conversion into Ryotwari) Regulation 1/1969.

The Regulation 1/1969 was enacted to abolish the Mahaldari System prevailing in the Agency Areas of erstwhile Nugur Taluk in Khammam District and came into force on 26 December 1970. The Director of Survey, Settlements and Land Records was appointed U/s 4(1) to carry out Survey and Settlement operations and to introduce ryotwari settlement in the Mahal villages.

The earliest reform introduced in the Nizam's Dominions was the Prevention of Alienation of Agricultural Land Act of 1349 F (1939–40). The Act applied to the non-Diwani territories also and empowered the government to notify from time to time what was described as the agricultural class. Members of this class were required to obtain the permission of the *taluqadars* to alienate agricultural land permanently. Tenants who were in continuous possession of land for a period of six years from 1932–1942 and who had personally cultivated those stretches of land during this period were afforded protection by the Agricultural Tenancy Act. These Acts were, however, not implemented effectively and hence the benefits to be extended under the Acts did not, in fact, materialize so far as the tenants were concerned and the dichotomy between ownership and cultivation of the land became more and more pronounced. The abolition of Jagirs in 1949, under the Hyderabad (Abolition of Jagirs) Regulation was a major reform undertaken by the Government of Hyderabad. The Hyderabad Tenancy and Agricultural Land Act 1950, based on the recommendations of the Agrarian Reforms Committee of 1949 provided for improvement of the status of tenant, limitation of the size of holdings, abolition of absentee landlordism, reduction of rents and imposition of restrictions on resumption of land for personal cultivation. The records of ordinary and protected tenancy rights were prepared and certificates were issued to approved tenants.

The other measures taken by the Hyderabad Government were the passing of an amendment to the Land Revenue Act of 1317 F (1907–08) in 1952, to provide right of ownership to *Shikmidars* in Ijara Izra and Banjara villages and the stoppage of cash grants like *Rusums* and *Mansabs* for institutions like the Deshmukhs and Deshpandes. The Hyderabad Abolition of the Inams Act of 1955, provided for the abolition of *inams* and conversion of their tenure into Ryotwari. This Act was, however, not enforced properly and hence the Andhra Pradesh (Telangana Area) Abolition of Inams Act of 1967 was passed.[23]

Abolition of Intermediaries and Operational Issues during Land Surveys

The land surveys carried out at various points of time ended with a provision for land rights to non-tribals in the Scheduled Areas of Andhra Pradesh. The land reforms, more particularly the abolition of intermediaries and settlement of land rights in favour of ryots, have turned out to be beneficial for the non-tribals.

Verrier Elwin, the anthropologist, who had warned about the possible dangers of the lack of proper maintenance of land records, had observed that 'in most of the inaccessible and ex-Zamindari areas no proper records of rights had been prepared'.[24] The unclear state of land records both in the initial stages of the survey and the settlement operations undertaken in the British period during 1932–35, and in the period following the plain area regular settlement operations, exacerbated the issue of land alienation in tribal areas. It is observed by the National Commission on Backward Areas (1981) that 'a significant consequence of the unsatisfactory state of land records was that the tribals were never legally recognized as owners of the land which they had cultivated, since they could only continue to occupy the area till a superior claim to the land was initiated'.[25]

Table 2.1

Laws Applicable to Agency Areas

S. No.	*Short Title or Subject*	*Year*
1.	The Ganjam Vizagpatnam Act	1839
2.	The Scheduled Districts Act	1874
3.	The Nugur Albaka and Cherla Laws and Cesses Regulations	1909
4.	The Agency Tract Interest and Land Transfer Act	1917
5.	The Andhra Pradesh Agency Rules	1924
6.	The Government of India Act	1935
7.	The Tribal Areas Regulations 1359 F	1949
8.	The Constitution of India	1950
9.	The Andhra Pradesh Scheduled Areas Land Transfer Regulations 1 of 59	1959
10.	The Andhra Pradesh Scheduled Areas Debt Relief Regulations	1960
11.	The Andhra Pradesh Mahals (Abolition and Conversion into Ryotwari) Regulation 1 of 69	1969
12.	The Andhra Pradesh Muttas (Abolition and Conversion into Ryotwari) Regulation 2 of 69	1969
13.	The Andhra Pradesh Scheduled Area Land Transfer Rules	1969
14.	The Andhra Pradesh Scheduled Areas Money Lenders Regulations	1970
15.	The Andhra Pradesh Scheduled Areas Land Transfer Regulations 1 of 70	1970
16.	The Andhra Pradesh Scheduled Areas Ryotwari Settlement Regulations 2 of 70	1970
17.	The Andhra Pradesh Scheduled Areas Land Transfer Regulations 1 of 71	1971
18.	The Andhra Pradesh Scheduled Areas Land Transfer Regulations 1 of 78	1978
19.	Panchayats Extension to Scheduled Areas Act (PESA)	1998
20.	Scheduled Tribes and other forest dwellers forest rights Recognition Act	2006

Table 2.1 shows historical evolution of laws and made aplicable to Scheduled Areas of Andhra Pradesh. The laws have been introduced to provide special governance in Scheduled Areas and protection of tribals and their rights over land and forest resources.

The entire system of private property introduced in the tribal areas with all its European revenue logic and mode of land recording process has further legalized the exploitative 'land relations as a legitimate process'. Thus, the very nature of the land legality has ignored the claims of the tribes and this continues to be the case till date.

The earliest step in the field of land reforms was taken in the form of the Madras Estates Land Act of 1908, which was enacted to ensure that as long as the tenant paid the share cultivation he could not be evicted from tenancy. This provision was made uniformly applicable to all areas and failed to make any special considerations regarding the tribal communities. The non-tribals who migrated to tribal areas took advantage of this provision of law during the land surveys carried out in 1902, 1932–35 and got surveyed the land in their favour as there is no specific bar on non-tribals for acquisition of lands in tribal areas. In 1934, in the Survey, 351 non-tribals were given land entitlements locally called *pattas* over 98,000 acres in East Godavari District Agency Area. By this time there were no stringent laws that protected the interest of the tribals from exploitation by the non-tribal groups. Tribals claim that more manipulations were found to have taken place during the survey conducted in 1934, rather than in 1919. Manipulations as incorporation of names of non-tribals as cultivators in land records had occurred. Subsequently, non-tribals claimed land rights on the basis of such land entries in the revenue accounts. These entries became hurdles in the implementation of tribal protective land laws.

Table 2.2

Typology of Land Tenures and Villages

Type of Land Tenure	*District*	*Taluks*	*No. of Intermediaries*	*No. of Villages*	*Areas in sq km*
Mahals	Kammam	Nugur	3	90	143.11
Muttas	East Godavari	Rampachodavaram	24	174	297.97
		Yellavaram	11	228	294.35
	Visakhapatnam	Chintapalli	5	358	356.67
Estates	Vizianagaram	Parvathipuram	–	254	228.73
		Palakonda	–	4	9.07
	Visakhapatnam	Paderu	–	1,373	888.58

Cont'd...

...Cont'd

	S. Kota	–	152	100.15
	Chodavaram	–	136	97.31
	Chintapalli	–	10	12.51
	Narsipatnam	–	3	3.15
East Godavari	Devipatnam	–	19	101.63
	Yellavaram	–	2	2.62
West Godavari	Polavaram and Buttayagudem	–	29	174.08
Khammam	Bhadrachalam	–	358	795.00
	Nugur	–	112	202.00

Source: Notes-Agency Settlement Regulation-Tribal Welfare Department-Government of Andhra Pradesh (1989).

Table 2.2 presents different land tenure systems which were prevailing before its abolition in the Agency Areas of North Coastal Andhra Pradesh.

The proprietors of land tenures like *Zamindari,* Muttadari, *Mahaldari, Mukhasadar,* were the principal intermediaries between the government and the cultivating peasants. *Zamindari, Muttadari, Mahaldari* systems were abolished in 1969–1970, while the *Mukhasa* system was abolished in 1989 in coastal Andhra and thereafter, its related Survey and Settlement Regulations were brought into force.

Survey and Settlement Regulations

After abolition of intermediary land tenure systems, survey and settlement operations work was undertaken in the Agency Areas of Srikakulam, Vizianagaram, Visakhapatnam, East Godavari, West Godavari, Nugur and Bhadrachalam taluks of Khammam District of the Andhra region.

The survey and settlement operations are covered by Andhra Pradesh Regulations 1/69, 2/69 and 2/70, to settle the land occupations of both the tribals and non-tribals. Three tenures, viz. *Malguzari, Muttadari* and Estate prevailing in these areas were converted into ryotwari. The intermediaries *Mahaldar, Muttadar and Zamindar* between the government and ryots were abolished. The three regulations are as follows:

- Andhra Pradesh Mahals (Abolition and Conversion into Ryotwari) Regulation 1969 (Andhra Pradesh Regulation

1/69): This Regulation was made for abolition of Mahals in the Scheduled Areas of Nugur, Albaka and Cherla in Khammam District and conversion thereof, into ryotwari land. It came into force with effect from 26 December 1970.

- Andhra Pradesh *Muttas* (Abolition and Conversion into Ryotwari) Regulation 1969 (AP Regulation 2/69): This Regulation was made for the abolition of *Muttas* in certain Scheduled Areas as Paderu in Visakhapatnam District and Rampachodavaram in East Godavari District. It came into force with effect from 26 December 1970. The purpose of the notification was to vest all rights and interests of *Muttadar* in the government, free from all encumbrances. The regulation provided that the government shall not dispossess any person of any agricultural land if he is prima-facie entitled to a ryotwari patta pending a final decision. The non-tribal ryot has to also prove that his possession and occupation over the claim land was not void or illegal under Andhra Pradesh Scheduled Areas Land Transfer Regulation 1959 (Regulation 1/59) or any other law. The tribal ryots in occupation of ryotwari holdings for a continuous period of not less than one year would be entitled to a ryotwari patta, whereas a non-tribal ryot is not entitled to a patta unless he is in lawful possession for a continuous period of 8 years immediately before the notified date and such possession and occupation was not attracted by tribal protective Land Transfer Regulations 1 of 70. This Regulation prohibits the transfer of land between tribals and non-tribals in the Fifth Scheduled Areas of the Constitution. No ryotwari patta would be granted for land that exceeds ten per cent gradient in respect of communal land. These regulations restrict the ryots from seeking patta over the forest land. The Government of Andhra Pradesh appointed Settlement Officers to conduct survey and settlement operations in the Pamuleru *Mutta* between 1970–76 and granted settlement pattas to tribals who had been in possession and enjoyment of land prior to the notified date of the regulations.
- Andhra Pradesh Scheduled Areas Ryotwari Settlement Regulation 1970 (Andhra Pradesh Regulation 2/70): This Regulation provides for the ryotwari settlement of certain land in the Scheduled Areas in the Andhra area in respect of

which no settlement has been effected, i.e. part of Khammam, Srikakulam, Vizianagaram, Visakhapatnam, East Godavari and West Godavari Districts. It came into force with effect from 1 July 1971.

All the Estates in the Scheduled Areas were brought under these Regulations. These Regulations say that no patta shall be granted in respect of land exceeding ten per cent gradient. The Regulations state that the Settlement Officer has to conduct an enquiry into the nature of all land in respect to which a patta is claimed, to decide in respect of which land the claim shall be allowed and the person entitled to ryotwari settlement patta. These Regulations, on one hand, end the feudal system of administration of land but, on the other hand, opened the floodgates of Scheduled Areas for non-tribals to claim legal rights over tribal land.

All the Settlement Regulations referred above, in fact, dilute the letter and spirit of Land Transfer Regulations 1 of 70 by enabling non-tribals to claim patta over land situated in the Scheduled Areas. It may be mentioned here that under the Land Transfer Regulations 1 of 70, it was legally presumed that unless and until contrary proved, the land in occupation of non-tribals would be deemed to have come from the tribals through a transfer.

The Expert Group on Prevention of Alienation of Tribal Land and its Restoration, of the Ministry of Rural Development, Government of India headed by the Planning Commission Member, B. N. Yugundar has also cast a serious doubt on the settlement patta throughout Fifth Schedule Areas. Similarly, the denial of pattas to the tribals is the other side of the coin of Settlement Pattas, which calls for a scrutiny of the rejection orders.[26]

As per the 1990 Report of Neerabh K. Prasad, an IAS officer, entitled 'Protection of Tribal Land', in the Settlement Regulations 2/69 and 2/70, it has been stipulated that the non-tribals had to prove eight years of continuous possession of land prior to 1969 and 1970, and an absence of any prohibited transfer as per Land Transfer Regulations, to be eligible for a grant of a *patta*. Further, it states that norms were openly flouted by the non-tribals. False receipts were created by the Mutta clerks or Estates clerks showing payment of taxes. The tribals were driven out by creating terror through organizing police raids, thus making it convenient for the non-tribals to get the tribal land measured in their names. In a specific case at Nelakota village of East Godavari District, the village abuts a huge inland tank by the name of Ramavarapu Ava and gets irrigation from the same. The non-tribal residents of the adjacent villages, especially Ramachandrapuram, had dubbed the tribals as Naxalites (past 1969 Srikakulam Naxalite Movement period) and organized police raids. The tribals now inform that they had to flee from the hill tops and that they stayed there for more than a month. This period was used by the non-tribals to get the land surveyed and settled in their favour. Land with rich forest growth was taken as patta even though tribals were never in occupation of the land; obviously with an intention to get the rich timber. The cases of Jangalthota and Chintalpudi of Y. Ramavaram Mandals of East Godavari District are glaring examples of these. The tribal claims were never properly examined and tribals were by and large unaware of the settlement operations. By the time the tribals realized that their land was being given as pattas to the non-tribals, it was too late for an appeal. As a result of these dubious measures, the landholdings of the non-tribals jumped from 9,805 hectares before 1969 to 16,789 hectares by 1976 in the Scheduled Area of East Godavari District.[27]

The non-tribals in three Agency mandals of West Godavari District are holding pattas over 53,719 acres, while tribals have pattas over 37,042 acres only in the Scheduled Area as per the Minutes of the Cabinet Sub-Committee circulated on 24 July 1997:

> Just before the abolition of the Estates, the landholders accelerated issuance of pattas in several cases even with regard to the waste land in the estates by receiving paltry sums. So the Settlement Officer is directed to reopen all the pattas that were granted till now under the provisions of Ryotwari Settlement Regulations 2 of 1970, observed by Justice B.S.A. Swamy while dealing with a case in relation to land disputes in West Godavari District Agency Areas.[28]

In Bhadrachalam division in Khammam District, 8,297 non-tribals were granted pattas in respect of 29,554.16 hectares of land according to the Report of Secretary to Government (1992). Expressing concern over the grant of ryotwari settlement pattas to non-tribals in the Scheduled Areas during the survey period, the Secretary to Government, Mr. Govindarajan (1992) reports:

> two cases have come to the attention of the Government during the course of verification by special officer for survey of tribal land and assignment to tribals in Khammam District in the month

> of July 1990. In one case, five non-tribals were granted ryotwari patta in respect of an extent of 30 acres of land while the tribals are in possession and enjoyment of the said land. In another case, non-tribals have obtained ryotwari pattas in respect of an extent of 101 acres where as the tribals are in continuous occupation and enjoyment of the said land.

There is another important legislation in respect of lands in the Telangana Area of the State. The Andhra Pradesh (Telangana Area) Tenancy and Agricultural Land Act of 1950 classifies all tenants into ordinary and protected tenants. The Act further stipulates that if the tenant personally cultivated the land continuously for a period of six years during a stipulated period, he/she shall be deemed to be a protected tenant and as a protected tenant he reserves the right to purchase the land from the owner. This Act was also in force in the tribal areas of Telangana region. The non-tribals who gained access to land from tribals through clandestine and dubious methods were protected by the legislation. There was no law strictly prohibiting the transfer of land between tribals and non-tribals till 1963 in the Telangana region, barring a revenue division Bhadrachalam in the Kammam District. The land reforms which were introduced by the State of Andhra Pradesh protecting the tenancy was made applicable to tribal areas without taking into cognizance the tribal interest.

During 1996–1997, when land disputes erupted in tribal areas of West Godavari District, one of the major contention of the tribals was that they should be given possession of land as per the 1902 Resettlement Register (RSR) and be made incumbent on the non-tribals who were occupying land classified as tribal or government in the 1902 Resettlement Register to prove that they had got hold of the land in a legal manner. The Resettlement Register of 1902 is even currently not available with the offices of the Commissioner, Tribal Welfare or the District.[29]

Land reforms focus on the individual *patta* while much of the tribal land is communally owned. It can, therefore, be declared State property according to the present law and taken away from tribals. Such alienation is clearly visible in the forest management system and development-induced displacement. Other processes of land transfers with the intervention of non-tribals supplement it.[30]

The state, by introducing the land record system, legalized the then existing land structures and relations, while ignoring the claims and prospects of the real 'owners'. Thus, in the process of alienation, not only has the land became alienated, but the state itself has become an 'alien' to tribals with its anti-tribal activities.[31]

Historical Evolution of Land and Forest Laws in Fifth Scheduled Areas

A brief overview of the legislations affecting the ownership and management of land and forest in Schedule Areas is essential to appreciate the pattern of the growing problem or the continued struggle for tribal land rights. It is important to have a critical assessment of the laws affecting land and forest in Agency Areas in a historical perspective, demarcating the major concerns and issues in two phases, viz. pre-Independence and post independence era.

Pre-Independence Period

George Russel, a member of the Board of Revenue, in the then Government of Madras, was appointed in the year 1822 to study the socio-economic situation in the tribal areas of Ganjam and Visakhapatnam Districts. The Ganjam and Vizagpatnam Act 1839,[32] was the result of the realization that tribal areas had to be administered separately. The responsibility for the administration of both civil and criminal justice was entrusted with the District Collectors as Agents to the state government. The areas that they governed were called 'Agency Areas'. However, the measures taken by the government in relation to the administration of the justice did not improve the situation in the tribal tracts. Several rebellions ensued. In the wake of widespread unrest in the tribal areas of northern-most districts of then Madras Presidency, the government enacted the Ganjam and Vizagpatnam Act 1839, under which the tribal areas were removed from the purview of general laws. The enactment was made to provide for the administration of justice and for collection of revenue in the Agency Areas. In view of the fact that certain doubts had arisen as to which Acts or Regulations were in force in some parts of British India, the Scheduled Districts Act XVI of 1874 came to be passed.

Land alienation as a pressing problem was first recognized during the British rule in India when the Schedule Districts Act XIV, 1874 was passed, aiming to protect tribals from the danger of further land (legal landholding) alienation and indebtedness. Exercising the power under Section 6 of the Scheduled Districts Act,

1874, the local government issued rules for the administration of the Agency Tracts and for regulation of the procedure of the Officers so appointed to administer them. Subsequently, the Agency Tracts Interest and Land Transfer Act 1917, (Act of 1917), came to be passed with the object of limiting the rate of interest and to check the transfer of land in the Agency Tracts in Ganjam, Visakhapatnam and Godavari Districts. By a subsequent notification, the Act was extended to the taluk of Bhadrachalam in the East Godavari District.

Under Section 2 of the said Act, Agency Tracts are defined to mean Scheduled Districts, as defined in the Acts XIV and XV of 1874. The ineffective implementation of protective legislations triggered movements in the tribal belt. Thus, the Lagarayi *fituri* began with a string of dacoities by a Koya-Kammaras, but the sympathies of at least one Muttadar was involved; in February 1917, Mottadam Virayya Dora, *Muttadar* of Gudem Patavidi, was deported to Visakhapatnam for complicity in the rising. This establishes that the Act 1917 was introduced due to this revolt. The object of Act 1 of 1917 is to limit the rate of interest and also to check the transfer of land in the Agency Tracts.

By the Agency Land and Interest Act of 1917, the Government of Madras made a belated attempt to protect the hill-men from indebtedness and land alienation. The Act prohibited contracts in which the rate of interest would exceed 24 per cent a year and forbade any transfer of immovable property in the Agency Tracts from a hill-man to an outsider without the Agent's prior consent. The bill was strongly opposed by the Indian Members of the Madras Legislative Council who threw back at the British their own shibboleths of 'progress' and 'development'. The District Association of Visakhapatnam, a forerunner of the District Congress Committee, urged that the eighty-year only distinction between the administrations of the Agency and the plains should be scrapped and free immigration into the hills be permitted. Its memorial claimed that contact with the plains' cultivators had already proved beneficial to the hill-men through the introduction of improved methods of agriculture.[33]

The 1918 Montagu and Chelmsford Report suggested that the backward area where the primitive people or tribals live should be excluded from the proposed political reform and the administration entrusted to the Governors of the provinces. Subsequently, the Government of India Act, 1919 divided these areas into two parts: 'wholly excluded and partially excluded areas'. The Simon Commission Report highlighted the twin dangers the tribal and hill-people were facing when exposed to the general laws, the risk of their agricultural land passing to more well-equipped and informed section of the population and the likely risk of them getting trapped by moneylenders. The Government of India Act, 1935,[34] dealt with excluded and partially excluded areas (classification of Scheduled Districts) and the administration thereof, was exclusively vested in the Governor of the Province. The Government of India (adoption of Indian laws) Order, 1937 repealed the 1874 Act and brought excluded and partially excluded areas directly under the governance of the Governor.

While alienation of revenue land among tribals was acknowledged during the colonial rule and by the founding fathers of the Indian Constitution, the right of tribals residing in the forest areas without any legal evidence was historically never acknowledged. The British Government finally decided on a policy of segregating the tribes into special areas where their lives and interests could be adequately protected and there would be less contact with non-tribal culture. For this purpose, an Act was passed in 1874 to specify tribal areas into 'Scheduled Districts'. These areas were reconstituted under Section 52 A of the Government of India Act of 1919, and finally, in 1935 more stringent provisions for a special treatment of tribal areas were incorporated by converting them into 'totally and partially excluded areas'.[35]

The loss of tribal control over land, both revenue and forest, was the principal reason for several tribal rebellions starting from the late 18th century through the 19th century, to the first few decades of the 20th century. Some of these tribal revolts were localized, while the others were more widespread. These rebellions focused and asserted the traditionally inalienable rights of the tribals on the local resources, land and forests. The imperialists as a colonial power created a new Zamindari and other feudal systems as the Mutta System, Mahals and Mukhasa in the tribal areas of Andhra Pradesh. These systems were historical offshoots of feudal landlordism. The imperialists in the pre-independence period encouraged the classes from outside tribal areas to exploit and forcefully bring tribal land resources into their personal ownership and control. The Adivasis expressed their dissent and protest in various forms against such feudal landlords.

The condition of the tribal population improved considerably as a result of the Rampa Rebellion. The various orders passed from time to time with the view to ameliorating the conditions of the tribal population of the East Godavari Agency were ultimately consolidated in a legislation known as the Agency Tracts Interest and Land Transfer Act of 1917. Similar to the position of tribals in the British Presidency, the tribals in Telangana Districts of Nizam rule in the State of Hyderabad suffered at the hands of land grabbers, landlords, unscrupulous traders and moneylenders. Whenever tanks were constructed or renovated during the Nizam's period, the non-tribals came to these tribal areas as contractors and started grabbing the land of the tribals by making transit stay. Some of the non-tribal labourers too settled as peasants, turning the tribal peasants into landless labourers. In short, the initiation or resumption of state's activity in the areas of excise, forest and revenue resulted in non-tribal immigration to the tribal areas and alienation of tribal land. Imposing heavy taxes on tribals and forcing them to retreat deep into the forest may be another reason for the rebellion.[36]

By the late thirties, the tribals of Adilabad District were subjected to a dual onslaught, one by the non-tribals who encroached on their agricultural land and the other by the forest officials who expanded the boundaries of the reserved forest at the expense of their traditional habitat. The resultant conflict culminated in the death of ten Gonds in a police firing in the 1940s.[37] The tribals in Adilabad District rebelled in 1940 under the leadership of the tribal, Komram Bhim following alienation of tribal land and forest reservation rules. The non-tribal settlers had managed to obtain title deeds for the occupied land which once belonged to the tribals. A large chunk of land which had been cultivated on Sivai Jamabandhi tenure (government land encroachments) and lying fallow at the time of demarcation was included in the Reserve. The policy of clearing large tracts of forest of all human habitations including the old, established villages inhabited for many generations led to armed resistance. Prof. Haimendorf, the Austrian born English anthropologist, was invited by the Nizam's Government to study the reasons for the unrest among the tribals.

The struggle ultimately resulted in the promulgation of the law known as Tribal Areas Regulation 1356 Fasli (1946 AD). This Regulation empowered the government to make such rules as appeared necessary or expedient to them for improved administration of any notified tribal area in respect of the tribals and of their relations with non-tribals. The substance of this regulation was incorporated in the Tribal Areas Regulation 1359 Fasli (1949 AD) and the rules giving effect to its provisions were issued by the Revenue Department under the title, Notified Tribal Area Rules 1359 Fasli on 16 November 1949.

The most important provision of this Regulation was that no court of law or revenue authority had any jurisdiction in any Notified Tribal Area in any dispute relating to land, house or house site occupied, claimed, rented or possessed by any tribal, or from which any tribal may have been evicted whether by process of law or otherwise, during a period of one year preceding the notification of such an area as a Notified Tribal Area.

In contrast, in the administration of adjoining provinces of British India, the Government of Hyderabad State had not provided for any special privileges for tribal communities till 1946.

Post-Independence Period

After the Constitution of India came into effect, the Fifth and Sixth Schedules were incorporated into the Constitution by the founding fathers. The Fifth Schedule designates power to the President of India to declare certain specified areas as Scheduled Areas. The Scheduled Areas (Part 'A' States) Order, 1950 and the Scheduled Areas (Part 'B' States) Order, 1950 were issued declaring certain specified areas as Scheduled Areas in Part 'A' and Part 'B' States respectively. Part 'A' States refers to the Scheduled Areas of Andhra region while Part 'B' States refers to Telangana region of Andhra Pradesh State. The provisions of the Fifth Schedule of the Constitution were made applicable to the Scheduled Areas of Andhra Pradesh. The Article 244 of the Constitution of India states:

> *Article 244:* Administration of Scheduled Areas and Tribals Areas. The provisions of the Fifth Schedule shall apply to the administration and control of the Scheduled Areas and Scheduled Tribes in any State other than (the States of Assam, Meghalaya, Tripura and Mizoram). The provisions of the Sixth Schedule shall apply to the administration of the tribal areas in the States of Assam, Meghalaya, Tripura and Mizoram.

The above Article provides that for administration and control of the Scheduled Areas in any State, other than the States of Assam,

Meghalaya and Tripura, the provisions of the Fifth Schedule shall apply. Clause (5) of the Fifth Schedule is to the effect that notwithstanding anything in the Constitution, the Governor may by public notification, direct that any particular Act of Parliament or of the Legislature of the State shall not apply to Scheduled Areas or any part thereof in the State, or shall apply to Scheduled Area or any part thereof in the State, subject to such exceptions and modifications as he may specify in the notification . The Governor may make regulations for the peace and good governance of any area in a State which is presently a Scheduled Area. In particular and without prejudice to the generality of the foregoing power, such regulations may,

1. Prohibit or restrict the transfer of land by or among members of the Scheduled Tribes in such area which is notified as Scheduled Area;
2. Regulate the allotment of land to members of the Scheduled Tribes in such areas;
3. Regulate the carrying on of business as moneylenders who lend money to members of the Scheduled Tribes in such areas.

All regulations made under this paragraph shall be submitted to the President forthwith and until granted his assent, shall have no effect. If there is a Tribes Advisory Council for the State, no regulation shall be made under this paragraph unless the Governor making the regulation has consulted such a Council. Therefore, the Governor may make a regulation for the peace and good governance of a Scheduled Area in a state. Such regulation can be made by the Governor after consulting the Tribes Advisory Council of the State if one already exists. Such a regulation will have effect when the President has given assent to the same.

With regard to the above, it is clear that the Governor can issue regulations in accordance with sub-para (2) of para (5), in particular, without prejudice to the generality of the powers, prohibiting or restricting transfer of land by or among the members of the Scheduled Tribes in such area; and regulate the allotment of land to members of the Scheduled Tribes in such an area. The Governor is empowered to make regulations or amend or repeal any law to provide peace and good governance to the Scheduled Areas.

Exercising the above power conferred by para (5) of Fifth Schedule, the Governor issued the Andhra Pradesh Scheduled Area Land Transfer Regulation, 1959 (Regulation 1 of 1959), which came into force on 4 March 1959, partially repealing the earlier Agency

Tracts Land Transfer Act of 1917. This was made to regulate the transfer of land in the Scheduled Areas of East Godavari, West Godavari, Visakhapatnam and Srikakulam. The Tribal Area Regulation 1359 Fasali (1949 AD) in the Telangana Districts was repealed in 1963 and got replaced by the Andhra Pradesh Scheduled Area Land Transfer Regulations 1 of 59 which came into force on 1 December 1963. As a result, the Andhra Pradesh Scheduled Areas Land Transfer Regulation, 1959 was made applicable to the areas in the Districts of Adilabad, Warangal, Khammam and Mahbubnagar as well. The regulation states that notwithstanding anything contained in any enactment, rule or law in force in the Agency Tracts, any transfer of immovable property situated in the Agency Tracts by a member of a Scheduled Tribe, shall be absolutely null and void unless made:

6. in favour of any other member of a Scheduled Tribe or a registered society as defined in clause (f) of Section 2 of the Madras Co-operative Societies Act, 1932 (Madras Act VL of 1932), composed solely of members of the Scheduled Tribes, or
7. with the previous sanction of the State Government, or subject to rules made in this behalf, with the previous consent of the Agent or of any prescribed officer in writing.

Although the protective Land Transfer Regulations had been in force, it was observed by several committees that the non-tribals were able to find ways and means to circumvent the provisions of the Land Transfer Regulation 1 of 1959 by entering into *benami* transactions and other clandestine ways with the uninformed tribals. As there was no check on transfer of land between the non-tribal settlers and other non-tribals, several transactions in relation to the immovable property situated in the Scheduled Areas were effected. As a result, non-tribal migration to Scheduled Areas increased and caused further tribal land alienation by new migrants through recorded or unrecorded clandestine transactions. The excessive exploitative conditions induced by external interventions, the ineffectiveness of the government response in prevention of tribal land alienation and restoration of alienated tribal land and the ineffective legislations triggered the Naxalite movement in Srikakulam region between 1968–70. The peasant uprising in Naxalbari in Darjeeling District of West Bengal[38] which prompted the tribals of the Srikakulam District to resort to armed struggle, started in October 1968. The Naxalite movement was not confined only to Srikakulam District but spread quickly to other areas of the state as well, particularly in the Warangal and Khammam Districts.[39] All the uprisings were defensive movements against state oppression. They were the last resort of the tribals driven to despair by the encroachments of outsiders on their land. The Srikakulam Naxalite movement again drew the attention of the state. Then the State felt that 'it would be absolutely necessary to create conditions for peace and maintain peace and prevent the new non-tribals from settling down in the Scheduled Area. If the alienations are permitted to the non-tribals there is a danger of large-scale exploitation by the new non-tribal again with the result peace will be disturbed in that area'.

It is only with a view to maintain peace and to govern the area effectively that Regulation 1 of 1970 was passed by the Andhra Pradesh Governor. A non-tribal who validly acquired the land title was not to be disturbed, but he would not be allowed to sell his land to a non-tribal which would inevitably mean new entrants into the Scheduled Area. The basic purpose was to ensure that the land of the tribals should not be frittered away to outsiders through transfer and that non-tribals should not be allowed to infiltrate into the Scheduled Areas by getting allotments of land made in their favour. In the case of a void transaction, the power to restore land to the tribal or his heirs, after evicting the non-tribal was vested with the government. Unless new entrants into the Scheduled Areas were prevented from settling down in the Scheduled Areas by purchasing properties either from tribals or non-tribals, it was not possible to prevent the exploitation of the tribals. It is only with a view to enforce the valid provisions of Regulation 1 of 1959, the Regulation, viz. Regulation 1 of 1970 was made. It was in the interests of the tribals and for their protection that Regulation 1 of 1970 was passed. It was so because without restricting or prohibiting the alienation of land in the possession of the non-tribals to other non-tribals, the objectives would not be achieved. The Regulations 1 of 70 state that notwithstanding anything contained in any enactment, rule or law in force in the Agency Tracts, any transfer of immovable property situated in the Agency Tracts by a person, whether or not such person is a member of a Scheduled Tribe, shall be absolutely null and void, unless such transfer is made in favour of a person, who is a member of a Scheduled Tribe or a society registered or deemed to be registered under the Andhra

Pradesh Co-operative Societies Act, 1964 (Act 7 of 1964) which is composed solely of members of the Scheduled Tribes.

Until the contrary is proved, any immovable property situated in the Agency Tracts and in the possession of a person who is not a member of a Scheduled Tribe, shall be presumed to have been acquired by such person or his predecessor in possession through a transfer made to him by a member of a Scheduled Tribe.

When a person intending to sell one's land is not able to effect such sale, by reason of the fact that no member of a Scheduled Tribe is willing to purchase the land on the terms offered, then the person may apply to the Agent, the Agency Divisional Officer or any other prescribed officer for the acquisition of such land by the State Government, and the Agent, Agency Divisional Officer or any other prescribed officer, as the case may be, may by order, take over such land on payment of compensation in accordance with the principles specified in Section 10 of the Andhra Pradesh Ceiling on Agricultural Holdings Act, 1961 (Act X of 1961), and such land shall thereupon vest with the State Government, free from all encumbrances and shall be disposed of in favour of members of the Scheduled Tribes or a society registered or deemed to be registered under the Andhra Pradesh Co-operative Societies Act, 1964 (Act 7 of 1964), composed solely of members of the Scheduled Tribes or in such other manner and subject to such conditions as may be prescribed.

If a transfer of immovable property is made in contravention of sub-section (1) the Agent, the Agency Divisional Officer or any other prescribed officer may, on application by anyone interested, or on information given in writing by a public servant, or suo motu decree ejectment against any person in possession of the property claiming under the transfer, after due notice to him in the manner prescribed, may restore it to the transferor or his heirs.

If the transferor or his heirs are not willing to take back the property or where their whereabouts are not known, the Agent, the Agency Divisional Officer or the prescribed officer, as the case may be, may order the assignment or sale of the property to any other member of a Scheduled Tribe or a society registered or deemed to be registered under any law relating to Co-operative Societies for the time being in force in the State, composed solely of members of the Scheduled Tribes, or otherwise dispose of it, as if it was property at the disposal of the State Government.

By virtue of the amended provisions, the transfer of immovable property situated in the Agency Tracts by a person, whether or not such a person is a member of a Scheduled Tribe, is made absolutely null and void unless such a transfer is made in favour of a member of a Scheduled Tribe or in favour of a Co-operative society which is composed solely of members of Schedule Tribes. Further, Clause (b) of Section 3(1), which was substituted by Regulation 1 of 1970 raised a presumption that the property situated in Agency Tracts in possession of a non-tribal shall be presumed to have been acquired by such a person or his predecessor-in-possession through a transfer made to him by a member of a Scheduled Tribe. In other words, if any non-tribal is in possession of the property situated in Agency Tracts, it is presumed that he or his predecessors acquired the same through a transfer made to him by a member of a Scheduled Tribe, which is prohibited. This is a rebuttable presumption. However, sub-section 2(a) of Section 3 of the Regulation, was not touched by the amendments made by regulation 1 of 70, which is to the effect that the Agent, the Agency Divisional Officer or any other prescribed officer may on an application by anyone interested, or on information given in writing by a public servant or suo motu decree ejectment against a person in possession under a void transfer, may restore it to the transferor or his heirs.

By further amendment to the Regulation, a new section 6-A and 6-B were incorporated, making any acquisition of the immovable property in the Scheduled Areas by non-tribals in contravention of tribal protective Land Transfer Regulations 1 of 59, as amended by 1 of 70 or continuing in possession of such property after a decree of ejectment is passed, as a cognizable offence. Andhra Pradesh has an exemplary Land Transfer Regulations 1 of 70. Despite such a strong legislation there are a large number of pending cases where land remains to be restored to the tribals.[40]

Many state governments having Scheduled Areas have not made use of the regulation making provisions under the Fifth Schedule. Partly, the implementation continues to be weak, either due to loopholes in the laws or due to inadequate implementation. Taking advantage of the loopholes in the laws, the exploitative forces circumvent the legislative provisions. The legal provisions have been inadequate in tackling the problem in all its dimensions and the implementation process has been weak so as to render them ineffective.[41]

The suo motu power given to the government to proceed against non-tribals without waiting for a complaint from a tribal seems to be an ideal arrangement, but in the given administrative culture, it has perhaps been more of a boon to the non-tribals than to the tribals. In proceedings taken up suo motu by the government, the non-tribal faces only the government. The government does not take the trouble of finding out who among the local tribals may have a claim to the land. It does not publicize the enquiry in the village. The officer hearing the cases, designated as Special Deputy Collector, merely looks into the documents provided by the non-tribal, and if they appear reliable, he approves the right of the non-tribal over the land.[42]

In practice, the orders being issued in favour of tribals are not being implemented by the enforcing authorities. Unsuccessful non-tribal parties continue their possession and enjoyment of land. As on 31 October 2005, the detected cases of non-tribal encroachments were about 70,000 which involved about 3,15,000 acres of land. But of this, only about one lakh acre was restored to the tribals, 35 years after the promulgation of the regulation. Over two lakh acres of disputed land is still in possession of non-tribals. The stark reality that stares one in the face is that about 50 per cent of the cultivable land in the Scheduled Areas of Andhra Pradesh is under the occupation of the non-tribals.[43]

As many of the newcomers were able to occupy the cultivable land, there can be no doubt that the minor revenue officials, and, in particular, the patwari and the revenue inspectors were won over by them as many were wealthy enough to pay large bribes to corrupt officials. The laws prohibiting the acquisition of tribal land by the non-tribals were obviously ignored. Otherwise, it would have been impossible for the recent migrants, with no claim to tribal status, to acquire house sites and arable land at the expense of the Gond tribals who lost all or most of their land within a span of a few years.[44]

The partially excluded areas comprise the East Godavari Agency, the Polavaram taluk of the West Godavari Agency. The tribes inhabiting these tracts are the Koya, Koya Dora and Hill Reddy. The tribes largely practice podu (slash and burn)

Table 2.3

Outcome of Cases Under LTR at SDC Courts as on 31 January 2010

S. No.	District	Cases Detected		Cases Disposed		Cases Decided in Favour of STs		Cases Decided in Favour of Non-STs		Land Restored to Tribals		Balance Cases at the End of the Month (col. 3–5 and 4–6)	
		Nos	Extent (Acrs)	Nos	Extent (Acrs)	Nos	Extent (Acrs)	Nos	Extent (Acrs)	Nos	Extent (Acrs)	Nos	Extent (Acrs)
1.	Srikakulam	462	1,100	453	1,024	296	538	157	486	250	522	9	76
2.	Vizianagaram	1,364	7,544	1,343	7,501	955	5,631	388	1,870	850	5,498	21	43
3.	Visakhapatnam	5,708	22,731	5,480	22,087	4,359	17,721	1,121	4,366	3,029	13,944	228	644
4.	East Godavari	8,485	49,637	8,264	48,768	3,751	19,667	4,513	29,101	3,392	17,685	221	869
5.	West Godavari	11,611	62,121	11,477	60,820	2,584	11,082	8,893	49,738	2,451	10,081	134	1,301
6.	Khammam	33,582	1,26,713	33,325	1,25,834	15,514	52,192	17,811	73,642	12,750	41,662	257	879
7.	Warangal	7,289	15,784	7,052	15,218	4,865	8,964	2,187	6,254	4,865	8,964	237	566
8.	Adilabad	8,245	54,008	7,564	51,543	4,175	27,839	3,389	23,704	3,305	23,606	681	2,465
9.	Mahabubnagar	16	61	15	57	13	49	2	8	13	49	1	4
10.	Total	76,762	3,39,699	74,973	3,32,852	36,512	1,43,683	38,461	1,89,169	30,905	1,22,011	1,789	6,847

Source: Office of the Commissioner of Tribal Welfare, Hyderabad, Admin. Report (January 2010).

cultivation. Crime is scarce and the tribals lead a simple life. The mechanism of justice followed therefore, needs to be simple.[45]

Of 76,762 cases covering an extent of 3,39,699 acres of land, 74,973 cases covering an extent of 3,32,852 acres were disposed of by the SDC Courts in the State of Andhra Pradesh by the end of January 2010. The courts decided 36,512 cases covering an extent of 1,43,683 acres of land in favour of the tribals. However, the enforcing machinery set up under the Regulations could only restore 1,22,011 acres of land pertaining to the 30,905 cases out of a total of 36,512. On the contrary, the non-tribal parties were able to secure orders in their favour in 38,461 cases and retained 1,89,169 acres of land in their possession.

Table 2.3 shows that the success rate for land acquisition is 49 per cent in the case of tribals and 51 per cent in the case of non-tribals. Tribals were able to regain land possession from non-tribals only to the extent of 43 per cent of the total extent of land, covered by cases disposed of, while the non-tribal could retain 57 per cent of the disputed land. Due to the failure of the implementing machinery in executing the orders passed by the SDC Court in favour of the tribals, only 85 per cent of the total cases were disposed of in favour of the tribals, and only 85 per cent of land extent was handed over physically to them. This shows the failure on the part of the administrative machinery in the execution of orders passed by the court in the favour of tribals. This resulted in continuation of non-tribals possessing land even when the eviction orders were passed against them.

The legal system in the Scheduled Areas is ostensibly designed to facilitate the passage of justice in the tribal dominated societies. In this cause, legal protection for the tribals has been formulated in the interest of their survival and livelihood. But, as K. Balagopal has pointed out,

> it is not enough if a disadvantaged class of people are endowed with legal rights. Legal instruments created for the benefit of the socially privileged can be expected to find their way to implementation without anything else. This is not the case with legal rights enacted for the benefit of the disadvantaged.[46]

Review of Judiciary Interventions

The concept of land as a commodity comes into conflict with the traditional concept of common property among communities, such as tribals, who have had no documented system of land ownership and hence, are unable to provide proof of ownership to claim compensation in case of displacement. The courts never consider this ground reality in dispensation of justice in the tribal land cases. The land is their most important natural, valuable asset and imperishable endowment from which the tribals derive their sustenance, social status, economic and social equality, permanent place of abode, work and living. It is a source of security and economic empowerment. Therefore, the tribes have formed great emotional attachment to their land. The land on which they live and till, assures them equality of status, and dignity of person and means to economic and social justice. It provides a means of economic empowerment in social democracy.[47]

The Supreme Court in the *P. Rami Reddy vs. State of Andhra Pradesh* held that the provisions of the Andhra Pradesh Scheduled Area Land Transfer Regulations 1 of 70 are constitutionally valid. A legislation, which in essence and substance aims at restoration of land to the 'tribals' that originally belonged to them but which passed into the hands of 'non-tribals' in the aforesaid background, certainly cannot be characterized as unreasonable. True, transfer by 'non-tribals' to 'non-tribals' would not diminish the pool. As a matter of fact, it would be unjust, unfair and highly unreasonable merely to freeze the situation, instead of reversing the injustice and restoring the status quo ante.[48]

The term 'transfer' under Land Transfer Regulation means mortgage with or without possession, lease, sale, gift, exchange or any other deal with immovable property. It should not be a testamentary disposition and includes a charge on such property or a contract relating to such property in respect of such mortgage, lease, sale, gift, exchange or other dealing. This means land transfers through execution of a 'will' by a testator are not covered by the word 'transfer' under the Land Transfer Regulations. However, the interpretation of the word 'transfer' by the High Court of Andhra Pradesh keeping in view of the expression 'dealing with immoveable property', includes acts of 'forcible dispossession and encroachment'. Thus, a dispossessed tribal is entitled to restoration of possession of his land.[49] The word 'other dealing' in the Regulation also includes allotment of shops at bus stands in Agency Areas by means of tenders and in the form of licences. The word 'licence' can be read under the general expression 'other dealings' used in Section 2(g) of the Regulation. Hence, even permitting non-tribal commercial establishments by the State is banned under the Regulation.[50] The Supreme Court while dealing with a case under 'Orissa Scheduled Areas Transfer of Immovable Property (by Scheduled Tribes) Regulation (2 of 1956) held that 'Transfer of immovable property' by Scheduled Tribes – Expression 'transfer' – includes any 'dealing' with such property. The word 'deal with' is not defined in the Statute. Its dictionary meaning, taken as safe guide, can be extended to achieve the legislative object of the Act: transaction or dealing with immovable property having effect of extinguishing title of a member of aboriginal tribe and vesting the same with the non-tribal. This can be construed as 'transfer of immovable property'.[51]

Further, the word 'exchange' in the definition of 'transfer' also includes exchange of shared immovable property among family members in the Scheduled Areas. Partition of family property is permitted but not exchange of property during the division of inherited family property by non-tribals.[52] The High Court of Andhra Pradesh further held that the word 'transfer' includes 'contract to sell'.[53]

The High Court of Andhra Pradesh held that even if the land classified as Gayalu or government, poramboke, the person who is in possession of such land, must be said to be dealing with such immovable property. Therefore, the same falls within the scope of 'transfer' as defined under Section 2(g) of the Regulation.[54]

The Supreme Court has held that the word 'person' in Section 3(1) would include both natural persons as well as juristic persons, and the Constitutional Government. The word 'person' would be so interpreted as to include State or juristic person, and corporate bodies. Transfer of land by juristic persons or allotment of land by State to non-tribals, is thus prohibited. This ruling restricts the power of the government to grant lease to non-tribals in Agency Areas for mining or any other such purposes. The Constitution of India, under Article 21, guarantees 'Right to life'. Right to life means far more than mere survival. Thus, tribals have the fundamental right to social and economic empowerment.[55]

The laws made applicable to the Scheduled Areas indicate an anxiety to safeguard the interests of tribals and to ensure that the land in the Scheduled Areas should remain in the possession of the tribals. The High Court of Andhra Pradesh held that the object seems to be that all immovable property in Agency Tracts, which was held by tribals at one time, as far as possible, must be restored back to them. Therefore, a non-tribal transferor, after the commencement of Land Transfer Regulations 1 of 70, cannot seek restoration of the alienated land to another non-tribal; nor can the non-tribal transferee claim retention of the land.[56]

Governments, from time to time, issued several orders for protecting the non-tribals landed interest in the Scheduled Areas, even after the 1 of 70 Regulations were promulgated by the Governor under the Fifth Schedule of the Constitution due to political pressures. Such among them were GO MS 129 dated 13 August 1979 directing the officers concerned not to evict non–tribal landless poor persons in occupation of government land in Scheduled Areas up to an extent of 5.00 acres of wet land or 10.00 acres dry land. This GO was questioned before the High Court of Andhra Pradesh. The High Court quashed the GO in the year 1984 as illegal and without jurisdiction.[57]

The subsequent GOs 41 in 1971 and GO 951 in 1974 prohibiting eviction of non-tribal Sivai Zamadars in occupation of government land in Scheduled Areas up to an extent of 21/2 acres wet or 5.00 acres dry land if they are in continuous possession of those land for a period of not less than 10 years, and preventing eviction of Sivai Zamadars belonging to the Scheduled Castes in occupation of government land up to an extent of 21/2 acres wet and 5.00 acres dry land, if they are in occupation of the land since 1969, were all quashed as they are against the provisions of tribal protective Land Transfer Regulations 1 of 70.[58] The High Court of Andhra Pradesh held that the land situated in the Scheduled Areas cannot be acquired under the Land Acquisition Act for providing house-sites even to Scheduled Castes *de hors* the Regulation.[59] The Land Transfer Regulation as amended by the Regulation 1 of 1970 prevails over the provisions of Regulation 2 of 1970 and no Ryotwari patta can be granted in violation of the provisions of Regulation 1 of 1970. Such a patta would not bind the authorities under Regulation 1 of 1970.[60]

The main purpose of the Andhra Pradesh Scheduled Area Land Transfer Regulations 1 of 59 is to invalidate any transfer of land situated in the Agency Tracts in favour of the non-tribal. In order to effectuate that intention, the Regulation set up a separate machinery. On the other hand, the Ryotwari Settlement Regulation 2 of 70 was enacted to provide for the ryotwari settlement of certain land areas in the Scheduled Area of Andhra Pradesh. Section 7 enacts that a non-tribal shall not be entitled to a ryotwari patta if his possession and occupation of the land is void or illegal under the Andhra Pradesh Scheduled Area Land Transfer Regulation 1 of 59. The proper course to read these two Regulations is to allow both of them to operate while giving primary importance to the operation of Regulation 1 of 59. Any decision under these Regulations by the authorities in determining rights over lands will prevail over the other laws. It means even a ryotwari patta granted to a non tribal against the provisions of Land Transfer Regulations would not give a better land entitlement to him. Thus, any decision made under Regulation 2 of 1970 can only be tentative and provisional and would be subject to the decision made under the Regulation 1 of 59.[61] The Land Transfer Regulations are superior and legally binding on the other legislations. The Supreme Court held that the prohibition against transfer and declaration of nullity enjoined under the Amended Land Transfer Regulation having been held to be an emanation of Para 5(2) of the Fifth Schedule to the Constitution itself, the determination of invalidity declared under the provisions of Land Transfer Regulations will have to be held as overriding any contrary determination under any other Regulation.[62]

Even the High Court of Andhra Pradesh is not inclined to apply the Principle of Res judicata to the tribal land alienation cases under the Regulations, and gives a restrictive frame for its application in tribal land cases. It is held that orders passed in the first proceedings initiated under the Regulation will not operate as Res judicata if the later proceedings are initiated by a third party or by the same party on the basis of any further material.[63] It was further held that the earlier proceedings of a case do not operate as Res judicate in the present proceedings if the land question involved in the earlier proceedings is distinct and different from the one on the basis of which the present proceedings are initiated.[64]

The mere fact that on the earlier occasion a petition filed under the Land Transfer Regulation 1959 was dismissed, does not confer any right on the non-tribal so long as the Statutory order subsists, viz. the void sale subsists. The statute prescribes that any transaction entered into between a tribal and non-tribal or between a non-tribal and a non-tribal, are void per se.[65]

However, judicial activism has put an obstacle to the very objective of Land Transfer Regulations. The Supreme Court of India held that the Andhra Pradesh Scheduled Areas Land Transfer Regulation (1 of 1959), Section 3 (as it stood before and after amendment in 1963 and 1970), prohibiting to transfer of immovable properties in Scheduled Area prospectively. This means the Regulations do not adversely affect completed transactions of transfer which have taken place prior to enforcement of Regulations.[66]

Dealing with a tribal land question situated in the Telangana area, the High Court applied the same principle and held that authorities acting under the said Regulation cannot interfere with the alienations effected prior to the commencement of the Regulation 1/1970. If the said transactions are illegal in view of any other provisions of law, it is for the appropriate forum to take action but they cannot be declared void by the Deputy Collector acting under Section 3 of Regulation 1/1970. The High Court held that the authorities under Regulation, while admitting the transfer to be prior to 1 December 1963, cannot set aside the same on the ground that it was by an unregistered sale deed and, therefore, not valid. There is no jurisdiction or power conferred on the authority to question the validity of alienation, otherwise than being in contravention of the regulation.[67] Therefore, these rulings have given a wider scope to non-tribals to escape from the clutches of tribal protective land laws, and manipulation of predated unregistered agreements and sale deeds.

The Tribes Advisory Council, a constitutional body under the Fifth Schedule of the Constitution, in its meetings held in 1984, recommended giving retrospective effect to the Andhra Pradesh Scheduled Area Land Transfer Regulations 1 of 59 from 1917 in the Andhra Region and in the Telangana Region from 1949. But the governments did not stick to the decision of the Tribal Advisory Council. Because of any such decision by ruling parties perhaps, would affect their non-tribal vote bank in the Scheduled Areas.

The ruling of Courts further weakened the unwilling state in enforcing the Land Transfer Regulations. The Regulations have provided suo moto power to initiate proceedings against the non-tribal occupants in the Scheduled Areas. However, the ruling of the Court has limited its power affecting the tribal land rights. The High Court of Andhra Pradesh held that exercising a *suo moto* power after a lapse of reasonable time would be arbitrary and contrary to the principle of 'Rule of Law' enshrined in the

Constitution and exercising such a *suo moto* power after 14 or 15 years would be ipso facto unreasonable.[68]

The legal system imposed by the British impinges on the customary land rights of the Adivasis. Tribals used to settle their land disputes only through customary law in many parts of the tribal areas before the introduction of the English common law which became the sole legitimate recourse for enforcing of land rights. Predictably, the usual difficulties with any *imposed* law – prolonged procedures, impractical rules of evidence, and delays in disposal of cases – hinder a verdict even in the simplest of cases. The tribals give more value to verbal rather than documentary evidence. However, the Indian Evidence Act gives more weightage to documentary evidence which is known to the non-tribal parties involved in the land issue and they have managed to document the land records favourably to gain advantage during court enquiries. Further, there is no scope for quick justice through established courts for settlement of cases. The courts usually take a longer period to pass judgements because the legal procedure is very comprehensive. In this backdrop, some of the tribals perhaps prefer the other forums which could settle their issues. Naxalites could be one among such forums. Indigenous communities, therefore, prefer the swift justice delivered by extremists such as the Naxalites and Maoists flourishing in the hinterland, over the procrastinated conventional court system to which they are unaccustomed. They thus, become ready recruits for extremist groups like the Maoists in Central and South India which promise protection of the tribes' natural rights in return for material and political support.[69]

Historical Evolution of Forest Laws and Restrictions on Tribal Entitlements

The evolution of forest laws and policy in India has been characterized by the progressive curtailment of the rights of tribals for sustenance and livelihood derived from the forests. The access of the tribals to forests and common property resources has been declining due to the progressive abrogation of their rights, largely by the state itself.

The establishment of a separate department to look after the 'forests' subject in 1864, with initial laws for administration in 1865 and the first Indian Forest Act of 1878, brought forests under the regulatory regime of the colonial government which resulted in the alienation of forest land from tribals. The Indian Forest Act, 1927, which provided the basic legal framework for management of forests in India, particularly the authority of the Executive to declare any forest or wasteland as reserved forest and regulate the use and transit of forest produce, was effectively used by the government to bring as much land as possible under government control for commercial exploitation. It conclusively established the right of the authority over forest and practically ignored the historical and traditional rights of tribals over the forests. This Act was invoked during the post-independence period as more areas were declared as reserved forests as princely states and fiduciary *zamindars* were merged with the Union of India. The non-recognition of the customary rights of tribals and other forest dwellers during the process essentially forms the backdrop of the current problem of alienation of forest land from tribals.

These legislations are the basis for the central and state forest laws. The basic premise established is that all forest land and wasteland is the property of the state and the state can make any provision with regard to its administration, use and alienation. The Forest Policy of 1894 was the first official move towards regulating the rights and concessions enjoyed by the forest dependent communities for centuries. The policy broadly recognizes the domestic bonafide rights of the people but restricts their free movement in the forests and brings their activities into close watch. At best, one can say that the policy converted the rights of forest dependent communities to privileges at the mercy of the state. The Debhar Commission noted that the full control of tribal communities over forest resources changed into merely to a few rights and concessions by the 1894 Forest Policy. To make matters worse, the National Forest Policy of independent India was not only merely an extension of the old policy followed during the colonial period, but it went a step further. Viewing the rights of tribals in the forests as a burden on the forests and an impediment in the scientific and economic exploitation of the forest resources, the rights and privileges of the tribal forest dwellers were converted into concessions.

The Indian Forest Act 1927, provides a comprehensive process and procedure for settlement of customary and traditional rights and privileges of the local forest dependent communities by the Forest Settlement Officer (FSO) before issue of final notification of the reservation of forests. No effective steps were taken to settle the rights of local communities over the forest land and the forest dwellers rights over the forests were not recognized in the absence of documentary proof to establish their claims. Further, Section 10 (5) of the Forest Act states that the practice of shifting cultivation shall in all cases be deemed a privilege subject to control, restriction and abolition by the State Government. However, under the Act, the Forest Settlement Officers are empowered to recommend to the State Governments, either to exclude such areas from final notification of reservation or to recommend allotment of alternate land for cultivation, based on the verification of claim and enquiry. But the provision was never used by Forest Settlement Officers to exclude areas under shifting cultivation from the forest notification. However, the British and Indian governments viewed shifting cultivation as a practice leading to the destruction of forests.

After independence, the national leadership in India considered it necessary to revise the Forest Policy of 1894 and brought in a new Forest Policy in 1952, aiming to evolve a system of balanced and complementary land use and maximum revenue. Tribal communities were granted certain concessions as collection of minor forest produce and grazing of cattle. The Dhebar Commission (1961) recommended that the Forest Policy of 1952 should be reconsidered and that subject to safeguards, tribals should be allowed to use forest land for cultivation, their needs should be met from outlying areas in the reserve forests and their requirements for grazing and shifting cultivation should be conceded. The purpose of the Dhebar Commission, appointed under Article 339 of the Constitution of India, was to get a report on the administration of the Scheduled Areas and situation of Scheduled Tribes.

The National Commission of Agriculture set up in 1976 further complicated the issue and recommended that the rights and privileges of communities had brought destruction of the forests and it was thus necessary to reverse the process. The Conference of State Ministers of Forests and Tribal Welfare on the 'Role of Forest in Tribal Economy', held in 1978, underlined that the tribals living in the forest villages should be given heritable and inalienable rights over the land which they cultivate without further loss of time. The conference further recommended that forest villages be abolished and the State should take immediate steps to convert them into revenue villages. The Report of the Committee on Forests and Tribals in India, Ministry of Home Affairs, Government of India (1982) says, 'Shifting cultivation has become a way of life of the tribals. As such change from shifting cultivation to settled cultivation has to be gradual, so that they are able to adjust themselves. The problem has social and cultural overtones and therefore, motivational approach through introduction of alternative programmes is recommended'.

However, contrary to the above referred, imposing the restrictions on the dereservation of forests and forest land for non-forest purposes, the Forest (Conservation) Act 1980 was introduced. An Advisory Committee was set up to advise the Central Government with regard to grant of approvals for forest clearances. This Act has become a weapon in the hands of forest officials who threaten and evict tribals who access forest land or retain land in their possession. However, the State is not aggressive in clearing the larger projects in tribal areas at the cost of ecological imbalance and loss of forest cover.

In historical context of forest policies in India, the Forest Policy of 1988 for the first time marks a great shift from the previous policies and ensures an integrated approach to the forest management through participation of the people.

The 29th Report of the Commissioner of Scheduled Castes and Scheduled Tribes of the Ministry of Tribal Affairs, Government of India in May 1990, issued a set of guidelines including dealing with regularization of land encroachment, review of disputed claims over forest land, regularization of pattas and leases and conversion of forest villages into revenue villages. However, the government has failed to implement these guidelines.

Forest Land Rights Deprivation among Tribals

Andhra Pradesh is the fifth largest State in terms of geographical area and the third largest state in terms of forest cover in the country. The state is a distinct geographical entity occupying the east central plateau of India with a long coastline. Of the 2,75,068 sq. km of geographical area, forests occupy 63,813 sq. km of land in the state. Rich in flora and fauna, the forests exhibit a wide range of types in composition and ecological status. About 3,695 Gram Panchayats in the state of Andhra Pradesh have forest interface covered by 20,32,303 acres of land as per the Report of the Tribal Welfare Department (2007).

There are 50.24 lakh tribals in the State as per the 2001 Census of which about 60 per cent live in Scheduled Areas. Around 62 per cent of the Scheduled Area in the state is covered by reserve forests and more than 60 per cent of reserve forests in the state are located in the Scheduled Areas which confirms that tribals and forests are closely interlinked.

Table 2.4

Forest Laws

S. No.	*Short Title or Subject*	*Year*
1.	Indian Forest Act	1865
2.	Revised Indian Forest Act (Act VII of 1878)	1878
3.	Indian Forest Act	1927
4.	Madras Forest Act (Andhra Area)	1882
5.	Forest Act for Hyderabad State	1900
6.	Revised Forest Act for Hyderabad State	1916
7.	Hyderabad Forest Act	1945
8.	AP Forest Act (Integration of Madras and Hyderabad Forest Acts)	1967
9.	Andhra Pradesh Minor Forest Produce (Regulations of Trade) Act	1971
10.	The AP Scheduled Areas Minor Forest Produce (Regulation of Trade) Regulation	1979
11.	The Forest (Conservation) Act	1980
12.	The AP Scheduled Area Minor Forest Produce (Regulation of Trade) Rules	1990

Table 2.4 presents historical evolution of forest laws in the country, during colonial and post colonial period.

In Hyderabad state, the forests were considered subservient to the interest of agriculture and were consequently administered by the district officials. A separate Forest Department was created in 1867 to protect exclusively certain plant species under a simple set of rules. The rest of the general forest produce and administration remained with the district officials. The revenue officials permitted cultivation in the forests. This system was considered unsatisfactory and the government took steps to gain control over the communities. In 1893, the government declared vast tracts covered by forest growth as protected forests and placed them under the sole charge of the Forest Department. To have legal control over forests, a Forest Act was enacted in 1900. Subsequently, it was revised and the Forest Act of 1916 was brought in. This Act, based on the lines of Indian Forest Act 1927, was repealed by the Hyderabad Forest Act 1945. The Madras Presidency formulated its own Act, viz., the Madras Forest Act 1882.

When the state of Andhra Pradesh was formed on 1 November 1956, the laws in force in the respective territories before the said date were continued in force by virtue of the States Reorganization Act 1956. Later, the Andhra Pradesh (Andhra Area) Forest Act 1882 (or Madras Forest Act 1882), and Andhra Pradesh (Telangana Area) Forest Act 1945 (or Hyderabad Forest Act 1945), were integrated and Andhra Pradesh Forest Act 1967 was formed for the protection and management of forests in the state of Andhra Pradesh. The Act empowers the state to constitute any land as a reserve forest and Forest Settlement Officers were appointed to determine the right of the local communities over such land. Each of these legislations has a distinct purpose. Thus, the Andhra Pradesh Forest Act is a consolidated legislation for all purposes including forest management and conservation of forests in the state of Andhra Pradesh.

According to the 1972 Report of the Task Force on Development of Tribal Areas, 'It is suggested that customary rights of tribals in land and forests may be recognized. It is inevitable that many of the customary rights of the tribals would require change in course of time for a larger national interest. The specific conditions to be considered are: communal ownership, land settled with the chief on behalf of the community, and individual ownership'.[70]

A special Chapter III-A (Preservation of Private Forests) contains Section 28-A to 28G in the Andhra Pradesh Forest Act 1967 and was made applicable to the Scheduled Areas in the year 1977, imposing restrictions to cut trees in the forest land owned by the communities and empowering the state to prohibit or regulate the removal of trees for any purposes, for the preservation of forests. Further, a notification was issued by the Governor of the State of Andhra Pradesh in 1979 excluding the right to claim ryotwari patta over the lands containing trees, shrubs, and coppice growth situated in land tenures of Mutta, Mukhasa, Zamindari and other government land. This notification has restricted the tribals to claim Settlement Pattas over the land in their occupation situated under these land tenures. They are denied rights ensured for seeking Settlement Pattas under the Ryotwari Settlement Regulations, introduced after abolition of other land tenures as the Mutta, Mukhasa, Zamindari, etc. in the Scheduled Areas of Andhra Pradesh.

Revenue and Forest Boundary Disputes

In the Andhra region, villages were surveyed excluding the forest areas. When a reserve forest adjoins the village boundaries, the boundary was demarcated by excluding the forest. However, in the Telangana region, the villages were surveyed including the forests in the villages. The forest blocks may lie in a single or more villages. In tribal areas the villages were initially surveyed to the extent of patta land, leaving out vast extents of hilly terrain. Subsequently, the gap areas between patta land of villages and Reserve Forest land were surveyed and maps prepared. In this regard, special survey units for tribal survey under Telugu Grameen Magani Samaradhan were created to survey the Reserve Forest boundaries by a team comprising both the revenue and forest officials with reference to the notified forest data. The gap areas lying between Reserve Forest limits and patta land of adjacent villages were surveyed to complete a survey of a village into two parts.

In 1987, the Government of Andhra Pradesh issued a Memo No. 26531/87 by the Ministry of Energy, Forests, Environment Science and Technology permitting the assignment of pre-1980 forest land occupations by tribal communities in the reserved forests. Based on this memo, D-Form Pattas were granted to tribals. However, during the implementation of the Joint Forest Management Scheme, the forest department brought such revenue patta land into the purview of the scheme and evicted the tribals, stating that the land is classified as 'forest' in their records. Such instances have been widely evidenced in the tribal areas of East Godavari District.

The conflict between the tribals and the Forest Department with respect to forest land and rights are not yet settled. A boundary of 21,210 km remains under dispute and 77,661 acres of land is recorded to be under cultivation by the tribals in reserved forests prior to 1980. These continued to be unregularized. This issue is an addition to recognition of land rights by revenue department in forest areas under Memo No. 26531/87.

Deforestation, mainly due to exploitation of forests for industrial purposes, is yet another manifestation of resource displacement. This has resulted in decreasing access to forest resources by the tribal communities. The non-recognition of customary and traditional rights of tribals over the forest land cultivation too is a major concern. The tribals are often evicted by the Forest Department from their forest land cultivations, being labelled as encroachers. Forest land to the extent of 13.43 lakh hectare is under encroachment in the country. In Andhra Pradesh alone 2,95,383 hectares of forest land is recorded as pre-1980 and post-1980 encroachments as on 31 March 2004.[71]

The baseline study conducted by the Integrated Tribal Development Agency in 1991 for the Andhra Pradesh Tribal Development Project funded by the International Federation for Agricultural Development (IFAD) project shows that 62,504 tribal households in four northern coastal districts, East Godavari, Visakhapatnam, Vizianagaram and Srikakulam are engaged in shifting cultivation as their only means of survival and livelihood on about 62,948 hectares of land.

There is no regularization process for these holdings to ensure entitlements in favour of tribal occupants. On the other hand, the forest department continues to evict tribal occupants of the forest land on the basis of the notification issued long back. The entire process is contrary to the statement made in the Common Minimum Programme that 'eviction of tribal communities and other forest dwelling communities from forests will be discontinued'.

The World Bank aided projects too are causing displacement of the tribals who depend on forest land for cultivation. The Forest Department in its Resettlement Action Plan document claims that with the financial support of the World Bank assisted Andhra Pradesh Forest Project, nearly 37,000 hectares of forests under encroachment in the tribal areas of Visakhapatnam have been voluntarily put under productive tree crops by the tribals who had encroached upon this land. This statement questions the rehabilitation provided to the displaced tribals. This clearly implies that tribals have been evicted from land under their occupation of podu or shifting cultivation land.

This is a clear violation of the World Bank's own policy towards indigenous people (OD4.30, involuntary settlement).

Offering a package and using NGOs to motivate social capital and compelling tribals to move out from the forest land is the hidden agenda of the Forest Department. The state has become an agent to implement the World Bank Projects. NGOs are systematically being co-opted by the state. Some of the NGOs act as a curtain to the state and World Bank to hide the displeasure or aggression of the target people. This is to reduce the pressure from the grassroots. This minimises the demand of tribals for regularization of their cultivation in the forest land. The forest department never recognized their rights over land and arbitrarily fixed the reserve forest boundaries in the tribal areas. The conflict between the tribals and forest department in respect of forest land is yet to be settled.

The State has come up with contradictory statements with regard to the extension of the forest land settlements covered by the Forest Rights Recognition Act 2006. The Secretary, Tribal Welfare, Government of Andhra Pradesh, issued guidelines for the implementation of the Act in the year 2008. The guidelines say that the Forest Department has informed that 2,36,355 hectares of land is under encroachment by forest dwelling tribals. This is only an indication and actual settlement of the land will be based on the claims accepted by the District Level Committee'. However, as per the reports of the Tribal Welfare Department, Government of Andhra Pradesh, presently 9,93,551 hectares or 24,838,79 acres of land is covered by Preliminary Notification under Section 4 of the Andhra Pradesh Forest Act, 1967. Preliminary Notification refers to a notification issued to the local public informing the intention of the government in declaration of certain areas as reserved forests. This notification is given under the 1967 Act seeking objections from the local people in the reservation process of land as reserve forest. A majority of this land has been under preliminary notification for at least the last two decades or even more. Both land and livelihood rights of lakhs of poor people have remained unrecognized on these deemed forests so far. If the rights of the occupants are settled under the Andhra Pradesh Forest Act it would restrict their rights to lay claim on their possession after the notification is issued.

However, the recent enactment of the Scheduled Tribes and other Traditional Forest Dwellers (Recognition of Forest Rights) Act 2006, which came into force in the year 2007, recognizes both the individual and community rights over the forest land. These laws are in addition to the existing rights ensuring land to the Adivasis in the Scheduled Areas. These laws facilitate to seek land entitlements through the recognition of their occupation of forest land. However, the state is claiming the process as distribution of land pattas to the tribals instead of recognizing the rights of tribals and other forest dwellers over the forest land.

The Forest Rights Recognition Act 2006, promises to be a pro-poor institutional reform and indeed, many poor people have already benefited from its implementation. However, the process has been severely anti-poor and so the pro-poor benefits have been restricted in many ways. It is surprising to note that the government has not distributed titles for community forest land claims but 100 titles were distributed to the Forest Department controlled Vana Samrakshna Samithis (VSS) in Adilabad District.

Tribal Land Rights Movements

Protests over tribal land rights are to be understood in the context of social, economic and political conditions during a specific period. Tribal revolts have generally been evoked by the struggle for survival. The revolts have generally been against the oppressive policies of both the government and the land proprietary institutions. As a consequence of these revolts, the efforts of the state were drawn to bring systems in place for special protection of the tribals. There were altogether 70 major tribal revolts during the 200 years of British rule in India.[72]

There are three phases which can be identified in the tribal movements:

1. During the British period most of the revolts were against the policies of the state affecting the traditional control of the tribals over their resources.
2. Political struggles against the exploitation by the non-tribals and appropriation of tribal land.
3. The opposition to the role of the state, particularly in the displacement of the tribals, and state-induced marginalization after the advent of globalization.

Tribal Struggles: Beginnings

The tribal revolts in Andhra Pradesh ensued on seven occasions. The first of the revolts led by Rambhoopati took place in 1802–1803. It is now popularly known as the Rampa Fituri, or Rampa Rebellion, named after Rampa near Chodavaram in the East Godavari District of Andhra Pradesh. A second revolt around 1862 was directed against the *Muttadars* (petty tribal zamindars), who supported the British. The third revolt around 1879 led by Chandraiah, Sambaiah, Thamman Dora and Ambul Reddy was also in the Rampa country. The fourth occasion on which a tribal uprising took place between 1922–1924 occurred under the leadership of Alluri Sri Rama Raju. While all these revolts had taken place in the coastal Andhra region, in the Telangana part of the Nizam's state, tribal revolts had taken place on two occasions. In 1842, Captain Blunt's troops were attacked by Baster Gonds forcing Captain Blunt to withdraw. Again, in 1941 a sporadic uprising of the Gonds and Kolam led by Komram Bheemu took place in the Adilabad District of the Telangana Area in the erstwhile Nizam's state.

Muttadars introduced new *abkari* (excise) regulations on account of which the local tribals were not allowed to tap toddy even for their domestic consumption. The imposition of several new taxes on the people led to a large number of litigation cases between the Zamindar, tribals and the Muttadars. In several cases the Zamindars obtained ex-party decrees and attached the property of the tribals. The police helped the Zamindars, and the confiscation of Muttas and the oppression of the people resulted in risings against Zamindar authority in 1859, 1861 and 1862.

Few forms of taxation could have affected the peasants of Rampa more directly than taxes on toddy. From March to June, when the podu (shifting cultivation) fields had been cleared and food stocks were low, the hill men would live upon palmyra and sago palm toddy. Not surprisingly, they reacted by refusing to pay the new taxes which was the last straw – the spark that fired the train of growing discontent with the *mansabdar's* regime. Almost at once, on 13 March 1879, the Rampa rebellion began.[74]

The revolt of the people of Rampa was clearly against the state's encroachment over their traditional rights over forest resources and those who had profited from their exploitation. Restrictions on podu, creation of forest reserves, increased axe tax, introduction of opium into the hills for revenue as well as for the subjugation of the tribals, prevention of the customary right to make toddy and collection of forest produce were the measures that drove the tribal people of Rampa to rebel repeatedly.[75]

Thus, one can see that peasant revolts occur when their traditional socio-economic order is under attack, when capitalist classes are either emerging from within the society or intruding on it from the outside. One finds precisely the same process at work in the peasant revolts of late-medieval Europe, and of colonial Burma and Vietnam in the early twentieth century.[76]

The observations of Haimendorf are worth noting here:

> From our point of view the history of Rampa Rebellion is important in two respects. It shows, firstly, that aboriginals, even if inherently not of warlike character, are capable of considerable efforts when driven to extremities, and secondly, that it is both inexpedient and dangerous to allow the control and exploitation of aboriginal population to fall into the hands of unscrupulous outsiders, who although not directly responsible to the government, are backed by the authority of the police and the law courts.[77]

In 1832, the disturbances in the district and in Parlakhemundi Zamindari of Ganjam rose to such severity that the government was compelled to appoint Mr Russel, a revenue board member as Special Commissioner to suppress the revolt, arming him with extraordinary powers and a large military force.[78]

According to Haimendorf, while in reality this insurrection cannot be called a tribal struggle or a popular revolt like the Rampa rebellion, it was nevertheless successful. The prolonged defiance of law and order by tribals in the hilly areas of Vishakhapatnam and East Godavari agencies opened the eyes of the government to the gravity of the problem in the area. It realized that the tribal people living in these areas required special protection. The British authorities decided once again to give special measures to the Agency people for their development. It was felt that they required a more protective approach rather than a merely administrative one. This led to the allocation of subjects of tribal legislation and tribal welfare from the centre to the state.[79] The Andhra Pradesh Agency Rules 1924, was made to govern the Agency Areas through the District Collector, designating her/him as an Agent to the Government.

An uprising of Gonds and Kolams in the Adilabad District of Hyderabad in 1940 occurred on account of the land and forest policy which ran directly counter to the needs and legitimate rights of the aboriginal people. By the late thirties, the tribals of Adilabad District were subjected to double oppression, one by the non-tribals who encroached upon their agricultural land, and the other, by the forest officials who expanded the boundaries of the reserved forest at the expense of their traditional habitat. The resultant conflict culminated in the death of ten Gonds in police firing in the 1940s.[80] The alienation of their land in the plains and the curtailment of their rights in the forests, were greatly resented by the tribals. The tyrannies and extractions of the subordinate government servants working in the forest and police departments further exasperated them.[81]

There are two main factors that can be traced to the tribal revolts that occurred in Andhra Pradesh and elsewhere in the country. There was a clash of economic interests between the tribals and non-tribals and secondly, exploitation and oppression led to the tribal revolts. The other major factor was the clash of cultures of the tribals and their non-tribal vested interests which often led to social oppression by the non-tribals, ultimately leading to militant tribal movements.[82]

Tribal Struggle in the Post-Independence Period

The non-tribal's hold over land continued unabated during the Nizam Government in the State of Hyderabad. Paradoxically, this took a new shape in the period 1947–57 with the dawn of the Telangana Peasant Movement (1946–51). This movement helped to bring a Tenancy Legislation protecting the interests of the tenant's land rights. The genesis of the peasant struggle in Telangana can be traced to the Srikakulam Movement of 1969 which was inspired by the Naxalbari Movement in West Bengal.

The Naxalite Movement in 1969 aimed to seize the state's power through an agrarian revolution. The Naxal Movement is said to have succeeded in regaining control over 3 lakh acres of tribal land in the five districts of Warangal, Karimnagar, Adilabad, West and East Godavari Districts in the state of Andhra Pradesh.[83] It may be mentioned here that the Tribal Protective Land Transfer Regulations 1 of 70 was promulgated after the Naxalite Movement in 1969.

Mass-based organizations affiliated to the left political parties with strong rural roots often took up the cause of tribals in land disputes in the post-1970s. Such organizations include the Raitu Coolie Sangham under the political party of CPI-ML New Democracy, which was earlier known as CPI-ML Prajapandha and involved in land issues in East Godavari. The Agency Girijan

Sangham frontal group of the revolutionary party CPI-ML, operating in both East and West Godavari. Andhra Pradesh Girijana Sangham, a splinter organization of CPI-M, began focusing on tribal land issues in the post-1990s in the Agency Areas of West Godavari District. These organizations have been involved in mobilizing the tribal communities for retrieval of their land from under the possession of non-tribals through land occupation movements.

The collective action of the tribals under the leadership of the Andhra Pradesh Communist Committee of Revolutionary (APCCR) created a scare among the non-tribal cultivators who had settled in the tribal areas. They could not approach the courts as they had illegally acquired tribal land. They began putting pressure on the state government to use police force to curb the collective action of the tribals on the plea that they were being led by the APCCR (Naxalite) cadres. As a result, the state government established police camps throughout the Agency Areas of East and West Godavari, Khammam and Warangal Districts. A police camp was also set up in Kondamodalu.[84]

The movement of tribals of Kondamodulu village which consists of twelve hamlets in Devipatnam Mandal of East-Godavari District in Andhra Pradesh focused on the land struggle against landlords who used to control tribal land through illegal means. Shivaiah Patrudu, a non-tribal landlord along with his other kinfolk, used to dictate terms in the Agency Area. The feudal lord's rule over the area was challenged by the 'Girijana Sangham' which was founded in 1967 by the tribals of the area, and is an outfit of the CPI (ML). The movement began in the year 1968 and gained momentum during the period between July 1981 and November 1982 when the tribals under the aegis of the Girijana Sangham, occupied the land controlled by the landlord and sowed paddy. Having vested control over 3,000 acres of land in that area, the movement has now spread to other areas as the neighbouring mandals of West Godavari District.

Post-1986, tribal areas of Devipatnam Mandal in East Godavari District witnessed land occupation movement by the tribals with the support of Andhra Pradesh Ryutu Coolie Sangham, a frontal group of CPI (ML) New Democracy. Tribals questioned the fraudulently obtained settlement *pattas* by non-tribals over their land during the survey and settlement period of 1970–76. The tribals occupied such land and restrained non-tribal settlement *patta* holders from entering a stretch of nearly 2,000 acres land.[85]

In 1996, the tribals in the area strongly put forward their claim that the entire land in Scheduled Areas belonged to them, while the non-tribals continued to show the title deeds of the land they held. This led to a controversy regarding the contradictory facts presented in the 1902 and the 1933 Resettlement Survey Register (RSR). Such controversies often took a violent turn during the struggle. Violent attacks on the non-tribals resulted in retaliation wherein both sections recorded loss of life. A civil war-like situation has resulted from this hostility. The incidents at Manugopala and Busarajupalli are illustrative of this. A group of non-tribals raided the tribal hamlet over a land issue in Manugopala village on 21 March 1996. On 5 August 1997, during a confrontation at Busarajupalli, the tribals scared the non-tribals by shooting arrows and thrashing a few men.[86]

A few NGOs as Laya and Sakthi, based in tribal area of East Godavari District have done considerable work in raising the tribal land question in coastal areas and parts of Telangana region in Andhra Pradesh through various tribal initiatives, without confining themselves to court litigation. The tribals are capacitated to articulate their land rights issues before the administrative authorities as the Mandal Revenue Officers, Revenue Divisional Officers and Project Officers. A section of the tribals is now equipped with the required knowledge and skills to understand the land records. This knowledge triggered a land movement which resulted in the state level officials agreeing to convene a meeting to settle all outstanding issues during the year 1997. Further, the land issues of Godavari District came under the consideration of Andhra Pradesh High Court on several occasions. One such case was Payam Gangamma and Vasudha Mishra and others (WP CC No. 1381/97). The High Court passed a land mark judgement agreeing with the concern of tribals and issued directions to be followed during the survey of lands to know the actual land possessors. The High Court directed the revenue authorities to conduct land survey in the presence of tribal stakeholders after furnishing the relevant land documents and maps. These changes have brought confidence in the tribal youth in resolving the land conflicts on their own.[87]

Even during the talks in 2004 with the government on the issue of land, the Peoples War Group (Maoists) and Janasakthi (CPI-ML) Group put forth several demands, as the lowering of the ceiling limits on land, distribution of surplus land, including the endowment and other land at the disposal of the government, to the poorer sections. The talks with the government pushed the state to constitute the Koneru Rangarao Land Committee to look into the land issues and study the land laws for recommendations to improve the agrarian situation. The Committee came up with several recommendations, protecting the interest of tribal land for effective implementation of tribal protective land transfer regulations and cancellation of settlement pattas obtained by non-tribals fraudulently. However, no amendments were made to plug the loopholes in the law. On the other hand, the circulars issued by the government for implementation are also not enforced.

Thus, the on and off movements for political contestation by the non governmental organizations and political parties for increasing access to land justice for tribals have created only a partial impact in enforcement of tribal protective land laws.

In the context of the above background, the phenomenon of both land and forest dispossession in the state of Andhra Pradesh, the study seeks to situate the land alienation problem in the Scheduled Area of East Godavari District and make an evidence based analysis from various sources by using descriptive, analytical data of land related information, case studies, and other methods.

Notes

1. Banerjee, Abhijit and Iyer, Lakshmi (2008) 'Colonial Land Tenure, Electoral Competition and Public Goods in India', Working Paper, January (www.hbs.edu/research/pdf/08-062).
2. Ellickson, R. (1993) 'Property in Land', *Yale Law Journal*, JSTOR, Lexis, Vol. 103, No. 6, pp. 1344–62.
3. Peters, P. (1998) 'The Erosion of Commons and the Emergence of Property: Problems for Social Analysis', in R.C. Hunt and A. Gilman (eds.), *Property in Economic Context*, University Press of America, Oxford, pp. 356–61.
4. See, e.g., Brockett, C.D. (1990) *Land, Power and Poverty: Agrarian Transformation and Political Conflict in Central America*, Unwin Hyman, Boston, pp. 23–26.
5. Saxena, K.B. (2006) 'Alternative Economic Survey, India 2005–06: Disempowering Masses, Development as Destitution', pp. 263–74. (http://www.daanishbooks.com/product_downloads/c/aes2005_06_20_kb_saxena_35543.pdf.).

6. Mohapatro, Prafullo Chandro (1987) *Land Revenue Administration in Tribal Areas in Economic Development of Tribal India*, Ashish Publishing House, New Delhi.
7. Jha, J.C. (1989) 'The Changing Land System of the Tribals of Chota Nagpur, 1771–1831', in Tarasankar Banerjee (ed.), *Changing Land Systems and Tribals in Eastern India in the Modern Period*, Subarnarekha, Calcutta.
8. Matlhy,T.J. (1918) *Ganjam Manual*, Madras, p. 139.
9. Sardesai, G.S. (1948) *New History of the Marathas*, Vol. II, Phoenix Publications, Bombay, p. 355.
10. Koraput District was part of Vizagapatam District of Madras presidency and was not included in Orissa till 1st April 1936 when the province of Orissa was newly created. The Ganjam District was also under the Madras presidency till this date.
11. Kumar, Dharma (ed.) (1982) *The Cambridge Economic History of India*, Vol. 2, Chapters I and II, Cambridge University Press, Cambridge.
12 Francis, W. (1907) *Madras District Gazetteers: Vizagapatnam*, Vol. I Government Press, Madras, pp. 310–11.
13. Dubey, S.N. and Murdia, Ratan (eds.) (1977) *Land Alienation and Restoration in Tribal Communities in India*, Himalaya Publishing House, Bombay, p. 140.
14. Senapati, N. and Sahu, N.K. (1966) *Orissa District Gazetteers, Koraput*, Odisha Government Press, Cuttack, pp. 70–71.
15. Francis, W. (1907) *Madras District Gazetteers, Vizagapatnam*, Vol. I, Government Press, Madras, pp. 318–19.
16. Rao, M.S.A. (1983) 'Non-tribal Colonisation and Tribal Deprivation in Andhra', *Social Action*, Vol. 33, July-September.
17. Furer-Haimendorf, op. cit., pp. 203–08; Hemingway, F.R. (1915). *Madras District Gazetteers: Godavari*, Government Press, Madras, p. 67; Thurston, E. and Rangachari, K. (1909) *Castes and Tribes of Southern India*, Vol. III and IV, Cosmo Publications, Delhi, p. 355 and pp. 64–65; Cain, Bhadrachellam and Rekapalli Taluqas, p. 33.
18. Arnold, David (1986) Committee of Circuit's Report, 1787, p. 4 cited in Ranajit Guha (ed.), *Subaltern Studies III*, Oxford University Press, Delhi.
19. Balagopal, K. (1989) 'Pitting the Tribals against the Non-tribal Poor', *Economic and Political Weekly*, May 27, pp. 1149–54.
20. Linga Murthy, N. and Sivaramakrishna Rao, C. (1985) 'Debt-Bondage in Tribal Areas: An Empirical Observation', in K. Murali Manohar, P. Ramaiah and C. Sivaramakrishna Rao (eds.), *Political Economy of Tribal Development*, Indian Institute of Public Administration, Warangal.

21. Report of the Study Team on Social Welfare and Welfare of Backward Classes (1959) Ministry of Social Welfare, Government of India, Vol. I.
22. Balagopal, K. (1989) 'Pitting the Tribals against the Non-tribal Poor', *Economic and Political Weekly*, Vol. 24, Issue No. 2, May 27, pp. 1149–54.
23. *A.P. District Gazetteers* (1976) Government of Andhra Pradesh Press, Hyderabad.
24. Elwin, Varrier (1963) *A New Deal for Tribal India*, Ministry of Home Affairs, New Delhi, p. 49.
25. National Commission Report on Backward Areas Development (1981) Ministry of Social Welfare Department, Government of India, June, p. 50.
26. J.M. Girglani Commission (2005) Committee Report of Ministry of Rural Development, Government of Andhra Pradesh Press, Hyderabad.
27. Trinadha Rao, P. (2007) *Persisting Alienation of Tribal Land*, A.P. Social Watch Report, Hyderabad.
28. P. Gangamma Vs. Vasudha Misra & another 1998 (2) ALD 35.
29. Note on Land Problems in Agency Areas of West Godavari (1997) Government of Andhra Pradesh, Social Welfare Department, Hyderabad.
30. Fernandes, Walter (1996) 'Land Reforms, Ownership Pattern and Alienation of Tribal Livelihood', *Social Action*, Vol. 46, October-December, p. 428.
31. Rao, B. Janardhana (1987) *Land Alienation in Tribal Areas*, Kakatya School of Public Administration, Warangal.
32. Presently Srikakulam, Vijayanagaram and Visakhapatnam Districts.
33. Arnold, David (1986) Memorial from Sec. Dist. Assoc., Vishkhapatnam, to Sec. Local and Municipal, 8 November 1916, L/P&J/6/408 cited 'Rebellious Hillmen: The Gudem-Rampa Risings 1839–1924', in Ranajit Guha (ed.), *Subaltern Studies III*, Oxford University Press, Delhi.
34. Based on Simon Commission Report.
35. For details see Ghurye, G.S. (1963) *The Scheduled Tribes*, Popular Press, Bombay, pp. 70–97.
36. Furer-Haimendorf, C. von (1985) *Tribes of India: The Struggle for Survival*, Oxford University Press, New Delhi.
37. Reddy, N. Subba (1988) 'Depriving Tribals of Land', *Economic and Political Weekly*, Vol. 23, Issue No. 29, July 16.
38. During May-July 1967.
39. Parthasarathy, G. (1979) *Peasant Movements and Changing Agrarian Structure in A.P.*, Department of Cooperation and Applied Economics, Andhra University, Visakhapatnam (mimeo).

40. Swaminadhan, D. (2004) 'Tribal Welfare and Development', Draft Policy Paper, Government of India, Delhi.
41. Karuppaiyan, E. (1990) 'Alienation of Tribal Land in Tamil Nadu', *Economic and Political Weekly*, Vol. 25, Issue 22, June 2, p. 1185.
42. Balagopal, K. (2007) 'Land Unrest in Andhra Pradesh III: Illegal Acquisition in Tribal Areas', *Economic and Political Weekly*, Vol. 42, Issue 40, October 6, p. 4031.
43. Reddy, N. Subba (2006) 'Development through Dismemberment of the Weak: Threat of Polavaram Project', *Economic and Political Weekly*, Vol. 41, Issue 15, April 15, pp. 1430–31.
44. Furer-Haimendorf, C. von (1985) *Tribes of India: The Struggle for Survival*, Oxford University Press, New Delhi.
45. A.V. Thakkar Committee (1947) Report of the Excluded and Partially Excluded Areas Sub-committee, August 18.
46. Balagopal, K. (2004) 'Foreword', in *Land Rights of Adivasis* by P. Trinadha Rao, Laya Publications, Visakhapatnam.
47. Samata Appellants vs. State of Andhra Pradesh & others with Ms. Hyderabad Abrasives & Minerals (P) Ltd. (Appellant) & State of Andhra Pradesh & other, Respondents, AIR 1997 Supreme Court 3297.
48. P. Rami Reddy & others vs. State of A.P. & another 1988 (22) Reports (SC) 364.
49. M. Suresh Bhargava & another vs. State of A.P. & others 1989 (2) ALT 516.
50. Adarsha Adivasi Mahila Samithi & others vs. Agent to the Govt., Khammam & others, 2003 (5) ALD 284.
51. Amrendra Prapat Singh (Appellant) vs. Tej Bahadur Prajapati & others, AIR 2004 Supreme Court 3782.
52. Ashok vs. Baba Rao & another 2002 (6) ALT 296.
53. Kakarla Nageswara Rao & other vs. Govt. of A.P. rep by its secretary (Tribal Welfare) Dept. Hyderabad 1995 (3) ALT 164.
54. Vuppuluri Veera Venkata Raju & others vs. Special Deputy Tahsildar, Tribal Welfare, Gangavaram (V&M), E.G. District & others 2007 (6) ALD 292.
55. Samata Appellants vs. State of Andhra Pradesh & others with Ms. Hyderabad Abrasives & Minerals (P) Ltd. (Appellant) & State of Andhra Pradesh & other, Respondents, AIR 1997 Supreme Court 3297.
56. Vemana Somalamma & another (Appl), Veera Sunkar Deo & another (Pet) vs. Deputy Collector (TW), Rampachodavaram, E.G. Dist, 1993 (1) ALT 409 (F.B.).
57. A.P. Girijan Welfare Students and Youth Union vs. State of A.P. W.P. No. 1755/90 dated 5 December 1984.

58. P. Gangamma vs. Vasudha Misra & another 1998 (2) ALD 35.
59. Koppula Saramma vs. Govt. of A.P. Social Welfare Dept. & others, 2001 (3) ALT 501.
60. Gadde Nagabushanamma vs. Govt. of A.P. & others 1999 (5) ALD 430.
61. Kandula Brahmaiah vs. The Deputy Collector (Tribal Welfare) Rampachodavaram, E.G. Dist. W.P. 2169/1981 dated 10 December 1986 (un-reported).
62. Samatha vs. State of A.P. AIR 1997 SC 3297.
63. N. Durga Rao & another vs. Special Deputy Collector (TW) Kota Ramachandrapuram W.G. Dist. & others, 2003 (6) ALD (NOC) 68.
64. Special Deputy Collector (TW), Rampachodavaram, E.G. Dist. & others vs. Datla Venkapathi Raju & others, 2003 (1) ALD 386 (D.B.). Similar view was taken by the court in G. Nageswararao @ China Nageswararao Vs. Government of A.P. & others, 2007 (6) ALD 621.
65. Ch. Satyanarayana vs. Agent to the Govt. & Dist. Collector, Visakhapatnam, W.P. 6065/1979 (un-reported).
66. Deputy Collector vs. Venkata Ramanaiah & another, AIR 1996 (SC) 224.
67. K. Mahalaxmi & another vs. Government of Andhra Pradesh & others, 2000 (5) ALD 588.
68. Kola Mahalaxmi vs. Agent to the Government, Khammam & others, 1999 (6) ALD 718.
69. See 'A Specter Haunting India', *The Economist*, 17 August 2006 (http://www.economist.com/world/asia/displaystory.cfm?story_id=7799247).
70. Prof. Vidyarthi Committee (1972) Report of the Task Force on Development of Tribal Areas, April 5.
71. Parliament Digest-Budget Session (2004) NCAS Publications, Pune, p. 53.
72. Raghavaiah, V. (1971) *Tribal Revolts*, Andhra Pradesh Adimjati Sevak Sangha, Nellore.
73. Raghavaiah, V. (1979) 'Unrest in Andhra Pradesh', in A.R. Desai (ed.), *Peasant Struggles in India*, Oxford University Press, Bombay, p. 176.
74. Sullivan to Chief Sec. 9 September 1879, ibid.; Joint Magistrate, Chodavaram, to District Magistrate, 18 March 1879, MJP, No. 313, 25 March 1879. In the Settlement of 1879–80, a small chigurupannu was incorporated in the Muttadars' 'kattubadi'.
75. Arnold, David (1982) 'Rebellious Hillmen: The Gudem-Rampa Risings 1839–1924', in Ranajit Guha (ed.), *Subaltern Studies I*, Oxford University Press, Delhi.
76. Hilton, op. cit., pp. 114–18; Scott, James C. (1976) *The Moral Economy of the Peasant Rebellion and Subsistence in Southeast Asia*, Yale University Press, New Haven; exp. Ch. 4 in Arnold, David (1982)

'Rebellious Hillmen: The Gudem-Rampa Risings 1839–1924', in Ranajit Guha (ed.), *Subaltern Studies I*, Oxford University Press, Delhi.

77. Furer-Haimendorf, C. von (1945) 'Aboriginal Rebellions in the Deccan', *Man in India*, Vol. 25 cited by Rao, P. Kamal Manohar and Rao, D.L. Prasad (1982) *Tribal Movements in Andhra Pradesh*, Ajanta Publishers, Delhi, pp. 353–72.
78. Francis, W. (1907) *Madras District Gazetteers: Vizagapatnam*, Vol. I, Government Press, Madras, pp. 318–19.
79. Raghavaiah, V. (1971) *Tribal Revolts*, Andhra Pradesh Adimjati Sevak Sangha, Nellore.
80. Reddy, N. Subba (1988) 'Depriving Tribals of Land', *Economic and Political Weekly*, Vol. 23, Issue 29, July.
81. See Furer-Haimendorf, C. von (1945) 'Aboriginal Rebellions in the Deccan', *Man in India*, Vol. 25, pp. 5–17.
82. Sivaramakrishana Rao, C. and Bobbili, A. (1985) 'Tribal Movements in Andhra Pradesh: A Short History', in K. Murali Manohar, P. Ramaiah and C. Sivaramakrishna Rao (eds), *Political Economy of Tribal Development*, Indian Institute of Public Administration, Warangal.
83. Report on Godavari Valley, Girijana Ryotanga Porata Charita, CPI (ML) 1977.
84. Jayaprakash Rao, P. (1985) 'The Struggle for Land: Tribal Revots in Two Villages', in K. Murali Manohar, P. Ramaiah and C. Sivaramakrishna Rao (eds), *Political Economy of Tribal Development*, Indian Institute of Public Administration, Warangal.
85. Trinadha Rao, P. (2007) 'Persisting Alienation of Tribal Land', in Fr. Thomas Pallithanam (ed.), *Rekindling Hope*, A.P. Social Watch Report, Hyderabad.
86. Kumar, Arun (2006) 'From Landlessness to Ownership: The Tribal Struggle for Property Rights', in Govinda Chandra Rath (ed.), *Tribal Development in India*, Sage Publications, New Delhi.
87. Trinadha Rao, P. (2007) 'Persisting Alienation of Tribal Land', in Fr. Thomas Pallithanam (ed.), *Rekindling Hope*, A.P. Social Watch Report, Hyderabad.

Chapter 3

Land Control by Non-Tribals in the Scheduled Areas of East Godavari District

Major Trends

The earliest records of land ownership dating back to the pre-independence period were based on rent system and land survey records. The British carried out a survey in 1902 and later in 1932, to create a register of what land the ryots controlled as well as to provide a basis for fiscal records. This was part of the individual cultivator-based land revenue tenure system (Ryotwari). In addition, the British adopted landlord-based land tenure systems as Muttadari, Mukhasadar and Zamindari in the Agency tracts. The land revenue systems and the tenure systems referred to the arrangement made by the British administration to collect revenue from land cultivators. A Land Register was developed which states the ryot's name, tenure, area and particulars of land assessment for the purpose of extracting feudal dues. No special protection was made for tribals to retain their land resources in the Scheduled Areas by imposing restrictions on the non-tribal Muttadars, Mukhasadars or Zamindars to transfer land to other non-tribals. This is the key factor for land alienation in the tribal areas.

The land ownership which was until then governed by oral tradition and collective understanding without formal records was disturbed. The introduction of an external agency to enumerate and recognize land ownership of the households made the community's control and role redundant by making an official, the ombudsman.

Subsequently, this resulted in land alienation in favour of the non-tribal immigrants. Power in the feudal system was vested in the institutional and legal structures that were put in place in the combined interests of landholders and the imperialist British State.

The Rampachodavaram division comprises most of what was in former times known as 'the Rampa country', from the village of that name which stands north of Chodavaram village. This Agency Tract is bound on the north by Bhadrachalam Taluk in Khammam District, on the west by Polavaram Taluk in West Godavari District separated by river Godavari, in the south by Rajahmundry Taluk and in the east by Yellavaram Taluk of East Godavari District as per the erstwhile recognized boundaries.

Early land tenural history recorded in Government Gazetteers says that only one village in the division is on the Ryotwari tenure, four villages are held as Mokhasas direct from the government, 50 belong to the zamindaris and the rest, some 300 in number, consist of hill Muttas held on the *kowl* tenure. The zamindari villages are said to have belonged long ago to Reddi chiefs, called the Reddi Razus, and have been sold by them, apparently before the permanent settlement of 1802–1803, to various lowland zamindars. Twenty villages belong to the Polavaram estate, four to Pithapuram, and two to Gutala, while the independent estates of Dandangi and Toyyeru and the disputed Mukhasa estate of Kondamodalu contain twelve, eight and four villages respectively. The hill Muttas, 24 in number, have a distinct history of their own.

The original Agency Tracts of Godavari consist of the whole of the old Mansabs (estates) of Rampa and Jaddangi, the more hilly parts of the old Peddapuram and Polavaram Zamindaris, the Dutcharthi and Guditeru Muttas of the Golgonda Agency transferred from Vizagapatam (Visakhapatnam) in 1881 and the Bhadrachalam taluk transferred from the Central Provinces. The Mansabs were disregarded as being unimportant, both at the time of the permanent settlement in 1802–1803 and during the settlement of 1861–1866. The land which formerly belonged to two zamindaris of Peddapuram and Polavaram is held either by the Muttadars or directly by the government. The zamindars came into prominence during the period preceding the transfer of this district to the British. The zamindars maintained retainers who helped them in the collection of revenue. They appropriated the entire revenue thus collected and themselves paid only a certain fixed sum to the government.

There is no operation of Rent Reduction Act in the erstwhile Mutta villages nor a system of collection of land revenue on the land in this area. The system in vogue here was the house-wise collection of 'Gadapa pannu'. The Muttadar used to collect fixed tax for every household in the Mutta villages, irrespective of landholdings of the households.

Administrative Areas under Land Tenure

Government Villages

The government villages, generally speaking, have not been surveyed or settled, but are rented out from year to year to the highest suitable bidder, who is debarred by the terms of his annual patta from raising the rent of the ryots. The auction is merely symbolic, as there is seldom any competition.

The settlement in the Agency Tract of government villages was carried as per the GOMs No. 2121, Revenue department dated 8 October 1931, as applicable to the upland areas of the East Godavari District, settled in the year 1899 along with certain modifications with regard to dry and irrigation sources. A land survey was also conducted in the year 1902. The rules covering the land survey of 1902 and 1935 did not have any specific legal protection to the land owned or occupied by tribals in the Agency Areas.

Mukhasa Villages

The Agency Areas also includes a few Mukhasa villages granted by the government on favourable terms for the services performed during the Rampa rebellion. Madhuveeti Yerram Raju was appointed as Mukhasadar of Nellipudi and Kuramagondi villages of Gangavaram Mandal by the virtue of *sanad* granted under GOMs No. 1239 dated 10 July 1907. The British government issued *sanad* annexing the tenures. The Sanads contain two conditions; firstly, that a stipulated annual quir-rent, including an *abkari* tax and a local fund cess, should be paid annually to the government; and, secondly, that the Muttadar should conduct himself loyally and peaceably, and should give every assistance to the government in maintaining law and order. A warning was added that if the Muttadar failed in his duties, his Mutta was liable to be taken over. There is no prohibition on transfer of land to non-tribals in the conditions of the Mukhasa Sanads. This is a major reason for the slipping of land to non-tribals in the Mukhasa land tenure villages.

Tribal Land Alienation in Scheduled Areas

Prior to Independence, the open invitation by proprietors or sanad holders of land tenures of Mukasha, Estate, Mutta to any person to own land on certain conditions is the key indicator for land alienation in the Scheduled Areas. The situation in government villages is altogether different, because even here there is no invitation or restriction on the occupation of land by non-tribals. After Independence, the state itself promoted colonization in the tribal areas in 1949 by inviting the plains people to settle here by offering land to them. The report[1] of the team of experts headed by the Special Agency Development Officer, R.S. Malayappan (1951) says that 'if necessary, after all the colonists are permanently settled and all the Government loans are repaid and after all the hill-men are brought to the level of the plainsmen, we can think of transferring the ownership of the land to the colonists'. The team of experts selected sites for colonization schemes in 34 places to settle plainsmen (non-tribals) in the erstwhile Agency taluks of Nugur, Bhadrachalam, Ellavaram and Gudem (Table 3.1).

Table 3.1

Colonization Schemes

S. No.	*Taluk*	*Extent Available for Land Coloni-zation (Acres)*	*Number of Families (Tribals and Non-tribals) to be Settled*	*Cost of Irrigation Scheme, if any (₹)*	*Concession Proposed to be Allowed to Settlers (Excluding the Interest Free Loan and Waiver of Land-revenue and Water–cess and Reclamation Charges) ₹*
1.	Nugur	10,750	1,245	1,77,44,000	1,74,075
2.	Bhadrachalam	12,450	1,525	1,42,38,000	2,21,175
3.	Polavaram	2,700	180	0	29,700
4.	Rampachodavaram	1,000	100	8,000	15,500
5.	Yellavaram	9,100	1,030	20,00,000	1,57,250
6.	Gudem	11,300	1,500	18,36,000	2,25,100
7.	Palakonda	1,000	200	3,60,000	29,000
		48,300	5,780	3,61,86,000	8,51,800

Source: Report of R.S. Malayappan (1951).

The state machinery and land proprietors are responsible for land alienation in the Agency tracts. The evidences can be traced from the report of Malayappan , which says:

> it is understood that the Taluk Officers are assigning Government land only to the plains settlers and do not even grant pattas to the hill-men although they have been cultivating the land for a number of years under *Sivayijama* right. It is said that a number of plains men have been granted land on *darkshats* up to 100 or 200 acres each. It is also brought to my notice that the Zamindars are disposing in large extents of waste land including the forests to plainsmen in anticipation of the abolition of the Zamindars and that bogus relinquishment and sale of hill-men's land are also taking place on a large scale.

In Rampa, a metalled road was built as far as Chodavaram in the early 1880s. By the 1930s it was possible to drive from there, 60 km away to Rajahmundry, in a few hours. The cart tracks from Chodavaram to the north and west were metalled and were reported in 1919 as having 'a great effect in opening up the country'. Two other important roads dating from the 1880s ran north from Yeleswaram, one through Dutcharti and Gurtedu Muttas and the other through Juddangi.[2] Perhaps, the purpose of construction of roads is associated with administrative convenience of the British Government to contain the unrest in the Agency Areas as also to open up the land and forest resources for its exploitation for the benefit of state revenue. This may be evidenced from R.S. Malayappan's Report which says that, 'It is proposed to form a road to Chintur in Bhadrachalam Taluk from Maredumilli and when it materializes the exploitation of these forests will be easy and large revenues will accrue to the Government.'

In the East Godavari region, massive invasion of tribal land by outsiders occurred after 1947. The Forest Department, in order to meet the raw material requirements of the Andhra Paper Mills and the growing demand for firewood and timber in the markets of the coastal plains, began the extraction of bamboo and timber from the forests of the northern hills on a large scale, starting in the early 1960s. The laying of roads in the hills to transport forest produce broke the isolation of many hill settlements, thereby facilitating increased land alienation.[3]

The Government of Andhra Pradesh granted leases in GoMs No. 352 for carrying mining operations to a company namely, Hyderabad Abrasives Limited on over 318 acres situated in Maredumilli reserve forest in East Godavari District, in the year 1974 for a period of 20 years. The company cleared the forests in 42 acres by the time the High Court intervened and directed to stop mining in WP 3,734 of 1993 as they were in violation of the Forest Conservation Act of 1980. However, the Supreme Court in *Samata Vs State of Andhra Pradesh* (1997) case, handing over of the lands in the Scheduled Areas to non-tribal owned companies was declared as illegal as per the provisions of Land Transfer Regulations 1 of 70. The Supreme Court passed Judgement when a mining lease was granted to a Perclase India Company over 120 acres in a village Nimmalapadu for exploiting calcite mineral in Paderu Agency Area of Viskahapatnam District. Thus, land alienation by the state for mining operations has had a negative impact on the ecology of the area.

Table 3.2 describes the total extent of land, mandal-wise, in the Scheduled Areas and the extent of land held by the tribals and the non-tribals.

Table 3.2

Mandalwise Data of Land in the Rampachodavaram Revenue Division

Name of the Mandal	*Land (in acres)*	*Land (in hectares)*
Rampachodavaram	1,52,829.59	61,848
Devipatnam	76,834.83	31,094
Maredumilli	2,23,224.54	90,344
Addateegala	1,52,476.14	61,705
Rajavommangi	1,14,955.71	46,521
Gangavaram	1,01,616.98	41,123
Y. Ramavaram	1,93,972.48	78,498
Total	10,15,910.27	4,11,133

Source: Office of Sub Collector, Rampachodavaram (2004).

The data reveals that of 4,11,133 hectares of land 1,33,585.32 hectares of land is under private ownership and Ryotwari pattas have been granted for the same. Of the total private ownership, 1,05,127.89 hectares is under tribal ownership while 28,457.43 hectares is under non-tribal ownership.

The total non-tribal households numbered 17,129 as per the 2001 Census. On an average, a non-tribal household has an extent of land 1.66 hectares. In the case of tribals, there are 35,478 households having an average landholding of 2.96 hectares. In fact, the legal and historical presumption says that the land situated in the Agency Tracts once belonged to tribals. If this were to be implemented, the tribals households in the Scheduled Areas of the district should have an average landholding of 3.76 hectares.

Land Administration and Ownership

The settlement operations were held in 1902 and 1932 in Rajavommangi and part of Gangavaram Mandal villages. All other areas in the Rampachodavaram Revenue Division were settled in 1975 under the Andhra Pradesh Muttas (Abolition and Conversion into Ryotwari) Regulation 1969 (Regulation 2 of 69) and the Andhra Pradesh Scheduled Areas Ryotwari) Regulations 2 of 70. The 2 of 69 Mutta Regulations were extended through an amended 1 of 89 Regulations to the unsettled 7 Mukhasa villages in Gangavaram and Rampachodavaram Mandals. The Mutta Regulations are intended to facilitate survey and settlement operations and determine the landholding rights of occupants. The Muttas are similar to Mukhasa land tenures. So the Survey and Settlement Regulations covering the Muttas were extended to Mukhasa land tenures in the year 1989.

The details in Table 3.3 show the extent of land settled in favour of both the tribals and non-tribals in the Scheduled Areas under 2 of 69 and 2 of 70 Ryotwari Settlement Regulations.

Table 3.3

Extent of Patta Land Under the Control of Tribals and Non-tribals in Mutta and Estate Land Tenure Villages

Status	*Regulation 2/69*		*Regulation 2/70*		*Total*	
	No. of Pattadars	*Extent in ha*	*No. of Pattadars*	*Extent in ha*	*No. of Pattadars*	*Extent in ha*
Tribes	15,246	40,450.39.0	1,454	3,986.36.0	17,600	44,436.75.0
Non-Tribes	419	2,487.72.0	1,237	2,829.10.5	1,656	5,316.82.5
Total	15,665	42,938.11.0	2,691	6,815.46.5	18,356	49,753.57.5

Source: Sub Collector's office, Rampachodavaram, 2004.

There are 394 habitations covered by Mutta areas in the Scheduled Areas of the district. The data shows that after the abolition of Muttas under 2 of 69 Regulations and during the survey period of 1970–76, the non-tribals numbering 419, could secure settlement pattas over the land of about 2,488 hectares which comes to 5.93 hectares on an average for each pattadar, while only 15,246 tribals could secure pattas over the land of 40,450 hectares which comes to 2.65 hectares on an average of each pattadar. It shows that during the Survey Settlement period, the non-tribals managed to get legal entitlements over the land situated in the Scheduled Areas, on which they did not have any legitimacy earlier.

As per the 1990 Report of Neerabh K. Prasad, an IAS officer, entitled 'Protection of Tribal Land', during the survey period 1970–1976, the landholdings of the non-tribals jumped from 9,805 hectares before 1969 to 16,789 hectares in the Scheduled Area of East Godavari District. This reveals that manipulation of land records took place to gain access to land.

There are 21 Estate villages in the Scheduled Areas of the district. In the case of Estate areas, after the abolition of Estates under 2 of 70 Ryotwari Settlement Regulations, 1,237 non-tribals were able to get settlement pattas over 2,829 hectares of land which comes to an average of 2.28 hectares for each pattadar, while 1,454 tribals could secure pattas over 3,936 hectares of land, which comes to an average of 2.74 hectares for each pattadar. The data clearly shows that the Regulations helped the non-tribals to get legitimacy to their occupations in the Scheduled Areas violating the letter and sprit of the tribal protective Land Transfer Regulations 1 of 70. The settlement process in favour of non-tribals during the period is an evidence of tribal land alienation in the Scheduled Areas.

The field study in the East Godavari District of Andhra Pradesh done by Laya during the year 1990, indicates that the forms of ownership of tribal land were never properly inquired into and the tribals were not completely aware of the implications of the Settlement operations. By the time a tribal realized that his land was given off to a non-tribal, it was generally too late to appeal.[4]

Table 3.4 shows the number of Mukhasa villages and extent of land held by the tribals and the non-tribals.

Table 3.4

Extent of Land Under the Control of Tribals and Non-tribals in Mukhasa Land Tenure Villages

S. No.	*Name of the Village*	*Total Sy. Nos*	*Extent in Acres*	*Total Land Under Occupation of Tribals*		*Total Land Under Occupation of Non-tribals*	
				No	*Ext (Ac)*	*No*	*Ext (Ac)*
1.	Vadapalli	98	640.14	97	640.14	–0-	–0-
2.	Nimmalapalem	140	881.21	96	881.21	–0-	–0-
3.	Dharamadugula	97	822.21	120	822.21	–0-	–0-
4.	Pandirimamidi	110	771.38	160	771.38	–0-	–0-
5.	Sirigindalapadu	52	450.79	74	438.32	10	12.47
6.	Kuramgondhi	46	812.00	46	812.00	–0-	–0-
7.	Nellipudi	503	7,307.79	74	132.91	726	7,174.88
		1,046	11,685.52	667	4,498.17	736	7,187.35

Source: Sub collector's office, Rampachodavaram, 2009.

Ac: Acre

There are seven Mukhasa villages in the Scheduled Areas of the district. The land tenure Mukhasa was abolished in 1989 and the 2 of 69 Mutta Regulations were extended for survey and settlement process. However, the land proprietor and sanad holder-Mukhasadar assailing the Survey and Settlement process initiated litigation in the higher courts. As such, no settlement pattas were granted either in favour of tribals or non-tribals. However, the survey figures of land show the extent of land occupation of non-tribals in Mukhasa villages. Of the 7 Mukhasa villages, huge extension of land is found in the hands of non-tribals in Nellipudi. Non-tribals hold 98 per cent of land in the scheduled village Nellipudi. This is due to transfer of the land by Mukhasadar to non-tribals by granting of Krishiki patta, an inalienable patta, on a condition to pay tax for the extent of the grant by the occupant. The Mukhasadar collects tax from the occupant. There is no condition that the Mukhasadar should give Krishiki patta only to tribals. As there is no prohibition in land transfers prior to the 1 of 70 Regulations between non-tribals, non-tribals were able to obtain antedated tax receipts along with Krishiki pattas from the non-tribal Mukhasadar.

There are 128 Government Revenue villages in the Scheduled Areas of the district. The total ryotwari land is 64,487 hectares of land, while the non-tribals are holding the land to the extent of 21,816 hectares, which comes to 34 per cent of the total land in the Government Revenue villages.

Table 3.5

Cultivable Land Under the Control of Tribals and Non-tribals in the Revenue Division, Rampachodavaram

Name of the Mandal	*Total Cultivable Area (ha)*	*Land with Tribals (ha)*	*Land with Non-tribals (ha)*
Rampachodavaram	12,323.04	1,295.97	230.08
Devipatnam	9,336.38	5,798.84	3,537.54
Maredumilli	5,863.52	5,863.52	-
Addateegala	36,333.75	27,820.66	8,513.09
Gangavaram	24,664.54	17,627.80	7,036.74
Rajavommangi	32,540.00	24,232.00	831.99
Y. Ramavaram	12,524.09	22,489.10	8,307.99
Total	1,33,585.32	1,05,127.89	28,457.43

Source: Sub Collector's office, Rampachodavaram, 2004.

Table 3.5 shows the pattern of land possession, not only the land covered by land tenures of Muttas, Estates, Mukhasas but also government land. The nature of land occupation will further give an understanding of landholdings of non-tribals in the Scheduled Areas and the extent of land alienation. Except in Maredumilli mandal, non-tribals hold land in all other Scheduled mandals in the Rampachodavaram Revenue Division.

The scheme of surveying the unsurveyed tracts in Scheduled Areas of the State and preparing up-to-date basic land records was taken up as a State Plan scheme by the Government of Andhra Pradesh during the VII Plan period as a part of the Integrated Tribal Development Programme aimed at general socio-economic development of tribals in the state. The Telugu Grameena Magani Samaradhana (TGMS) survey conducted between 1986 to 1996 reveals the extent of land alienation among tribals. There were 6,781 non-tribals controlling 15,521.17 hectares of land in the Scheduled Area of East Godavari District.[5] An inference can be drawn from the TGMS survey data that the process of land alienation took place without any official check.

Therefore, the total extent of land covered by Survey and Settlement operations in favour of non-tribals in all major land tenure systems in the Scheduled Areas of the district was 27,419 hectares. An extent of 80 per cent of land was surveyed and settled by the year 1932 itself in government villages, followed by 19 per cent settled during Survey and Settlements between 1970–1975 in both Mutta and Estate land tenures and one per cent of land is yet to be settled in favour of non-tribals in Mukhasa tenures.

The estimation of landholdings in the hands of non-tribals is a difficult task. Land transfers are dynamic in nature. Most of the private land transactions held between tribals and non-tribals or among the non-tribals are unregistered and oral in nature. So the extent of land covered by such private land deals is unrecorded in the revenue records. The extent of land in the possession of non-tribals by virtue of unauthorized land transfers is also unknown unless a detailed survey is conducted village-wise. The revenue records do not reflect the extent of land and names of actual cultivators as per the ground situation. The name of the pattadar is carried as the enjoyer of that land in the column of 'enjoyer' in Adangal records. The encroachments on government land by non-tribals are not registered in the revenue records separately. So the extent of land held by such government land is also not covered by the analysis.

Landholding Pattern in Agency Area: 1995–96 to 2005–2006

This data is to understand the landholding patterns among the tribals and the non-tribals. There have been significant changes in the landholding among the non-tribals, especially between 1995–1996 and 2005–2006. Changing patterns in the landholding among the tribals and the non-tribals and the land situation in the Scheduled Areas are discussed here.

Table 3.6

Landholding Patterns of Tribals in A Decade Period (1995–96 to 2005–06)

Size of Landholdings	*ST Landholding in 1995–96*		*ST Landholding in 2005–06*	
	% of Holdings	*% of Extent (Ac)*	*% of Holdings*	*% of Extent (Ac)*
Large	2% (330)	8% (11,633.54)	1% (391)	8% (13,959.96)
Medium	12% (3,202)	33% (45,699.01)	12% (3,982)	32% (56,023.30)
Semi medium	25% (6,778)	32% (45,517.38)	26% (8,301)	33% (56,041.17)
Small	26% (6,956)	18% (25,086.78)	28% (8,935)	19% (31,976.41)
Marginal	35% (9,350)	9% (12,561.23)	33% (10,546)	8% (14,387.02)
Total	100 (26,616)	100 (1,40,497.94)	100 (32,155)	100 (1,72,387.86)

Source: Data computed from Agricultural Census Handbook: East Godavari District, Statistical Office, Kakinada.[6]

Ac: acre

Figure 3.1

Landholdings of Tribals by 1995–96 to 2005–06

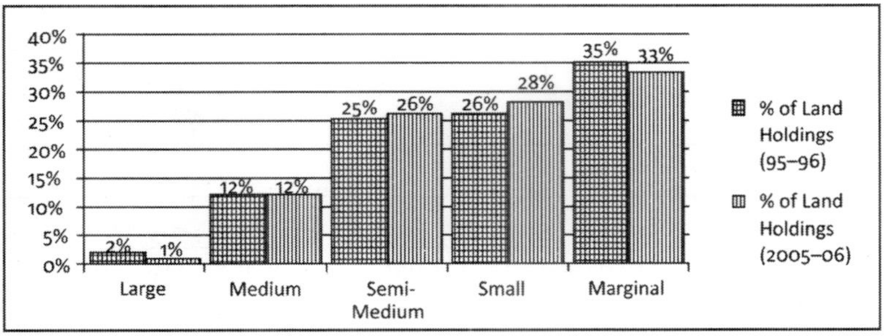

The data shows that the extent of landholding in respect of large tribal farmers has diminished from two per cent to one per cent. Similarly, the landholdings of marginal farmers have declined from 35 per cent to 33 per cent. However, the number of small farmers has increased from 26 per cent to 28 per cent, as well as semi-medium farmers from 25 per cent to 26 per cent during the period 1996–2006 (see Table 3.6 and Figure 3.1).

Figure 3.2

Operational Area of Tribal Farmers (1995–96 and 2005–06)

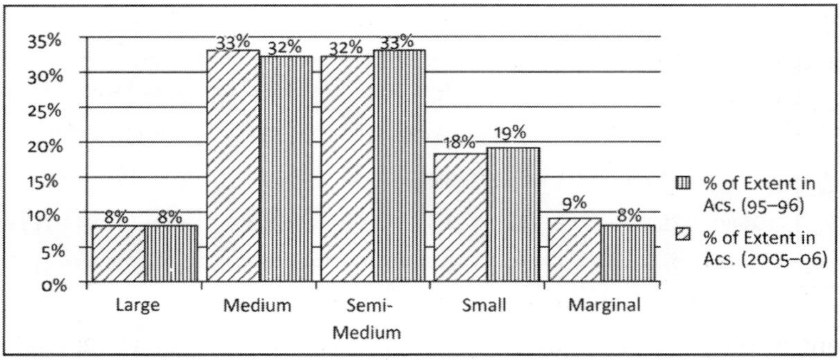

The data in Figure 3.2 shows that the operated area of larger families are intact, while the extent of land has decreased to one per cent in case of medium and marginal farmers, but there is an increase of one per cent in the case of semi-medium and small farmers.

Table 3.7

Landholding Patterns of Non-tribals in a Decadal Period (1995–96 to 2005–06)

Size of Landholdings	*NT*		*NT*	
	1995–96		*2005–06*	
	% of Holdings	*% of Extent (Ac)*	*% of Holdings*	*% of Extent (Ac)*
Large	2% (132)	17% (5,095.96)	1% (86)	11% (3,262.01)
Medium	9% (561)	26% (8,002.05)	8% (558)	26% (7,941.38)
Semi-medium	20% (1,204)	27% (8,283.97)	19% (1,270)	28% (8,526.06)
Small	25% (1,506)	18% (5,494.47)	27% (1,802)	22% (6,396.18)
Marginal	44% (2,667)	12% (3,670.87)	45% (2,982)	13% (3,954.40)
	100 (6,070)	100 (30,547.32)	100 (6,698)	100 (30,079.03)

Ac: acre

Table 3.7 shows a decline in the landholdings by one per cent in the case of large non-tribal farmers. Similarly, in the case of medium and semi-medium farmers, there is an increase of two per

Figure 3.3

Landholdings of Non-tribals (1995–96 to 2005–06)

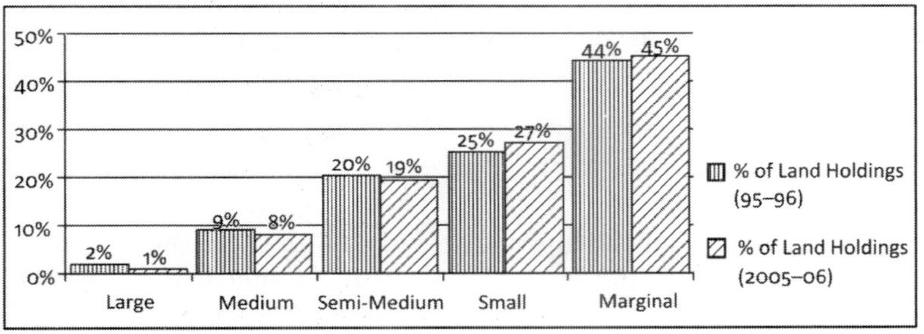

cent in the case of small farmers and one per cent in the case of marginal farmers (Figure 3.3).

Figure 3.4

Operational Area of Non-tribal Farmers (1995–96 and 2005–06)

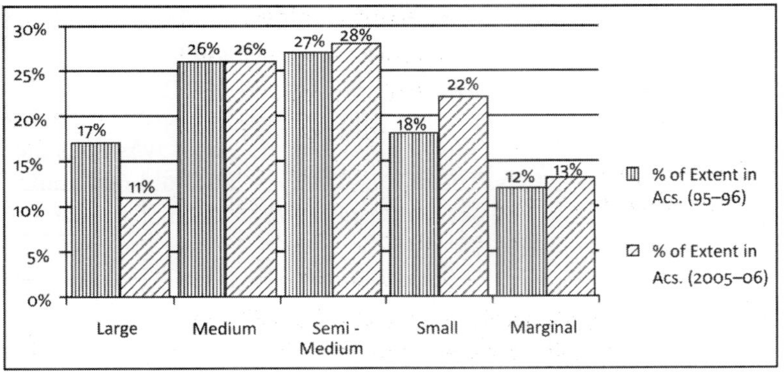

The data reveals that the operated area of non-tribal landholders has decreased to 6 per cent in the case of large farmers. However, there is an increase of one per cent in the case of semi-medium and marginal farmers while four per cent in the case of small farmers (Figure 3.4).

Landholdings

The total non-tribal landholdings numbered 6,070 and had an operating area of 30,547 acres in 1995–1996. The number increased to 6,698 with an operating area of 30,080 acres in the year 2005–06. This shows that the non-tribals had lost their grip over the land to the extent of 467 acres, which is a marginal decrease in a decadal period.

But in the case of tribals, the number of landholdings was 26,616, with an operating area of 1,40,498 acres of land in the year 1995–1996. There is a sign of increase of landholdings to 32,155 with an operating area of 1,72,388 acres. Therefore, these figures clearly indicate that during the period of a decade, there was an increase of landholding in the case of tribals, which is not necessarily to be understood as being due to the land restored from the holdings of non-tribals. It may perhaps be the greater extent of Government Assigned land. In fact, the two major sources for acquisition of land by tribals are either recovery from non-tribals or access to government land.

There is an increase of one per cent of marginal non-tribal farmers from 1996 to 2006, while there is a trend of two per cent decrease in the case of tribals. The small farmers, among both the tribals and the non-tribals, have increased by two per cent. There is a one per cent decrease of non-tribal, semi-medium landholders from 1996 to 2006, but there is an increase of one per cent in the case of tribals. Again, there is a decrease of one per cent of medium non-tribal holders from 1996 to 2006, but the status was the same in the case of the tribals. The status of larger landholdings diminished to the extent of one per cent from 1996 to 2006, in the case of both tribals and non-tribals.

Operating Area

The operating area of tribals in the case of large farmers saw no increase between 1995–1996 and 2005–2006, but in the case of non-tribals, there was a decrease of 6 per cent. The operating area of tribal medium farmers decreased to one per cent while there was no change in the case of non-tribals. There was an increase of one per cent in the operating area of semi-medium, tribal landholders. The same situation holds for the non-tribals. The operating area increased to one per cent in the case of small tribal farmers, while 4 per cent in the case of the non-tribals. There is a decrease of one per cent in the operating area of marginal tribal farmers, but there is an increase of one per cent in the case of the non-tribals.

Implementation of Land Transfer Regulations and Outcome

The Special Deputy Collector (Tribal Welfare) Court was set up in 1976 to conduct enquiries into the petitions filed under Land Transfer Regulations in order to restore the tribal alienated land from the possession of non-tribals. This court is at the preliminary level to conduct enquiry into petitions filed by tribals or Special Deputy Tahsildars appointed to represent the interest of tribals, seeking restoration of lands from the illegal possession of non-tribals. The Special Deputy Collector Court issued a notice to the non-tribal land occupants, calling for their appearance with adequate proof to show as how they got the land in the Scheduled villages. Under the law, the onus of proof lies on the non-tribals to establish that their land occupations are in accordance with the provision of Land Transfer Regulations and that they did not get the land in their possession through transfer effected from tribals. The Special Deputy Collector Court has the machinery of Special Deputy Tahsildars whose task is to identify non-tribal land occupations, which are against the provisions of Land Transfer Regulations. The Special Deputy Collector Court can also initiate proceedings on their reports known as suo moto, and tribal petitioners or any other interested person.

The following data shows the outcome of the implementation of the Land Transfer Regulations through setting up of special courts manned by the Special Deputy Collectors.

Of 9,012 cases, covering an extent of 52,494 acres of land, 8,325 cases covering an extent of 49,130 acres were disposed of by the Court. The Court decided 3,812 cases covering an extent of 20,029 acres of land in favour of the tribals. However, the enforcing machinery set up under the Regulations could restore only 17,685 acres of land pertaining to the 3,392 cases out of 3,812. On the contrary, the non-tribals parties were able to secure orders in their favour in 4,513 cases and retained the land of 29,101 acres in their possession.

Table 3.8 shows that the success rate for land restoration is 46 per cent in the case of tribals, and 54 per cent in the case of the non-tribals. The tribals were able to regain the possession of land from the non-tribals only to the extent of 41 per cent of the total extent of land covered by cases disposed of, while the non-tribals

Table 3.8

The Outcome of Cases Under Land Transfer Regulations from the Inception of SDC Court in 1976 to 30 April 2011 at Rampachodavaram

S. No.	*Total Cases Booked*		*Total Disposed*		*Decided in Favour of STs*		*Decided in Favour of NTs*		*Restored to Tribals*		*Total Remaining*	
	Nos.	*Extent/ Acres*	*Nos.*	*Extent/ Acres*	*Nos.*	*Extent/ Acres*	*Nos.*	*Extent/ Acres*	*Nos.*	*Extent/ Acres*	*Nos.*	*Extent/ Acres*
1.	9,012	52,493.92	8,325	49,130.34	3,812	20,029.34	4,513	29,101	3,392	17,685	687	3,363.58

Source: Office of Special Deputy Collector (Tribal Welfare), Rampachodavaram.

were able to retain the remaining 59 per cent of the disputed land. Due to the failure of the implementing machinery in enforcing the orders passed by the Special Deputy Collector Court in favour of the tribals, only 89 per cent of the total cases were disposed of. These covered an extent of 88 per cent of land which was handed over physically to the tribal parties. This shows the blatant neglect in the implementation of orders passed in favour of the tribals. The machinery set up for the restoration of the alienated tribal land failed to meet the ends of justice. The non-tribals influencing the officials who are responsible for implementation of the orders on one hand, and on the other hand, approaching the higher Courts and getting orders for stay of the operation of the orders, are the key factors for failure of land justice to tribals.

Strength of Enforcing Machinery

The enforcing machinery in place shows its commitment (or lack of it) towards the implementation of Land Transfer Regulations 1 of 59 as amended by 1 of 70. Table 3.9 shows the period of occupation and vacancy of the position of the Special Deputy Collector (TW).

Table 3.9

Vacancy Position of SDC Post

S. No.	*Position of the Post/Name of the SDC*	*From*	*To*	*Working Period (Months)*	*Vacant Period (Months)*
1.	R. Sankar	7–4–99	9–1–01	20	
2.	Post vacancy	10–1–01	14–2–02		13
3.	G. Krishna Kishore	15–2–02	31–12–04	34	
4.	Post vacancy	1–1–05	28–8–06		19
5.	I. Prasad	29–8–06	30–6–08	22	
6.	Post vacancy	1–7–08	24–3–11		32
7.	V. Sugunakumari	25–3–11	Still working		
				76 (54%)	64 (46%)

Source: Table developed based on the information at SDC office, Rampachodavaram.

The post of Special Deputy Collector (TW) had no appointment for 64 months, while the officer worked on the post for 76 months during the period from April 1999 to March 2011. The post has not been functional for half the period.

Table 3.10

Vacancy Position of Office Staff of the SDC Court at Rampachodavaram as on 30 April 2011

S. No.	*Name of the Post*	*No. of Posts*	*Presently Working in the Office*	*Vacancy Position*	*Persons went on Deputation*
1.	Spl Dy Collector	1	1	0	0
2.	Spl Dy Tahsildars	6	3	0	3
3.	UDRIs	3	0	3	0
4.	Sr Asst's	1	0	1	0
5.	Jr Asst's	1	1	0	0
6.	Typist	1	0	1	0
7.	Driver	1	0	1	0
8.	Attenders	9	4	4	1
	Total	23	9	10	4

Source: Special Deputy Collector's Office, Rampachodavaram.

The vacancy position of office of the Special Deputy Collector Court will show the importance being given to the implementation of Land Transfer Regulations in the Scheduled Areas (Table 3.10). Of the 23 posts related to the implementing machinery, only 9 staff members were working. Out of 6 Special Deputy Tahsildar posts, three Tahsildars went on deputation to work in other departments, leaving their critical role in the implementation of the Land Transfer Regulations. In fact, the key role of the Special Deputy Tahsildar is to detect cases against the non-tribals who have been in possession of land in violation of Land Transfer Regulations and file these before the Special Deputy Collector. In addition, the Special Deputy Tahsildars have to hand over the land in the cases decided in favour of the tribals by evicting non-tribal occupants.

Forest Land Rights Deprivation

The land administration is concerned with the administration of rights, restrictions and responsibilities over land. This clearly overlaps with the environmental concerns regarding land use or rights over resource use because environmental concerns can arise from the way people choose to exercise their rights, restrictions and responsibilities over land.

The process of reservation of forests of Rampa country was a halted affair. There were serious protests in the late 19th century against the extension of the Madras Forests Act, 1882. The situation grew serious enough to lead to the framing of the Rampa Country Forests and Transit Rules in 1894.

The process of the reservation and notification of the protected and reserved forests started way back in the year 1891 and continued till 1978 in the Agency Division of Rampachodavaram. This resulted in the forest land alienation from the control of the tribals.

Table 3.11

Extent of Reserved Forests in Pre- and Post-independence Period in the Scheduled Areas of the East Godavari District

S. No.	*Range*	*1891–1941 (Pre-Independence) ha*	*1966–1978 (Post-Independence) ha*	*Total ha*
1.	Eleswaram	25,546.82	2,276.90	27,823.72
2.	Sudikonda	13,600.64	761.88	14,362.52
3.	Maredumilli	2,470.19	93,048.22	95,518.41
4.	Addateegala	28,059.11	10,827.03	38,886.14
5.	Rampachodavaram	27,916.46	29,369.36	57,285.82
6.	Tuni	3,494.04	0	3,494.04
7.	Gokavaram	1,737.08	5,878.12	7,615.20
	Total	1,02,824.34	1,42,161.51	2,44,985.85

Data computed from the reports of District Forest Officer, Kakinada, 2010.

Table 3.11 and Figure 3.5 shows the government imposition of restrictions in usage of larger tracts of forests by the tribal communities through reserved forest notifications. Around 42 per cent of the total forest cover was already notified in the pre-independence period while 58 per cent was declared as protected and reserved forests after independence. During the notification period, the rights of the tribal communities were not settled and their customary rights were abrogated by the forest settlement officers.

Figure 3.5

Extent of Reserved Forests in Pre- and Post-Independence Period in the Scheduled Areas

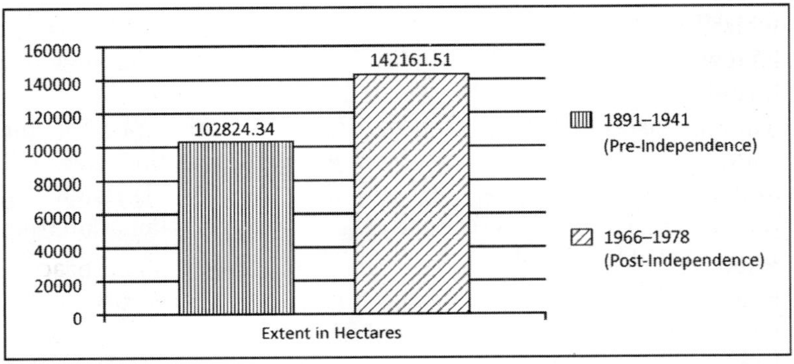

The notification issued proposing reserve forests over 4,708 hectares of land covering two blocks, namely, Anguluru and Purushuottapatnam in the Gokavaram forest range, was pending for finalization from the year 1968 till 2010. The tribals were deprived of their rights during the notification period as they were not aware of the said notification.

On the other hand, the resource destruction started when the Andhra Pradesh Paper Mills was given forest areas for the extraction of wood for the paper mill. Subsequently, in the year 1974, the government permitted the mining company to excavate laterite minerals from 318 acres of reserve forest land of Maredumilli Mandal. Further, after the promulgation of 1 of 70 Land Transfer Regulations, the government gave forests for the Godavari Plywood Factory at Rampachodavaram to fell soft wood trees for manufacturing of plywood.

Further, the tribals were dispossessed from the forest land due to implementation of forest development programmes and compensatory afforestation programmes. The tribals were dispossessed from the forest land occupation in the name of Joint Forest Management Schemes. When the Forest Conservation Act came into force in 1980, there was indiscriminate eviction of all people including the tribals from the reserved forests. No consideration was shown to even those tribals who had been practising podu (shifting cultivation) cultivation prior to this date. There was hardly any consideration shown to the impact of such an action on tribals for whom no alternative livelihood sustenance had been provided. There are no legislative provisions for the protection of the rights which the tribals had enjoyed for centuries. Thereby, a great deal of land which had in former years been cultivated on podu tenure, was included in the reserve. The tribals were thus deprived of its future use and rights. According to the legal principles of forest reservation, the forest settlement officer should look into the objections of the cultivators of the land and their land is not to be included in the reserved forest unless the cultivators are compensated elsewhere. The tribals stay in the forest villages. In practice, however, land held by tribals was included in the reserved forest, without compensation being granted. The dispossessed tribals hardly have evidence to claim their rights over podu land under the subsequent Forest Rights Recognition Act.

Subsequently, the Forest Rights Recognition Act 2006 came into force to reverse the historical injustice meted to the tribals. Due to the inherent gaps in the implementation of the Act, the tribals in the district have not been able to secure forest rights entitlements as per their claims.

Table 3.12

Status Report on Implementation of Individual Claims Under Recognition of Forest Rights Act as from its Enforcement in 2006 to 5 November 2010

Status of Convening Gram Sabhas in Forest Interface Gram Panchayats		*Individual Claims*		*Outcome-Title Deeds Granted*		*% of Claims*	*% of Extent*
No. of Gram Panchayats having Forest Interface	*Extent of Forest Land Under Occupation (in acres)*	*No. Received*	*Extent in Acres*	*No. of Individual Titles*	*Extent in Acres*		
120	1,20,141.57	12,448	31,269	5,887	24,870.28	47	79

Source: ITDA office, Rampachodavaram, 2010.

Only 47 per cent of the claims covering an extent of only 79 per cent of the land were allowed by the district level committee in the Rampachodavaram Division. In fact, the tribals are to be ensured forest rights over 1,20,142 acres of land, since the land has been in their occupation. If this land is also taken into consideration, the tribal occupants only received 21 per cent of the total land under their occupation. The data reveals that the tribals are denied forest rights and are displaced from their traditional occupations (Table 3.12).

Table 3.13

Community Claims Received from VSSs and Title Deeds Granted to VSSs in the Name of Community Claims from the Inception of Act 2006 till 2010

Name of the District and Mandal	*Community Claims Received from VSSs*		*Title Deeds Granted to VSSs in the Name of Community Claims*		*% of Claims*	*% of Extent*
	No. Received	*Extent in Acres*	*No. Received*	*Extent in Acres*		
Rampach-odavaram	287	2,09,850	287	2,09,850.1	100	100

The Government of Andhra Pradesh granted pattas for community forestry rights to Vana Samarakshna Samithi formed by the Forest Department for implementation of the Joint Forest Management Programme aided by the World Bank instead of granting community land rights in the village as such. The grant of pattas to the Vana Samrakshna Samithis is in violation of the provisions of Forest Rights Recognition Act 2006 which ensures that only community rights over the forests be allowed in favour of the community in the village. The Sarpanch of Pamuleru in Maredumilli Mandal of East Godavari District challenged the decision of the government in granting community rights to the Vana Samarkshna Samithi before the High Court of Andhra Pradesh in WP No. 21112/2010, which is pending for consideration. The data further reveals that the rights ensured under the Recognition of Forest Rights are not recognized properly while 100 per cent claims were allowed in favour of the Vana Samarakshna Samithi (Table 3.13).

Table 3.14

Title Deeds Granted Under Recognition of Forest Rights Act to the Community as on 5 November 2010

Name of the District and Mandal	*Community Claims Received*		*Title Deeds Granted to Community*		*% of Claims*	*% of Extent*
	No. Received	*Extent in Acres*	*No. Received*	*Extent in Acres*		
Rampachodavaram	533	407	82	158	15	39

The data reveals that the community rights which are to be ensured were denied to the tribal communities over the forest land. Only 15 per cent of the land claims covering 39 per cent of the area were allowed. In fact, the community claims which were allowed in name of Vana Samarakshna Samithi should have been issued to the tribal communities (Table 3.14).

Case Studies: Dispossession of Tribal Land

Four case studies are being discussed here to give a comprehensive picture of the process of land alienation and the various factors involved in it. The cases were selected as they illustrate varied dimensions of land dispossession through transfer and subsequent struggle for land retrieval.

Case Study 1: Land Alienation in Estate Village, Manturu

Manturu village consists of 364 households with a population of 1,050. Men number 519 while 531 are women.

Manturu Estate formed part of the Rampa country and was declared subsequently as an Agency Area in 1879 (Fort St. George 1879; Gazette P. 462). Manturu, Penikalapadu, Madipalli, Mallavaram, Kachuluru and Moolapadu villages, which originally formed part of Manturu Zameen Estate, presently fall under the Devipatnam Mandal of East Godavari District. These six villages are notified as Scheduled villages. The Estate Abolition Act 1948 came into force in 1949 in the plain areas, but for the Estates situated in the Scheduled Areas, the Estates Regulations were extended in 1951. The Manturu Estate was taken over by the government in 1952. Though the estate of Manturu was taken over by the government as early as in 1952, no survey and settlement was conducted as the Regulations do not contemplate rules to conduct survey and settlement. In order to conduct survey and settlement in all the Estate villages in the Scheduled Areas of the State, Andhra Pradesh Scheduled Areas Ryotwari Settlement Regulations 2 of 70 were promulgated which came into force on 1 July 1971. After survey and settlement, these villages have become Ryotwari villages.

Litigation of Landholder

The landholder of Manturu Estate, Kruttiventy Perraju Pantulu filed WP 652/52 challenging the notification issued by the government to take over six villages in 1952 under the Estate Abolition Act 1948, without giving an opportunity to him to contest the notification. His main contention is that Manturu is not a Zameen estate within the meaning of Section 3 of Estate Land Act 1908. The High Court passed an order in 1957 in Writ proceedings directing the government to hear his objections. The government heard the objections of the landholder and held that declaring Manturu Estate as a Zameen Estate is correct. The unsuccessful landholder filed a civil suit OS No. 61/67 in the District Court, Rajahmundry, contesting that the six villages are not Zameen Estate and sought for a decree for delivery of property situated in all six villages including land, forest, mines, hills, hillocks, all natural streams, waterways and finally succeeded in the litigation. The court declared that these villages cannot be abolished under the Estate Abolition Act and taking over these villages under the Government GO 258 dated 18 February 1964 is illegal and inoperative. This judgement was challenged by the District Collector and he filed an appeal in 236/73 before the High Court of Andhra Pradesh. The High Court upheld the judgement of the District Court. The notable point is that the representatives of the government in the litigation failed to argue that the District Court, Rajahmundry, has no jurisdiction to adjudicate civil disputes arising out of the Agency Areas and that the civil courts constituted under Andhra Pradesh Agency Rules 1924 are alone applicable.

Intervention by Tribals

Madakam Ganganna Dora and 64 tribals of Manturu village filed a Writ Petition 12317/91 in the High Court questioning the District Court's decree, as the land covered by the decree of the court is in their actual possession. The High Court finally dismissed their Writ

Petition on the ground that there was no representation at the time of hearing.

Execution of Decree by Landholder

The landholder filed an Execution Petition (EP) for the execution of decree passed in his favour before the Additional District Court, Rajahmundry. The Execution Petition is made for delivery of the property. The Execution Petition is still pending before the court, as the High Court of Andhra Pradesh passed an interim stay in 2009 staying the proceedings on the ground that the District Court, Rajahmundry, has no jurisdiction to adjudicate civil disputes arising out of Scheduled Areas. The successors of the proprietor of Manturu Zameen Estate are continuing their legal struggle.

Survey and Settlement Operations

The Survey and Settlement authorities, unmindful of the litigation subsisting since 1952, carried out a survey and settlement operation under 2 of 70 Regulations and granted pattas for both tribal and non-tribal cultivating ryots.

Manturu Patta Details

As per Fair Adangals, the total extent of land is 1,156.83 hectares. The classification of wet land is 43.62 hectares, dry land 902.37 hectares, while Poromboke is 210.84 hectares. The tribals are questioning even the settlement pattas granted in favour of non-tribals under 2 of 70 Regulations.

Displacement Under Polavaram Project

All six villages in Manturu Estate are being submerged under the Polavaram Project. The Land Acquisition Authorities in Ref. 542/2009 issued proclamation notices for acquisition of land of Ac.373 covering Manturu village block 1 and 2. The land title over the area is still under dispute before the High Court as well as the District Court, Rajahmundry.

Case Study 2: Land Alienation in Mutta Area

The Muttadar of Rampa Mutta was Chitukula Reddy, a Konda Reddy tribe. After his death his second wife Yesodamma became the Muttadarini of the Mutta. The government granted permission to Muttadarini Sankura Yesodamma to lease out Mutta land of 600 acres located in Rampa Mutta villages in a GO Ms 2,932 Rev. Department on 13 November 1950 to one non-tribal Karri China Venkat Reddy who belonged to the upper caste Reddy community. As per the conditions laid down in the GO, it is a conditional lease for a period of 25 years, from 1 February 1951 to 31 January 1976. The non-tribal Karri China Venkat Reddy came to Agency Areas to operate liquor business from Pandalapaka village near Anaparthi, 90 km away from Rampachodavaram before 1950. He developed a social relationship with the family of Yesodamma, a Konda Reddi woman and gained access to the land. After introduction of the Andhra Pradesh Gram Panchayat Act in 1964, the son-in-law of the landlord Harichandra Reddy contested elections for the post of Samithi President to the Rampachodavaram Samithi, a middle tier of the Panchayat Raj Institution. However, he lost the seat. The non-tribal landlord family became an influential political power centre in the Agency Area. This helped to gain strength to retain land in tribal areas.

Land Settlement During 1970–76

In fact, after the abolition of Muttas in 1969, the non-tribals claimed settlement patta for the land over 600 acres located in Rampa, Rampachodavaram and the surrounding villages, but the Settlement Officer granted patta for only 340 acres on 13 November 1973.

Irregular Enquiry

The applicant made an application on 12 November 1973. On the same date, notice was issued to the Tahsildar of Rampachodavaram and the applicant too, for enquiry on the very next day for the hearing. The case was adjourned from 13 to 15 November, again at the request of the applicant. On 15 November the case was heard and orders were issued on 23 November 1973. The hurriedness in passing the order shows that there was no elaborate enquiry into the claim of the non-tribals. As per settlement rules, one week prior notice is supposed to be given to the parties before initiating enquiry into the matter. Therefore, it shows that the Settlement Officer had a predetermined view to grant patta to the non-tribals without following the rules.

Cancellation of Order by Director of Settlement

On an appeal by another sublease, the non-tribal holder, Alapati Bapiraju, challenged the order of the Settlement Officer, Rajahmundry. The Director of Survey Settlement set aside the order of the Settlement Officer and demanded a fresh enquiry in 1974, holding that the Settlement Officer had bypassed the survey and settlement procedure for the grant of the pattas.

Disallowing of Claim by Commissioner of Settlements

The unsuccessful non-tribal filed an appeal before the Commissioner of Survey and Settlements challenging the order of the Director of Settlements. The Commissioner dismissed the appeal in 1981. Then the non-tribal filed a Writ Petition in 7,487/81, assailing the order of the Commissioner of Settlements. The High Court allowed the claim of the non-tribal landlord for patta, setting aside the order of the Commissioner of Settlements. Then, government filed an appeal which was dismissed in 1990. Further, a second appeal was filed before the Supreme Court by the Forest Department, objecting that the land also included forest cover. The Supreme Court remanded the matter to the Commissioner of Settlements and ordered for fresh enquiry in 1991. Finally, the Commissioner of Settlements allowed the claim of the non-tribal to the extent of 197 acres in 1995 and ordered the grant of the pattas.

Tribal Struggle

The tribals who were landless, started a land occupation movement with the support of Ryutu Coolie Sangham, a frontal group of the CPI (ML) New Democracy and erected flags in the land by showing symbolic occupation of land in the year 1995. The movement was further intensified in the year 2000. A complaint was lodged by the non-tribal against the tribals. An enquiry was held by Sub Divisional Magistrate, Rampachodavaram. However, the Magistrate failed to confirm names of those who were in the actual possession of the land.

Official Collusion

The Special Deputy Tahsildar filed a case against the non-tribals pattadars under LTR 1 of 70 for restoration of the land to the government. In fact, the land has been in actual possession of tribals who gained access to the land through a land occupation movement. The plan of both the non-tribal and the official was to seek another order from the Special Deputy Collector, to create legal problems for the tribal occupants. However, after learning of the colluded litigation, tribals joined the case and objected to the proceedings as the land is not in the possession of non-tribals. As such the provisions are not applicable to the case. Finally, the court dismissed the petition given by the Special Deputy Tahsildar, observing that the tribals are in the possession of the land.

Land Purchase by Government

Knowing fully well that the land is in actual possession of the tribals, the government came forward to purchase 95 acres of land at the instance of non-tribal landlords who received political support from the ruling Congress Party. The government paid compensation of ₹ 41,80,000 to the non-tribals. Then the tribals who were in possession of the land moved the petition before the High Court and obtained stay orders against their eviction from the land.

Attempt to Displace Tribals

The government purchased the land by paying huge compensation to the absentee non-tribal landlord in order to give the said land to the displaced tribals under Bhupathipalem reservoir near Rampachodavaram. This act is nothing but to displace the existing tribals who are in actual possession of the land and eking out their livelihood from it. The government created a social conflict between these tribal sections. It made plans to get tribals to occupy the land by granting Ryotwari pattas to them. The tribals made a futile bid to enter the land. The actual possessors again filed a case against the government seeking injunction not to evict them. The court passed an order not to evict the tribals occupying the land without due process of the law.

The non-tribals took the money and left the village. The tribal oustees for whom this land was offered by the government have been left with no other option but to enter into the land The actual tribal possessors of the land are under legal protection granted by the High Court. The government failed to show the solution both to the tribal oustees and the present tribal occupants of the land.

The land alienation was caused due to the intervention of the State itself in the year 1950 by approving the lease deed for 600 acres of land in favour of the non-tribals. Ultimately, the state itself showed a path to gain huge monetary benefit to the non-tribals over 197 acres of land.

Case Study 3: Land Alienation under Polavaram Project

This case study examines the tribal land question in one of the mandals in the Scheduled Areas of the study district, Devipatnam which faces threat of submergence due to the Polavaram Project. Indira Sagar, the ₹ 8,000 crore gigantic dam proposed at Polavaram in West Godavari District in Andhra Pradesh, promises to transfer 80 thousand million cubic feet (TMC) water to the Krishna basin via a 174 km long right canal and to Visakhapatnam District via a 181.53 km long left canal. The project, it is promised, will irrigate 7.21 lakh acres in Krishna, Godavari (East and West) and Visakhapatnam Districts, and generate about 960 MW of electricity. However, over 276 tribal villages in the Agency Areas of East and West Godavari Districts and Khammam District are expected to be submerged. According to the 2001 Census, 2,37,000 people will be displaced and as many as 53.17 per cent of the displaced will be tribals. Tribals and Dalits account for 65.75 per cent of the displaced people. The natural resources, cultural systems, traditional knowledge of all these communities are closely tied to the land they inhabit. With the loss of the land, minor forest produce, tubers, leaves, indigenous medicinal systems, common property resources that support human population and livestock, the very existence of these communities will become unsustainable. The Government of Andhra Pradesh began the land acquisition and other rehabilitation work, even without any constitutional and statutory clearances from the concerned Ministries for the construction of the Polavaram Project. However, the government succumbed to the pressure of tribal groups and later started applying for the necessary clearances.

The inhabitants of 276 habitations spread over 9 mandals in three Districts of East, West and Khammam Districts face displacement due to the Polavaram Project. Devipatnam, a mandal in the East Godavari District, is one amongst them. The project would affect 43 tribal villages and displace 12,000 people who constitute 9.81 per cent of the total population in the Devipatnam Mandal. The area likely to be submerged under the project is 8,328.50 acres. It belongs to 1,687 tribals and 1,011 non-tribals. About 1,687 tribals are holding land to an extent of 5,844.35 acres.

Of the total tribals landholdings, the settlement patta land comprises an extent of 3,212.57 acres while 718.62 acres is assigned land. About 451.66 acres is occupied government land. Further, the tribals hold possession and enjoyment of other land to an extent of 1,461.50 acres. This land once belonged to the tribals. Later, non-tribals managed to obtain settlement pattas during the Survey and Settlement period between 1970–76. The tribals regained possession of some of the land about 15 to 20 years back from non-tribals settlement patta holders through mass-based land struggles with the support of Rytu Coolie Sangham and Agency Girijan Sangham, saying that non-tribals had obtained settlement pattas over the tribal land in connivance with the settlement officials.

The Government of Andhra Pradesh has initiated land acquisition process in the name of providing land-to-land compensation and houses for proposed tribal oustees under the Polavaram Project. In fact, the government can acquire the land for the stated purposes under the Land Acquisition Act. But for the Polavaram Project, the state has adopted a different process for land acquisition under the provisions of the Andhra Pradesh Scheduled Area Land Transfer Regulations 1 of 70 in the Scheduled Areas of Devipatnam Mandal in the study district.

The 1 of 70 Regulations are intended to protect the land rights of tribals in the Scheduled Areas of Andhra Pradesh. These Regulations prohibit the transfer of land not only between tribals and non-tribals but also among the non-tribals in the Scheduled Areas. Unless the contrary is proved the land in possession of the non-tribals shall be presumed to have been acquired through a transfer from tribals under the law.

The 1 of 70 Regulations permits the non-tribal landholders to give their land to the government for acquisition on the terms of payment of compensation, if the tribals are unwilling to purchase the land from them or unwilling to purchase it on the terms being offered by the non-tribals. These provisions are not intended for acquisition of land by the state. This provision is misinterpreted by the government and is being invoked for acquisition of land at a massive scale for the purpose of the Polavaram Project, unmindful of the tribal rights involved in the said land. This land acquisition process is questionable and a serious threat to the tribal land rights.

As per the provisions, more specifically Rule 15 and 16 of GOMs No. 763 dated 11 August 1969, which are known as the Andhra Pradesh Scheduled Areas Land Transfer Rules 1969, if no tribal comes forward to purchase the land offered for sale by a non-tribal, then the non-tribal may apply to the Agency Divisional Officer (Revenue Divisional Officer), Agent to the government (District Collector), offering to give his land on payment of compensation. Then the acquisition authority has to give public notice by beating of tom-tom in the respective Gram Panchayats, seeking objections from the local inhabitants for the proposed acquisition of land from the non-tribals. The notice must be made available at the concerned Police Station, Gram Panchayat and other conspicuous places in the village. Fifteen days after the notice an enquiry has to be held under the provisions of Land Transfer Regulations 1 of 59 as amended by 1 of 70, to determine the rights of the tribals.

The acquisition authorities purchased a total land area of 595.66 acres situated in the Scheduled Areas of Addateegala, Gangavaram and Devipatnam mandal in East Godavari District from the non-tribals in the name of the Polavaram Project Rehabilitation programme, through 49 land transactions by paying them more than ₹ 2 crore in utter violation of laws, more particularly, in violation of the spirit of the Tribal Protective Land Transfer Regulations 1 of 70. The unscrupulous non-tribals availed the opportunity to dispose off their land acquired earlier through dubious and clandestine transactions from the tribals. Some of the non-tribals have fictitious titles, while some have managed to acquire titles even over the government land situated in the Scheduled Areas in violation of the Land Transfer Regulations 1 of 70.

The authorities purchased the land from the non-tribals through nominal and sham transactions without considering the fact that several tribals have been in possession and enjoyment of such land since several years. The tribals also made a representation on 13 April 2006 to the Project Officer, Integrated Tribal Development Agency, seeking his intervention. The Project Officer, Integrated Tribal Development Agency, East Godavari District, in his letter in reference No. T8/Grievance/2006 dated 13 April 2006, stated that tribals have been in possession and enjoyment of the land for the past 12 years and directed the acquisition authority not to buy such land from the non-tribals. But the acquisition authority did not obey the instructions of the Project Officer, Integrated Tribal Development Agency, Rampachodavaram. On the other hand, the non-tribals in connivance with the revenue staff, got land records prepared, incorporating their names as cultivators in recent adangals, even though the land was in the possession of tribals. Making available the land which is already in possession of tribals, to the project affected tribal land losers under the Rehabilitation Scheme, would certainly cause land conflicts among the tribals. The tribals opposed to this move are slapped with police cases and sent to jail.

In one instance, the authority purchased land of 10.92 acres covered under S. No. 175 and 177 from the non-tribals which is classified as 'Government Land' in the Indukuru revenue village under Devipatnam mandal. This land is in possession of tribals since a long time. The same acquisition authority, Revenue Divisional Officer, who is in charge of the post of Special Deputy Collector (TW), an enquiry authority under Land Transfer Regulations 1 of 59 as amended by 1 of 70, passed orders in favour of the non-tribals to give legitimacy to illegal non-tribal landholdings for the S. No. 175 and 177 of Indukuru Village and also for S. No. 89/1 in LTRP No. 61/05 and LTRP No. 62/05. The tribals initiated legal proceedings questioning the legal title of the non-tribal sellers before the Additional Agent to Government Court/PO (ITDA), Rampachodavaram. The Court upheld the contention of the tribals and found fault with acquisition of government land from the non-tribals and paid monetary compensation for such land.

From the viewpoint of those who lost land, land to land compensation for tribals under the Rehabilitation scheme is a mirage. The government purchased the land from the non-tribals to assign such land in favour of tribals under the Indira Sagar Project Rehabilitation Scheme. In fact, some of the land covered by such sales is unfit for cultivation. The land is stony and undulated. Some land is classified as burial grounds, streams, *puntha* (cart track), tanks and roads.

The land acquisition authority purchased land to an extent of 37.50 acres covered by R. S. No. 247 in Pothavaram village in Devipatnam mandal from a non-tribal who is a retired Deputy Collector. Another loop is that the land is covered by the Land Ceiling proceedings and the government declared the land to being surplus and some of the land as already under the possession of the tribals. The tribal possessors objected to the eviction process of the government and the handing over of such land in compensation to tribal land losers under the Polavaram Project. This process of the Revenue Authorities has thus created a social conflict among the tribals by promoting land conflicts among the tribals.

The Government of Andhra Pradesh purchased the land measuring an extent of 17.80 acres in Marripalem village in Gangavaram Mandal covered by RS. Nos. 36/2,178/1,199/2, 69/3,72 from a non-tribal, Thonda Venkat Rao. The land title of the non-tribal is in question. Similarly, in many cases non-tribals have no legal title over the land covered by sales, strictly under the provisions of 1 of 70 Regulations.

Some of the non-tribals are absentee and non-resident landlords. The tribals say that even they do not know the boundaries of the land. During the survey and settlement period, the non-tribals managed to get settlement pattas over the land situated in the Scheduled Areas in violation of the Survey and Settlement Regulations 2 of 70. The Settlement Pattas covered by such sales to the non-tribals, particularly in Devipatnam mandal are still under challenge before the Survey and Settlements Authorities. Such disputed land is being given to the tribals who are likely loose their land under the project.

The concerned legal provisions are not followed. Land acquisition in the Scheduled Areas is governed by the Panchayats (Extension to Scheduled Areas) Act 1996 (Act 40 of 1996), enacted by the Parliament. The Executive instructions issued by the Government of India under the Act, Part VI-A of the Andhra Pradesh Panchayat Raj Act enacted by the State Legislature through the amending Act 7 of 1998, which follows the mandate of the Parliament's Act 40 of 96. Section 4 of the Act says that every Gram Sabha or Panchayat at the appropriate level shall be consulted before taking acquisition of land in the Scheduled Areas for the development projects. Under Section 242 F of the Andhra Pradesh Panchayat Raj Act, the Mandal Parishad shall be consulted before taking acquisition of land in the Scheduled Areas. The combined effect of these instructions and the statutory provisions was due for consideration by the Honourable Court of Andhra Pradesh.[7] The High Court was pleased to hold that before land acquisition could be done in the Scheduled Areas, the proposal shall be placed before the affected Gram Sabhas for their consent, which must be in the form of resolution. Thereafter, the proposal shall be placed before the concerned Mandal Parishad for its opinion. The government is not following the required procedures for land acquisition. Gram Sabha resolutions were passed in the affected tribal villages and sent to the higher ups, questioning the land acquisition procedure adopted by the acquisition authorities.

A former Sarpanch of Indukuru Village under Devipatnam Mandal, Komaram Veeraswamy and Convenor, Tribal Land Rights Protection Committee, Tellam Venkata Rao, who are both tribals, filed a Public Interest Litigation (WP No. 18283/2006), before the High Court of Andhra Pradesh questioning all 49 land transactions held by land acquisition authority in East Godavari District and sought a declaration that all such sale transactions are declared to be illegal. At the first instance, the High Court directed the tribal petitioners to implead all the 49 non-tribal land sellers in the proceedings. The petitioners impleaded all the 49 non-tribals parties in the proceedings. Then the High Court admitted a Writ Petition and ordered a notice to all non-tribal sellers and also the government seeking explanation.

Summary

The case study shows how tribals are being displaced from their land under big projects as the Polavaram. It further reveals how the tribals, even though they are not covered by the project, are evicted from the land which is in their possession, due to acquisition of such land from the absentee non-tribal land lords. The case study further reveals the procedure adopted for rehabilitation and compensation for tribal land losers under the project.

Case Study 4: Spurious Scheduled Tribe Caste Certificates

This case is a typical example of how outsiders control the tribal areas as well as their land with the support of spurious Scheduled Tribes caste certificates. The two non-tribal families Padala and Anantha of Ellavaram village in Addateegala Mandal are controlling land of 197 acres in the tribal villages.

In 1987, the issue of false certificates emerged to the fore during the local elections for the Mandal President of Addateegala Mandal. One of the defeated tribal candidates challenged the elections of strong Congress (I) elected candidate, Anantha Chakra Rao who had contested the elections on the basis of Konda Kapu,

Table 3.15

Land Acquired by the Revenue Divisional Officer, Rampachodavaram U/S3(1)(C) of APSALTR 1959 and Rule 15 of APSALTR Rule 1969 under R&R Package of Indira Sagar (Polavaram) Project

(1) Gangavaram Mandal

S. No.	Name of the Village	Survey No.	Extent in Acres	Name of the Ryot (NT) who sold away to Government	Amount paid through Cheques (₹)	Nature of the Purchased Land
1.	Kamavarapupadu	9	5.28	Rajeti Sreedharacharyulu S/o Ranga Charyulu	1,84,800	Hillocks, Streams, Scurby Jungle, Undulated stony land and unfit for cultivation.
2.	Kamavarapupadu	12/P	3.86	Cherala V.M. Deekshita Srinivasa Rao	7,71,750	Hillocks, Streams, Scurby Jungle, Undulated stony land and unfit for cultivation.
		18/2	2.54	S/o Bapayya Pantulu		
		21/2	2.03	Cheerala Bapayya Pantulu		
		22/2	0.29			
		25	4.33			
		12/P	9			
3.	Nela Donelapalli	36	26.95	Sayyaparaju Srihari Raju, Sayyapuraju Meherbaba S/o Seetarama Raju	9,43,250	Unfit for cultivation.

Cont'd...

...Cont'd

4.	Konndalampalem	12	5.72	D.V.V. Satya Prasad,	9,39,050	Land covered by S. no 10/2 – are forest land and stream land. Some lands are in possession of tribals and holding D pattas.
		8	5.16	S/o Butchirama Sambaiah		
		10/2	5.18			
		9/1	5.94			
		15/2	2.96			
		14	1.87			
5.	Konndalampalem	16/1	17.1	D. Veeranna Chowdari	7,63,350	Land covered by S. No. 16/1 are forest land and remaining land in the said survey number are in possession of tribals.
		10/1	4.71	D. Pattabhi Rama Rao S/o Subarayudu		Land covered by S. No. 10/1 are in tribals possession and holding D'Form pattas.
6.	Marripalem	36/2	2.57	Tonda Venkata Rao	6,23,000	Burial ground land in S. No. 69/3 and, etc. remaining land under other S. No streams, scurby, etc. Some lands are in possession of tribals. Non-tribal has no valid title.
		178/1	1.95	S/o Bullabai		
		199/2	2.76			
		69/3	3.21			
		72	7.31			

Cont'd...

...Cont'd

7.	Yetipalli	115/1	9.26	Annabattula Muralikrishna S/o Late Nageswara Rao	3,24,100	Tribals are in possession of land.
	Total		129.98		45,49,300	
				(2) Devipatnam Mandal		
1.	Indukuru	96/1	11.31	N. Srinivas Reddy S/o Harinath Reddy	3,95,850	Tribals are in possession.
2.	Pothavaram	275	7.50	B.L. Narasimha Rao S/o B.V.M.R. Sarma	2,62,500	Tribals are in possession.
3.	Pothavaram	247	37.50	B.L. Narasimha Rao S/o B.V.M.R. Sarma	13,12,500	Land ceiling land (Surplus Land taken over by the Government). Some portion of the land is a stream land while the other portion of the land is a tank and road. The remaining portion of the land is in the possession of Tribals.
4.	Indukuru	175	5.00	Badireddy Srinivasrao S/o Suraiah		Government, waste land as per fair adangal (CMA 4/2006 pending in PO Court-writ appeal is also pending in High Court. Tribals are in possession.

Cont'd...

...Cont'd

5.	Indukuru	177	5.92	Polapalli Krishna Murthy S/o Seetharamaiah		Government waste land as per fair adangal (CMA 4/2006 pending in PO Court-writ appeal is also pending in High Court) Tribals are in possession.
6.	Indukuru	89/1	11.01	Pasumathi Mangaraju S/o Subbarao		(CMA 5/2006 pending in PO Court-writ appeal is also pending in High Court) Tribals are in possession.
7.	Indukuru	139/2 143/4	11.31 7.90	Pasumarthi Ammani @ Subha Raju, W/o Subharao	6,72,350	Tribals are in possession.
8.	Peddabhim-palli	47/P	4.59	Badireddy Satya Subhalakshmi W/o late Venkanna dora	1,60,650	Road, Heap of stones, Stony land.
	Total		102.04		28,03,850	

Data computed from the office records of Subcollectors and ITDA offices, ITDA, Rampachodavaram.

Scheduled Tribe certificate in OP No. 32/1987. The Election Tribunal held in April, 1989 that Anantha Chakra Rao is a non-tribal and belongs to the Kapu caste and not to the Scheduled Tribe Konda Kapu, and set aside the elections. Ironically, a month before this historic judgement, he was shot dead allegedly by the Naxalites belonging to the Peoples War Group.

Anantha Udaya Bhaskara Rao is the son of deceased Anantha Chakra Rao. He contested the elections for the post of MPTC of Doramamidi and was elected as the President of Mandal Praja Parishad, Addateegala, on the basis of his caste certificate in 2005. The District Collector, East Godavari District cancelled his caste certificate in 2008 after several legal halts created by Bhaskara Rao. His paternal grandfather, Anantha Veeraju was elected as Samithi President of Addateegala, a position which was reserved for the Scheduled Tribe community. He had obtained the certificate as a Scheduled Tribe member from the District Collector of East Godavari in the year 1967. His maternal great grandfather, Padala Veeraju, was elected thrice as the Samithi President of Addateegala Panchayat Samithi as a Scheduled Tribe candidate. Padala Veeraju also served as the Munsif of the village. So, all the land records were under his control and made it easy to manipulate land records in their favour. Padala Veeraju similarly obtained a caste certificate in 1955 from the District Collector. The issue of caste certificates by the Collector was seriously questioned by the Election Tribunal which observed, 'It is not clear what made such a high authority as Collector of District to issue caste certificates, that too invalid ones, while much lower authorities have the power to issue the certificates. The family relations of Padala family from where his maternal grandmother came were only for plains Kapu with no relationship to the agency'. The Election Tribunal further held that, it seems that there is an organized well-planned effort on the part of Revenue authorities to block any enquiry on the caste of 'Padala' family and so repeat ad nauseam the same invalid reports/Judgements based on irrelevant criteria ... a deliberate attempt to colour Padala family as 'Konda Kapu'. The proceedings of the District Collector cancelling the caste certificate obtained by Ananta Udaya Bhaskar, also assert that Padala Suranna was a native of Yeleswaram in the erstwhile Prathipadu Taluk. Thus, it proves that they migrated from the plains and are settlers in tribal areas.

The enquiry conducted by the Tribal Cultural Research Training Institute, the Government of Andhra Pradesh reveals that 'all the matrimonial relations of the family members of Anantha Chakra Rao were performed with plain Kapus, that their family members do not belong to Kondakapu and their caste was recorded as Kapu in the birth registers of Ellavaram village pertaining to the year 1942 and 1950, but still they are getting constitutional benefits meant for real tribals'.

Though all the enquiries clearly reveal that the family members of Anantha and Padala belong to the Kapu and not to the Konda Kapu Scheduled Tribe, the successors of the families Anantha Uday Bhaskar continue as members of the Scheduled Tribe, obtaining stay order from the High Court of Andhra Pradesh in Election Petition No. 15/2009, stalling the operation of his caste certificate cancellation proceedings by the District Collector.

Table 3.16

Landholdings of Padala and Anantha Families

S. No.	*Name of the Person*	*Extent (Acre)*	*Village*
1.	Padala Veerayamma (died)	18	Ellavaram
2.	Ananth Eswararao	18	Gondolu
		5	Ellavaram
3.	Anatha Mangaratnam	8	Ellavaram
		16	Gondolu
4.	Anantha Rupulamma	12	Gondolu
5.	Padala Jaggarao	16	Godolu
6.	Sons–2	16	Gondolu
7.	Padala Ganiraju	8	Ellavaram
		8	Gondolu
8.	Padala Chinna Jaggarao	10	Ellavaram
9.	Padala Janardhanarao	10	Ellavaram
10.	Padala Suryanarayana	12	Ellavaram
11.	Padala Baburao	8	Ellavaram
12.	Padala Venkateswararao	8	Ellavaram
13.	Padala Veereswararao	12	Ellavaram
14.	Padala Veerabadrarao	12	Ellavaram
	Grand Total	197	

These two non-tribal families acquired the land in the Scheduled Areas on the basis of caste certificates declaring them as members of the Scheduled Tribe, Konda Kapu. There is no prohibition of land transfer either from non-tribal to tribal or among the tribals under LTR 1 of 70. The maternal grandfather happened to be the village munsif which further helped to control the land records and their names got incorporated in the land revenue accounts. The land occupation movement of Naxalites belonging to the Peoples War Group from 1984 onwards fetched tribals of Chenupakalu and Gondolu to gain access to land of 60 acres. But for the Naxalite pressure, the government granted assignment pattas during the year in 1995–96 in favour of the tribals. Thus, the fake caste certificates obtained by the plains area non-tribals, was also one of the contributing factors for tribal land alienation.

Case Study 5: Eviction from Forest Land

Lakkonda is a predominantly Kondareddis village in Gangavaram Mandal. Around 70 tribal families are cultivating the 300 acres of land in Survey No. 1 of Lakkonda village. Among them some of the families were granted 'D' Form Patta during 2004 and others are yet to be granted pattas. However, they are all cultivating the said land by growing fruit-bearing trees and have been living here for the past 30 years.

The threat of dispossession of tribals from the land started with the transferring of land of 220 hectares by the District Collector in 2001. A further 10.10 acres of land in the same survey number in the year 2004 was transferred under the compensatory Afforestation Programme in lieu of loss of forest land due to the construction of Bhupatipalem Reservoir near Rampachodavaram, East Godavari District. Forest land transfers were effected on paper, ignoring the tribal rights over the land without any prior notice. The land records show that the land classified as 'Poromboke', was reclassified as forest land after entrustment to the Forest Department. Later, the Forest Department started the threat of eviction of tribal families from the land. On verification of records it was noticed that no such final notification was given that declared the land in question as forest land. But the records show that there is correspondence between the forest officials proposing for notification of land as forest land. In the year 2010, the Forest Department dispossessed tribals in part of the cultivable land high handedly and arbitrarily. The forest rights claims made by the tribals under the Forest Rights Recognition Act 2006, are kept pending without finalization of rights. As there was no option left for the tribals, they filed a petition seeking intervention of the High Court of Andhra Pradesh claiming their right of possession over the forest land, which is yet to be decided.

Notes

1. Malayappan, R.S. (Reprinted 1984) Report of the Special Development Officer, Govt. of A.P., Hyderabad, p. 8.
2. Arnold, David (1986) Agent Godavari, to Chief Sec. 29 July 1884, G.O. 2618, Jdl. 27 September 1909, Godavari Statistical Appendix, pp. 413–14 cited in 'Rebellious Hillmen: The Gudem-Rampa Risings 1839–1924', in Ranajit Guha (ed.), *Subaltern Studies III*, Oxford University Press, Delhi.
3. Jayaprakash Rao, P. (1985) 'The Struggle for Land: Tribal Revolts in Two Villages', in K. Murali Manohar, P. Ramaiah and C. Sivaramakrishna Rao (eds), *Political Economy of Tribal Development*, Indian Institute of Public Administration, Warangal.
4. D'Souza, Nafisa Goga (1991) 'Land Holding Systems in Tribal Areas', *Social Action*, Vol. 41, No. 1, January-March, ISI, New Delhi, pp. 345–50.
5. Government Records (1986) Sub Collector's Office, Rampachodavaram, East Godavari District.
6. Large farmers: Land holdings of Ac. 10–20; Medium farmers: Ac. 4–10; Semi Medium farmers: Ac. 2–3; Small farmers: Ac. 1–2 and Marginal farmers: Ac. 0.50–1.
7. Sarapu Chinna Pothuraju Dora vs. District Collector, East Godavari District, 2002 (1) ALT 699.

CHAPTER 4

Land Alienation in Villages

A Political Ethnography

This chapter captures the profile of tribal respondents and their perception of the problem of tribal land alienation. It also describes the extent of increase in the landholdings of the non-tribals over a period of time in the sample villages. The primary data is supplemented here by the secondary data. A political ethnography method is used to elicit information from the respondents and case studies of the sample villages are presented, articulating the land alienation and its causative factors.

Sample Village 1: Veerabhadrapuram

Social Demography

The total households of Veerabhadrapuram number 186, with a population of 669 persons. As per the 2001 Census, of the total population, the tribal population is 198 and the remaining 471 individuals are non-tribals. The study covers interviews with 63 representatives covering all the tribal households to elicit their perceptions on various dimensions of land alienation.

The major tribes inhabiting the village include the Konda Reddi, Koya Dora and Konda Kammara. This reflects the representation of the tribes in the region as well.

The majority of respondents are women. Only 33 per cent are males. All respondents are married.

Age background of the respondents shows that 60 per cent are below 45 years. All age categories above 20 years are represented.

Figure 4.1

Distribution of Tribal Communities (Veerabhadrapuram)

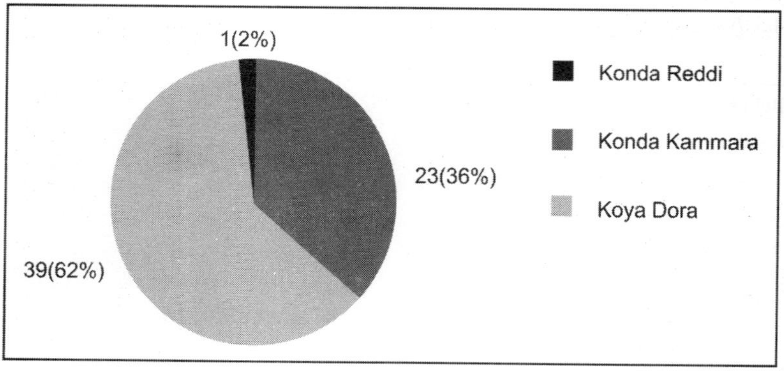

Figure 4.2

Agewise Distribution of Tribal Respondents

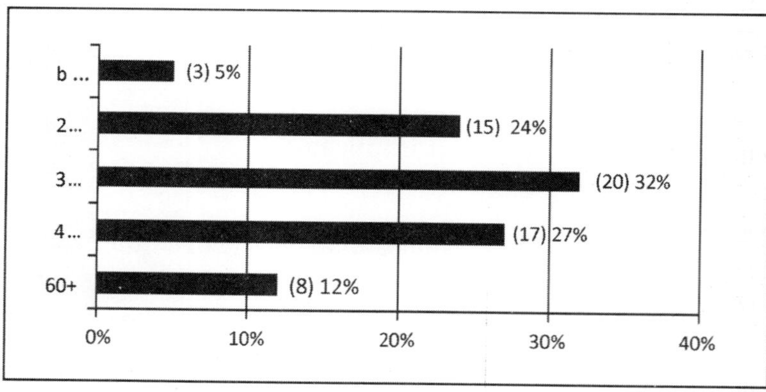

About 76 per cent of the respondents are illiterate. Interestingly, the literate persons belonged to the age group of below 45 years. The education pattern of the family members indicates that as many as 17 per cent are entirely illiterate, more so in the case of sons than daughters. Another 22 per cent have completed studies only up to Standard IV. Only 16 per cent have studied beyond the Standard X.

The average size of the family is three. The age profile indicates the following pattern: about 20 per cent of the family members in the sample family are above 21 years old, 62 per cent are between 6–20 years and only 18 per cent are below 5 years.

Table 4.1

Age-wise Distribution of Children of Respondents

Age (years)	*Sons*		*Daughters*		*Total*	
	No.	*%*	*No.*	*%*	*No.*	*%*
Below 5	6	13	7	26	13	18
6–10	8	17	3	11	11	15
11–20	21	46	13	48	34	47
21–35	10	22	4	15	14	19
36–50	1	2	0	0	1	1

Source: Field Data.

Table 4.2

Education of Children of Respondents

Education	*Sons*		*Daughters*		*Total*	
	No.	*%*	*No.*	*%*	*No.*	*%*
Illiterate	9	19	3	11	12	17
Up to Std. IV	10	22	6	22	16	22
V–VII	6	13	2	7	8	11
VIII–X	10	22	9	33	19	26
X+	7	15	5	19	12	16
Not Specified	4	9	2	8	6	8
Total	46	100	27	100	73	100

Source: Field Data.

The marital status of the family members shows that only 7 per cent are married.

Table 4.3

Marital Status of Children of Respondents

Marital Status	*Sons*		*Daughters*		*Total*	
	No.	*%*	*No.*	*%*	*No.*	*%*
Married	4	9	1	4	5	7
Unmarried	42	91	26	96	68	93
Total	46	100	27	100	73	100

Source: Field Data.

The activity profile of the family members reveals that as many as 19 per cent are engaged in cultivation, 14 per cent in agricultural or casual Labour and 35 per cent are students. The distribution of family members by their activity is characteristic of the roles prevalent among the tribal communities in the district in accordance with their age.

Table 4.4

Activity Profile of Children of Respondents

Occupation	*Sons*		*Daughters*		*Total*	
	No.	*%*	*No.*	*%*	*No.*	*%*
Cultivation	13	29	1	4	14	19
Agricultural Labour/Casual Labour	6	13	4	15	10	14
Job	1	2	1	4	2	3
Student	14	31	12	44	26	35
Any other	1	2	1	4	2	3
Not Specified	11	24	8	29	19	26
Total	46	100	27	100	73	100

Source: Field data.

Pattern of Land Ownership and Dispossession

The following table shows the steady increase of non-tribal population from 1961 to 1991, while it only decreased marginally in 2001 as per the Census Reports. The migration of non-tribals to the study village has become a phenomenon in order to gain access to land without any hassles. The decrease of non-tribal population after 1991 may be due to land struggles against the non-tribals in the area and adverse actions of government officials.

Year	*Total*	*Non-Tribal (NT)*	*Scheduled Tribe (ST)*
1961	393	255	138
1971	497	328	169
1981	600	391	209
1991	704	486	218
2001	669	471	198

Source: District Census book, Statistical Office, East Godavari District, Kakinada.

The pattern of land ownership and possession held by both tribals and non-tribals is necessary to understand how the land appropriation process occurred and the way in which the tribals of this village were alienated from their own land. The study village had witnessed the land survey in the year 1902, during the British period. Till today, the tribals in the village are not aware of what actually the land survey was intended for. According to hearsy, the evidence of the tribals is that the land was originally tilled by the tribals and the land survey in the name of non-tribals resulted in the degradation of their status from original tillers to labourers in their land. Thus, the non-incorporation of names of original tribal tillers in the land survey records presents a distorted picture of land ownership among the tribals. The primary objective of the land survey was to assess the landholdings and generate land revenue from the cultivators. The following table presents the pattern of land ownership recorded during the land survey of 1902.

Table 4.5

Landholdings of Tribal and Non-Tribal Families

S. No.	*Name of the Family*	*Scheduled Tribe (ST)/ Non-Tribal (NT)*	*No. of Landholdings*	*Extent (Acres)*
1.	Padala	NT	5	38.95
2.	Kaki	NT	1	2.55
3.	Chikkala	NT	5	18.34
4.	Marisetty	NT	2	7.64
5.	Diviti	NT	2	12.65
	Total	5	15	80.13
1.	Bachala	ST	1	1.61
2.	Allam	ST	1	1.51
	Total	2	2	3.12

Source: Data computed from 1902 Survey Registers at MRO office, Addateegala.

The holdings of non-tribal by the year 1902 are recorded to the extent of 80.13 acres while the tribal occupation is only to the extent of 3.12 acres. Thus, the land shown in the name of tribals in the land survey registers provides a distorted picture of land ownership.

The following table presents land records of a further land survey held in the year 1932. This is the last land survey during the pre-Independence period in the study village. The land ownership recorded in the name of the tribal and the non-tribal communities reflects the reality.

Table 4.6

Particulars of Ryotwari Landholdings of Tribal and Non-Tribal Families

Name of the Family	*No. of Families*	*Caste*	*As per 1932 RSR (Ac) Ryotwari Landholdings*	*Percentage*
Choppara	2	Non-Tribe	119.77	
Yejju	1	Non-Tribe	35.90	
Chikkala	2	Non-Tribe	13.37	
Adimula	1	Non-Tribe	40.01	
Kaki	1	Non-Tribe	15.42	
Hoda	1	Non-Tribe	7.17	
Gorsa	1	Non-Tribe	16.12	
Nagabatla	1	Non-Tribe	4.82	
Chennada	1	Non-Tribe	11.76	
Gaddam	1	Non-Tribe	6.59	
Korakanti	1	Non-Tribe	2.16	
Total	13		273.09	86%
Bendraju	1	Konda Reddi	22.19	
Chendraju	1	Konda Reddi	23.21	
Total (2)	2		45.40	14%
Grand Total	15		318.49	100%

Source: Data Computed from 1932 Survey Registers, MRO office, Addateegala.

The nature of land ownership in the village has not changed much but the number of cultivating non-tribal families rose from 5 to 13 in the year 1902. The extent of landholdings increased from 80 acres to 273 acres between 1902 and 1932. Non-tribals controlled almost 86 per cent of the total land in the villages by the year 1932. The landholdings of tribal families increased considerably from 3 acres to 45 acres but it is negligible if compared with the recorded land ownership of the non-tribals. The landholdings constitute 14 per cent of the total recorded landholdings. Thus the non-tribals, during the period, had complete control over the land available in the village.

Table 4.7

Present Possession of Land Held by Tribals

Name of the Family	*No. of House-holds*	*Caste*	*Tribal*			
			Government Land		*Ryotwari Land (Ac)*	*Total (Ac)*
			Without Patta (Ac)	*D Patta*		
Madem	3	ST	0		2.85	2.85
Kanem	5	ST	0		5.24	5.24
Karu	4	ST	0		3.04	3.04
Jartha	1	ST	0		0.82	0.82
Kunjam	1	ST	0		1.28	1.28
Vedurupalli	1	ST	0		0.95	0.95
Bandaru	4	ST	1.89		0.22	2.11
Chintoju	1	ST	0.50		0	0.50
Gorla	1	ST	0.50		0	0.50
Teegala	3	ST	3.22		0	3.22
Nasam	1	ST	0.98		0	0.98
Bendroju	1	ST	6.14		14.13	20.27
Bhusari	2	ST	0		1.90	1.90
Avevala	4	ST	0		4.09	4.09
Pallala	1	ST	1.65		0	1.65
Badugula	4	ST	0		3.95	3.95
Barnaja	1	ST	0		0.95	0.95
Neram	1	ST	0		1.55	1.55
Total	39		14.88		40.97	55.85

Data Computed data from Record of Rights, MRO office, Addateegala.

The position of the landholdings of the tribals and non-tribals in the village are uneven. The following table explains the pattern of land ownership and the changing relations among them. The data is as per the Record of Rights maintained by the Revenue Department during the year 2009–2010.

Table 4.7 presents the number of cultivating tribal households which is 39, and an increase in number from 3 in 1932 to 39 in 2010. But their total ryotwari landholdings decreased from 45 acres in 1932 to 41 acres in 2010. The fragmented landholding of tribals also indicates the decreasing size of landholdings and increasing number of tribal landless poor. Seven tribal families hold land without any tenural security.

Table 4.8 presents the pattern of land ownership among non-tribals.

Table 4.8

Possession of Land Held by Non-Tribals by 2010

Name of the Family	*No. of House-holds*	*Caste*	*Non-Tribal*			
			Government Land		*Ryotwari Land (Ac)*	*Total (Ac)*
			Without Patta (Ac)	*D. Patta*		
Mosuri	1	NT-BC	0.98		0	0.98
Bodapalli	1	NT-Kapu (oc)	0.50		0	0.50
Adimula	6	NT–BC	1.29		77.93	79.22
Tiragatti	1	NT–Kapu (oc)	0		0.95	0.95
Majjupureddy	1	NT-BC	0		0.95	0.95
Kosunuri	1	NT-Kapu (oc)	1.81		3.45	5.26
Magalapudi	1	NT-BC	4.12		0	4.12
Chikkala	1	NT-Kapu (oc)	0		17.05	17.05
Kokkera	1	NT-BC	0.50		0	0.50
Katta	1	NT-BC	0		4.22	4.22
Devudu	1	NT-BC	0		2.16	2.16
Donapudi	1	NT-BC	0		0.53	0.53
Sanapathi	1	NT-Kapu (oc)	9.52		0	9.52
Adabala	1	NT-Kapu (oc)	0		4.20	4.20
Dasamsetti	1	NT-Kapu (oc)	7.98		6.20	14.18
Sarakani	1	NT-Kapu (oc)	0		0.70	0.70
Palivala	4	NT-BC	18.87		0.67	19.54
Neeli	2	NT-Kapu (oc)	4.60		2.97	7.57
Komakula	3	NT-Kapu (oc)	11.42		4.29	15.71

Cont'd...

...Cont'd

Pedireddy	2	NT-Kapu (oc)	0	6.22	6.22
Punyamathula	1	NT-Kapu (oc)	0	9.04	9.04
Vuggirala	3	NT-Kapu (oc)	0.42	3.00	3.42
Rasamsetti	1	NT-Kapu (oc)	30.61	2.89	33.50
Padala	1	NT-Kapu (oc)	0.25	0	0.25
Indiradevi	1	NT-Kapu (oc)	1.28	0	1.28
Total	39		94.15	147.42	241.57

Data computed from Record of Rights, MRO office, Addateegala.

The size of the total registered Ryotwari landholdings of the non-tribals decreased from 273 acres in 1932 to 147 acres in 2010. The number of cultivating non-tribal families increased from 13 to 39. The reason for the decrease in the size of the recorded landholdings can be attributed to the land struggles and administrative steps taken for implementation of Land Transfer Regulations 1 of 70. But almost an equal extent has been recovered and is in occupation of the non-tribals without any legal entitlements. The landholdings of the non-tribals in the study village is over 94 acres without any patta and indicates the continued control over land in the study village. This land may be a part of the court litigation cases. Thus there is only a marginal difference of 31 acres in the total landholdings from 273 acres in 1932 to 242 acres in 2010.

Thus, 81 per cent of land in the village is under the control of the non-tribals, while 19 per cent of the land only is held by tribals. This shows that the gravity of tribal land alienation situation is high. The notable point is that non-tribals are controlling the land to an extent of 94 acres without any legal entitlement. Another significant point is the influx of a larger number of non-tribal population in the Scheduled village itself. It shows the failure of the implementation of Land Transfer Regulations. No mechanism is put in place to control the infiltration of non-tribals which is also the causative factor for land occupation. The imperialist land revenue policy for land survey in the years 1902 and 1932 paved the way to obtain land in favour of the non-tribals. The caste composition and the land ownership of non-tribals indicate that the upper caste 'Kapu' are in considerable number among the non-tribals castes, followed by the Other Backward Communities.

Table 4.9

Landholding Pattern among Tribals and Non-Tribals

Category of Landholders	*Tribal (No.)*	*Extent (Ac)*	*Non-Tribals (No.)*	*Extent (Ac)*
Large (10–20)	1	20.27	6	127.55
Medium (4–10)	0	0	12	73.25
Semi-medium (2–4)	1	2.73	8	28.24
Small (1–2)	9	11.39	3	4.96
Marginal (below 1)	28	21.46	10	7.57
Total	39	55.85	39	241.57

The pattern of landholding among tribals and the non-tribals clearly indicates a trend that is proportionally marginal, and small tribal farmers are more in number in the case of tribals, while large, medium and semi-medium farmers are on the higher side in the case of non-tribals. This reflects the high extent of tribal landlessness in the village.

Table 4.10

Trends of Land Alienation

1902 (Extent-Ac)	*1932 (Extent-Ac)*	*2010 (Extent-Ac)*
80 (5 Non-tribal families)	273 (13 Non-tribal families)	242 (39 Non-tribal families)

The number of five landholding families in 1902 increased to 13 in 1932 and further to 39 in 2010. This is an indication that there is a trend of increasing non-tribal cultivating families in the village. The extent of landholdings of 80 acres in 1902 enormously increased to 273 acres during the land survey in 1932. The settlements of the non-tribals in the study village benefited them to get surveyed land named in their favour during the land survey of 1932. The study village is on the way to Addateegala Mandal headquarter. The immigration of non-tribal settlers in the pre-Independence period may be due to the road construction activity which intended to counter the Alluri Seetharamaraju movement in the mandal. Thus, the land survey in pre-Independence period is the cause of land alienation. The size of landholdings decreased from 273 acres in 1932 to 242 acres in the year 2010. This gradual trend of slow process of land alienation may be largely due to varied changes in the later years. The land struggle of the Peoples War Group in the area against acquisition of land by non-tribal settlers and government action for assignment of land in favour of tribals altered the change of ownership of the non-tribals in the later period.

All the tribal households were interviewed in the study village. The primary data of the village shows that out of 63 tribal households, 32 are landless. In fact, only 34.80 acres of land is under actual cultivation although the land revenue accounts shows that 56 acres is in their name. The analysis of the landholdings shows an unequal ownership among the tribals and the non-tribals. More than 40 per cent of the present tribal respondents are immigrants from other tribal villages. These tribals are not in a position to state the precise causative factors which contributed to the process of land transfer from the tribals to the non-tribals during the pre-Independence period 1947. The law permits any tribal to question the occupation of land held by the non-tribals, but the immigrant tribals are not equipped with any documentary or oral proof to strengthen their arguments for land restoration. The original tribal families who tilled the land moved to other tribal villages as they were dispossessed from the land by the non-tribals. The mobility of tribals from one village to another village helped non-tribal occupants of land to substantiate their land claims before the administrative authorities. The elders in the village say that they have no confidence that they will ever get back the alienated land from the possession of the non-tribal occupants in the given situation. The revenue authorities do not help them in retrieval of the alienated land. Thus, the problem of land alienation is acute in the village and the situation is not favourable for the restoration of land from the control of the non-tribals.

Land Struggles

Land struggles against the non-tribals were started in the year 1983–1984 by the Peoples War Group. The violent acts of Naxalites, including a killing of the non-tribal landlord of Tiragati family and kidnapping of Peddapuram Revenue Divisional Officer in the area made non-tribals to involuntarily surrender some of their land to the government. The government distributed such land of 20 acres to the tribals, says a tribal woman Lakshmi of the study village. Perhaps the influence of the land movement in the study village has created an impact in articulation of their land concerns on the women. The women are vocal and were ready to answer the questionnaire during the field study because some of them are also pursuing legal cases through court of law for restoration of their land. The extent of 67 per cent of women respondents attending the interview in the study village may be an indication of their level of understanding of land issues and decisive nature in fighting for land rights. The women here are more vocal compared with the other sample villages.

Process of Land Alienation

Case 1

- *Forced Dispossession:* Neram Bhadra Rao belonging to the Konda Kammara Scheduled Tribe community, says that he owned 1.55 acres of land prior to 2002. The Mandal Revenue Authorities of Addateegala granted an assignment patta for 0.81 acres in favour of his wife in the year 2002. This land was occupied forcibly by a non-tribal, namely, Peddireddy Suribabu. Since 2003, Neram Bhadra Rao has been pleading with the revenue authorities for the restoration of land from the possession of the non-tribal, Peddireddy Suribabu. So far he has not got back the land.

Case 2

- *Failure in Enforcement of Order/Patta in absence of Land Possession:* Nalamati Rajulamma belongs to the Kondareddi Scheduled Tribe, and is a widow. Earlier, a petition was filed by the Special Deputy Tahsildar on behalf of tribals in the village under Land Transfer Regulations against a non-tribal for restoration of 0.80 acres of land covered by S. No. 9/10. After an enquiry, the Special Deputy Collector of Rampachodavaram passed an order for the restoration of the said land to the government as the possession was illegal, with a direction for onward assignment of the land to the tribal. Later, the revenue authorities granted patta on such land to

Rajulamma in the year 2002 in Ref. No. 172/2002. This patta was granted under the land distribution scheme. The revenue officers did not physically hand over the land except handing out the land entitlement. The non-tribal, Badra Rao, is still continuing his possession over the land, in spite of an order passed against him by the Special Deputy Collector Court. The patta holder Rajulamma is pleading with the Mandal Revenue Officer for possession of land for the last nine years. But her pleas are not being attended to by the revenue authority. The case of Rajulamma shows that having land entitlement is different from the actual possession of the land covered by the said patta. So her landless situation continues irrespective of the distribution of land pattas to the eligible tribals. Further, there is failure on the part of the enforcing authorities in evicting non-tribals from the land, even though a clear direction was given by the courts.

Case 3

- *Tribal Land Leased Out:* Busari Lova Lakshmi belongs to the Kondareddi Scheduled Tribe, a widow with three sons. She says that her grandfather cultivated the a land stretch of 3.00 acres. This land was leased out by him 40 years back to one Ch. Veera Krishna, a non-tribal, in order to overcome financial crisis. The land was further transferred by Krishna to another non-tribal, Ramaswamy. The purchaser, Ramaswamy, managed to incorporate his name in the revenue records. Ramaswamy was reluctant to give back the land although the tribals were prepared to clear the debts. A case in LTRP No. 11/2007 was enquired into at the instance of the Special Deputy Tahsildar. But it ended in favour of the non-tribals. The court held that earlier an enquiry was held for the same land. As such, it attracts the legal principle of Res judicata and no enquiry will be held. Busari Lova Lakshmi says that the non-tribal manipulated land records in his favour and obtained title deeds from the revenue staff. Now her family has become landless and is living on daily wage earnings. Thus, it is an established fact that the process of land alienation was due to the tribal's indebtedness. The transactions are oral in nature without any support of documentary proof, as such, there is difficulty in proving the cases in courts.

Case 4

- *Police Intervention:* Adimulam Kantham belongs to the Kondakammari tribe. She has an ancestral property of 1.95 acres in S. No. 26/2 and 22 acres situated in Veerabhadrapuram village. The tribal woman did not cultivate the land for some years after the death of her husband. Meanwhile, a non-tribal Siva, occupied the land. She pleaded for the land. But he did not give over the possession of the land to her. She filed a case in LTRP 311/2004 for the retrieval of land from the illegal possession of the non-tribal. But the court was not inclined to take up the case, holding that a case with the same subject matter of dispute was pending for consideration before the Agent to Government's court, Kakinada. Adimulam Kantham approached the Tahsildar, Addateegala in 2007, who said that Siva had no legal right and she could enter the land and cultivate it. With the support of her son Ramana, Adimulam Kantham ventured to enter the fields and started cultivating the land. Meanwhile, Siva filed a false complaint in the police station at Addateegla. The police of Addateegala illegally detained her son for two days and threatened to file a case against them. Kantham says that the non-tribal Siva has been cultivating the land without any obstruction from any enforcing authorities of the Land Transfer Regulations.

In fact, police interference is unwarranted in civil matters. There is a clear direction from the Director General of Police in circular No. 695/L&O/2007 that 'the subordinate staff is not to interfere on behalf of non-tribals and against tribals in land disputes in the Agency Areas'. This circular was issued following the recommendations of the Koneru Land Committee, set up by the Government of Andhra Pradesh to look into land disputes. Thus the case shows that the intervention of the police is helping non-tribals to possess the land although it is against the provisions of the Land Transfer Regulations.

Summary

In 1932, 13 non-tribal families held land of 273 acres. The number of non-tribal families jumped to 39 and they were able to increase their retention upto 242 acres of land till the year 2010 in the study village. But their landholdings were only 80 acres in the 1902 land survey. Except for two non-tribal families, the remaining 23 new non-tribal families gained access to land only after 1932. But, in fact, only 5 non-tribal families were holding land in 1902. Similarly, land was held by 10 non-tribal families in 1932. The names of original non-tribal landholders were not found in land records maintained for the further period. This was made possible as there was no restriction to transfer land among the non-tribals till the commencement of 1 of 70 Land Transfer Regulations. The land from the non-tribal land occupants in 1902 changed hands to other non-tribals in 1932, and further to new non-tribal entrants in the village as a continuous process. This is due to the flexibility in law enforcement system which facilitated infiltration of non-tribals to tribal areas and gain access to their land. The private land transactions over the land eroded the community ownership over the resources held by the tribal communities.

These land transfers erased the native land disputes of tribals who lost the land owned by their ancestors. The evidence in respect of tribal land claims is erased or removed during the Court enquiries. The Special Deputy Collector Court allowed the claims of non-tribals on the basis of documentary transactions without any elaborate enquiry regarding the field situation. Thus, the tribals hardly received justice due to lack of documentary proof.

The British land revenue policy which was unmindful of the tribal or the non-tribal distinction in determining the landholdings, has become a major set back for the restoration of alienated land. The tribals were unaware of the value of land registrations engineered by the land administration during the British period in the name of land survey. The subsequent tribal protective land laws have failed to reverse the historical injustice meted to tribals during the land survey itself. This is evident from the fact that there was an increase in the population of the non-tribals and their landholdings in the village since 1902. Further, the penetration of the non-tribals into the village to gain access to and to occupy land easily is the causative factor of land alienation. No official check has been put in place to check or control the influx of non-tribal population. The oral evidences of tribals in the study village show their inability to get back the land lost to the non-tribals through oral transactions. According to the legal principles, even the land registered in the name of non-tribals in 1932, per se does not create any title under the Andhra Pradesh Agency Area Land Transfer Act 1917, which prohibits the transfer of land between the tribals and the non-tribals. Thus, the burden of proof always lies on the non-tribal who has to establish that the land in possession did not come through any transfer from a member of the Scheduled Tribe. The legal presumption made under the Land Transfer Regulations 1 of 70 is that the land situated in the Scheduled Areas originally belonged to the tribals, unless the contrary is proved. If such being the case, there is no record in favour of the non-tribals prior to 1932 to show that they had been in continuous possession of the land from the inception of the Andhra Pradesh Agency Tracts Land Transfer Act 1917, till the enquiry initiated by the court.

Figure 4.3

LTR Implementation and Outcome

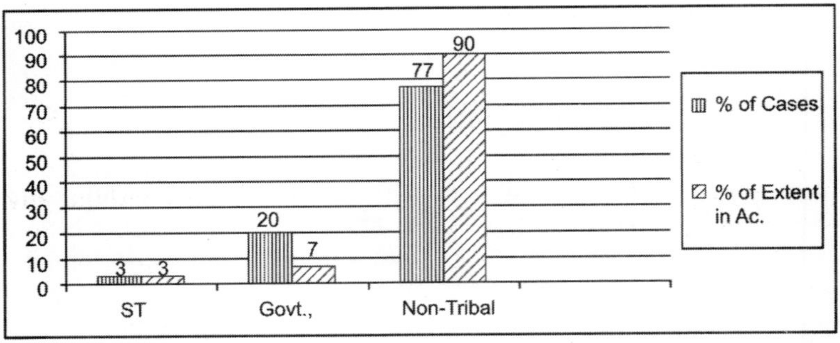

A total of 38 cases were booked under the Land Transfer Regulations 1 of 59 as amended by 1 of 70 before the Special Deputy Collector's Court at Rampachodavaram, covering an extent of 277 acres of land. Only a single case, covering an extent of 8.28 acres, was decided in favour of the tribals, while cases decided in favour of non-tribals covered an extent of 224 acres. Of these, 6 cases covering an extent of 17 acres, were decided in favour of the government. If the cases decided in favour of the government too are added to the cases of tribals, then a total of 7 cases would cover a land area of 25 acres. The tribals won only 22 per cent of cases covering an extent of 10 acres of the disputed land. The outcome of the legal process at the preliminary level enquiry court indicates the trends of land alienation.

Sample Village 2: Nellipudi

Social Demography

There are 868 households in the village, covered by a population of 3,511. Of this, the tribal population is 388 only. The remaining population of 3,143 comprises the non-tribal population as per the 2001 Census. The study covers the interviews of 75 representatives from all tribal households to elicit their perceptions on various dimensions of land alienation. The village Nellipudi includes its hamlet village, Chinnampalem.

The major tribes in the village are Konda Reddi, Konda Dora, Koya Dora and Konda Kammara. The distribution of communities in the village is also representative of the tribes in this region as well.

Figure 4.4

Distribution of Tribal Communities

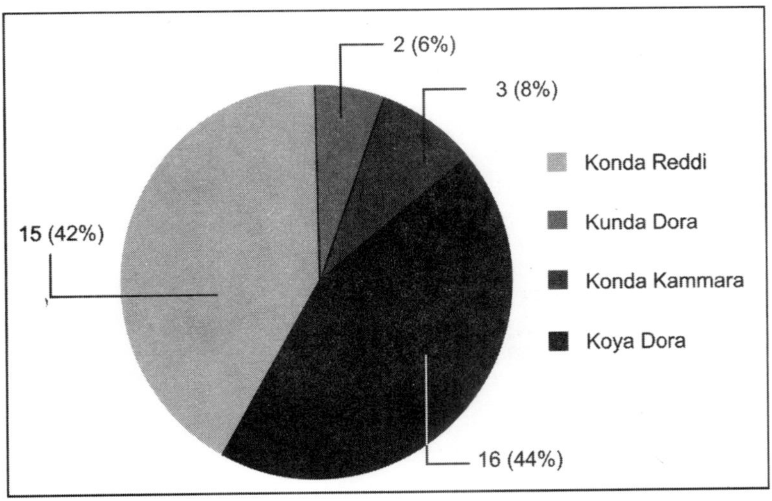

The majority of respondents are females. Only 42 per cent are males. All the respondents are married.

The majority of respondents are females. Only 37 per cent are males. The Konda Kammara women are sufficiently articulate to explain the land issues, unlike the Konda Reddi women. All the respondents are married. The age background of the respondents shows that 73 per cent are below 45 years. All age categories above 20 years are represented.

A majority of the respondents, about 47 per cent are illiterate. Interestingly, all the literate belonged to an age category of below 45 years.

Figure 4.5

Distribution of Tribal Communities

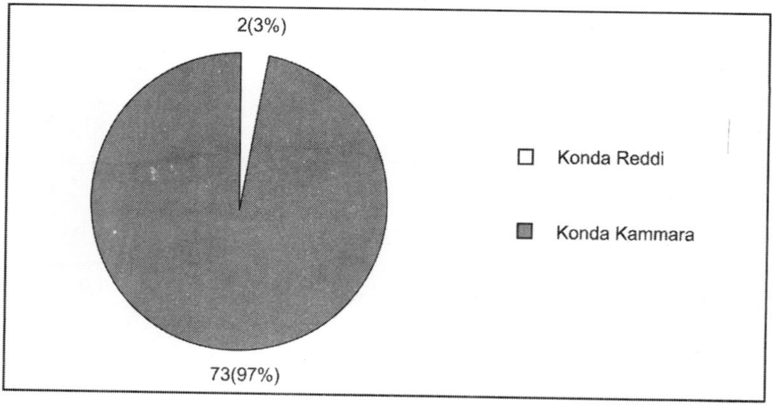

Figure 4.6

Age-wise Distribution of Tribal Respondents

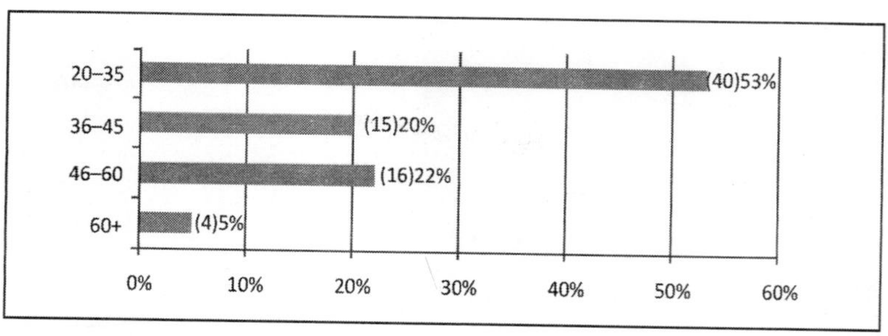

The average size of the family is 3. The age profile indicates the following pattern: about 13 per cent of the family members in the sample family are above 21 years old, 64 per cent are between 6–20 years and only 23 per cent are below 5 years. The age background of sons and daughters of respondents is presented in Table 4.11.

The education pattern of the family members indicates that as many as 4 per cent are totally illiterate (all were sons). Another 25 per cent have completed their studies only up to Standard IV. Only 25 per cent have studied beyond Standard X. The education of sons and daughters of respondents is presented in Table 4.12.

Table 4.11

Age-wise Distribution of Children of Respondents

Age	*Sons*		*Daughters*		*Total*	
	No.	*%*	*No.*	*%*	*No.*	*%*
Below 5	8	17	13	29	21	23
6–10	3	7	12	27	15	16
11–20	26	55	18	40	44	48
21–35	10	21	2	4	12	13
36–50	0	0	0	0	0	0
Total	47	100	45	100	92	100

Source: Field Data.

Table 4.12

Education of Children Respondents

Education	*Sons*		*Daughters*		*Total*	
	No.	*%*	*No.*	*%*	*No.*	*%*
Illiterate	4	9	0	0	4	4
Up to Std. IV	9	19	14	31	23	25
V–VII	7	15	8	18	15	16
VIII–X	12	25	6	13	18	20
X+	12	25	11	25	23	25
Not Specified	3	7	6	13	9	10
Total	47	100	45	100	92	100

Source: Field Data.

The marital status of the family members shows that 16 per cent are married. Of them the details of the marital status for boys and girls among the respondent households is presented in Table 4.13.

The activity profile of the family members reveals that as many as 10 per cent are engaged in cultivation, 3 per cent are in agricultural or casual labour and 66 per cent are engaged in studies. The distribution of family members by their activity is characteristic of the roles they play according to their age which also reflects the general prevalence among the tribal communities in the district.

Table 4.13

Distribution of Children of Respondents by their Marital Status

Marital Status	*Sons*		*Daughters*		*Total*	
	No.	*%*	*No.*	*%*	*No.*	*%*
Married	11	23	4	9	15	16
Unmarried	36	77	41	91	77	84
Total	47	100	45	100	92	100

Source: Field Data.

Table 4.14

Activity-wise Distribution of Children Respondents

Occupation	*Sons*		*Daughters*		*Total*	
	No.	*%*	*No.*	*%*	*No.*	*%*
Cultivation	9	19	0	0	9	10
Agricultural Labour/Casual Labour	2	4	1	2	3	3
Job	1	2	0	0	1	1
Student	30	64	31	69	61	66
Any other	0	0	0	0	0	0
Not Specified	5	11	13	29	18	20
Total	47	100	45	100	92	100

Source: Field Data.

Land Ownership and Possession

The village is held on Mukhasa tenure. The village was formerly part of the Rampa Mansabdar's property. It was given to the father of the late Mukhasadar, Bhupathi Dev in recognition of his services to the government. He died in 1906. After his death, his grandson was given a sanad in 1907.

Of all the 75 tribal households covered by the study in Nellipudi and its hamlet, Chinnampalem, 30 households are landless. The remaining 45 households have cultivable land to the extent of 93 acres. Of the 93 acres, the tribals own land to the extent of 30 acres. The podu land extends to 5 acres. Four tribal families cultivate land on lease to the extent of 7 acres. The tribals say that several tribal families were compelled to move to other tribal villages during the Rampa disturbances during the British period.

Table 4.15 presents the land ownership pattern of the tribals as per the Record of Rights maintained during the year 2009–2010. The data reveals only the land in the government records and does not include Mukhasa land.

Table 4.15

Land in Possession of Tribals in 2010

Name of the Family	*No. of House-holds*	*Caste*	*As per 2010 ROR 1B Land-holdings*	*Tribal*			
				Government Land		*Ryotwari Land*	*Total*
				Without Patta	*D Patta*		
Pathara	1	Tribe	2		6.10	5.20	11.30
Towdoju	1	Tribe	1		3.00		3.00
Boraga	1	Tribe	1		3.00		3.00
Annika	1	Tribe	1		8.43	1.05	9.48
Chattada	1	Tribe	1		10.20		10.20
	5		6		30.73	6.25	36.98

Source: Data computed from Record of Rights (IB) Register 2010, MRO office, Gangavaram.

Table 4.16

Landholding of Non-Tribals as in 2010

Landowner		*Patta land-Extent/Acres*	*Land without Patta/Extent/Acres*	*Total Extent-Acres*
Government		*Not Applicable*	*Not Applicable*	*66.51*
OC 6	Kamma 1	3.36	0	22.82
	Rajulu 5	16.53	2.93	
BC 8	Gollalu 6	21.60	0	30.36
	Chakali 2	8.76	0	
SC 3	Mala 3	15.96	0	15.96
17		66.21	2.93	135.65

Five tribal households have 'D Form Patta land' to the extent of 31 acres which is classified as government land. The Ryotwari pass books issued, reflect that land was given only to the extent of 6 acres.

Table 4.16 presents the pattern of land ownership and caste composition of the non-tribals in the study village.

The non-tribal landholdings are to the extent of 66 acres as per the Record of Rights. The remaining land of 67 acres is considered to be government land as per the Record of Rights. Among the non-tribals, 6 families belong to the upper caste of the Kamma and the Rajus.

The land particulars collected in the field and details under the Record of Rights may vary due to the reason that the final Survey and Settlement did not take place in Nellipudi. The unregularized land occupations in the study village have been maintained in separate Mukhasa Amarakam accounts. The extent of land occupation in Mukhasa land tenure in Nellipudi shows an alarming extent of land alienation situation among tribals.

The Mukhasa Amarakam accounts maintained during the year 1945 show the landholdings of the cultivators. The landholdings are registered as per the grant of Mukhasadar to the cultivating tenants on payment of tax. The grant of Mukhasadar to a cultivator is on condition that such land shall not be given away further to others. But there is no restriction to the Mukhasadar to the extent of the land to be given to a non tribal.

Table 4.17 presents the total landholdings of both tribals and non-tribals in the village.

Table 4.17

Landholdings of Tribals and Non-Tribals (1945)

S. No.	*Category*	*No. of Landholdings*	*Extent (Ac)*	*% Of*
1.	Non-tribal	372	1,997.80	96.53
2.	Tribal	25	71.96	3.47
	Total	397	2,069.76	100

Source: Mukhasa Amarakarm Register 1945, MRO office, Gangavaram.

The data shows that the extent of landholding with the non-tribals in 1945 was 1998 acres, which comes to 96.53 per cent of the total holdings, while the tribals landholding was recorded as 72 acres which comes to 3.47 per cent. However, the delay in the abolition of Mukhasas resulted in the increase of land alienation.

As per the land records maintained by the Sub Collector's office, Rampachodavaram, of the 7,307 acres of Mukhasa land tenure, 736 non-tribal holders control 7,175 acres which constitutes 98 per cent, while 74 tribal occupants have land only to the extent of 132 acres in their occupation. This was the situation at the end of 2009. Therefore, the extent covered by the landholdings in the case of the non-tribals jumped from 1998 acres in 1945 to 7,175 acres in 2009. While in the case of tribals, it increased from 72 acres to 132 acres only. This shows that land alienation among tribals in Nellipudi increased alarmingly. The policy of land settlement in Mukhasa Tenure triggered the expansion of land occupations by the non-tribal communities.

Process of Land Loss

The penetration of the non-tribals to Nellipudi is a major factor for land alienation. Table 4.18 demonstrates the steady increase of the non-tribal population in the village.

Table 4.18

Decadal Population of Tribals and Non-Tribals

Nellipudi Village				
Year	*Total*	*NT*	*ST*	*Total House Hold*
1961	2,015	1,814	201	407
1971	2,034	1,723	311	385
1981	2,020	1,776	244	411
1991	2,772	2,349	423	575
2001	3,511	3,123	388	868

Source: District Census Book, Statistical Office, East Godavari District, Kakinda.

The total population in the village as per the 2001 Census is 3,511, covered by 868 households. The Scheduled Tribe population is 388 only. The Scheduled Caste 'Mala' population in the village is 1,330, which is the highest among the non-tribals, constituting 43 per cent of the total non-tribal population. The enquiry in the study villages with regard to the presence of high population of Scheduled Caste reveals an interesting point. The inflow of non-tribal Schedule Caste population of Mala caste to Agency Areas in general is attributed to the flexible policy of the then Madras Presidency Government. The Revenue Department issued GO Ms No. 1318 in 1931 including the Malas/Agency Malas and Valmikis in the list of 'Hill Tribes'. Again, in 1932 the 'Malas' alone were included in the list through GO Ms No. 1091, 1939. But the inclusion of the Mala caste in the list of Scheduled Tribe list was discontinued after the enforcement of the Constitution of India. The 'Hill Tribe' status given to the Malas in the earlier period prompted their infiltration. The population of non-tribal caste 'Golla' too is high in Nellipudi. These non-tribals are a nomadic community who moved from the plain areas of the district to Nellipudi during the pre-Independence period, to facilitate the grazing of their cattle in the tribal areas. During drought season these communities migrated to tribal areas and later settled in the village. Thus, the emergence of outsiders and their inroads in the study village resulted in various changes in land relations.

The fundamental reason for land alienation in Nellipudi was that there was no prohibition of land transfers from Mukhasadar to non-tribals till the introduction of the Land Transfer Regulations 1 of 1970. Further, the Mukhasa land tenure continued till its abolition in 1989, much later than the abolition of other land tenure systems in the district. No control was exercised by the government over such Mukhasa land, which further resulted in a huge chunk of land transfer. Presently, the non-tribal occupants are claiming legitimacy over such occupations.

The following case helps to understand the different strategies adopted by the non-tribals to retain the land in their control.

Genesis of Land Titles

In 1919, one Pasumarthi Maridi Raju, a non-tribal, purchased land of 41.43 acres situated in the study village, Nellipudi, in an auction conducted by the Assistant Commissioner, Rampa Agency. Another non-tribal, Kancharla Veeranna took land on lease initially from Maridi Raju, and purchased it subsequently. The possession of land of Kancharla Veeranna was challenged by the Mukhasadar. The Mukhasadar of Nellipudi muchasa filed a case in CC No. 138/1939 before the Sub Magistrate, Yellavaram, against Veeranna. However, the Court confirmed the land title of Veeranna over the land. The dispute between the Mukhasadar and Veeranna ended.

Keeping Tribal Women as 'Mistress' to Retain Land

The son of Veeranna namely Venkatarao, was married and had children. He took a tribal woman Kosu Buchamma and kept her as his mistress. Venkatarao claims before the court that his father Veeranna gifted the land of 41.43 acres to Kosu Buchemma in the year 1961 due to Venkatrap's marital relationship with her. However, the tribals in the village disagree with this statement and say that the marriage with Kosu Buchamma by Venkatarao is part of a systematic attempt to hold the land by the non-tribal Veeranna. Otherwise, it was difficult for non-tribals to retain land in the Scheduled Areas. Further, the villagers say that tribal Kosu Buchamma was already married to a tribal named Bapanna Dora. The gift of a huge piece of land to a tribal woman, Buchamma by a non-tribal, Veeranna shows his intentions to escape legal complications under the Land Transfer Regulations and to sustain landed interests.

Land Conflict with Non-Tribals

The land litigation continued further. Mukhasadar Madhuveeti Yerramraju issued a Krishiki patta over the land in favour of another non-tribal, Maddipati Kondayya in 1965 to cultivate the land on the condition to pay Mukhasa tax. Based on this Krishiki Patta, Maddipati's family members stepped into the land of Kancharla Venkanna in the year 1985 for cultivation. Then Kancharla Venkanna filed a civil suit in OS No. 109/98 in the court of Agent to Government (District Collector), East Godavari District, seeking eviction of Maddipati's family members from the land.

During subsistence of the proceedings before the Agent to Government (District Collector), Kosu Buchamma was brought to litigation to strengthen their case and a case was filed before the Special Deputy Collector (Tribal welfare) Court, Rampachodavaram in LTRP No. 41/2001 to seek restoration of land from the possession of the non-tribal landlords, Maddipati Prasad and others, under the provisions of LTR 1 of 70. The Special Deputy Collector's Court decided the case in favour of Kosu Buchamma and passed orders evicting the non-tribal Maddipati Prasad. The unsuccessful non-tribal filed an appeal before the Additional Agent to the Government Court. The Court dismissed his appeal in CMA No. 23/2003. However, the non-tribal, Maddipati Prasad continues his possession of 43 acres land by filing a Writ Petition in the High Court and its related Revision Petition No. 1312/L2/06 which are pending for finalization. The case study shows the vicious ways by which non-tribals retain their hold over the land in the Scheduled Areas.

Figure 4.7

Nellipudi: Implementation of Land Transfer Regulations and Outcome

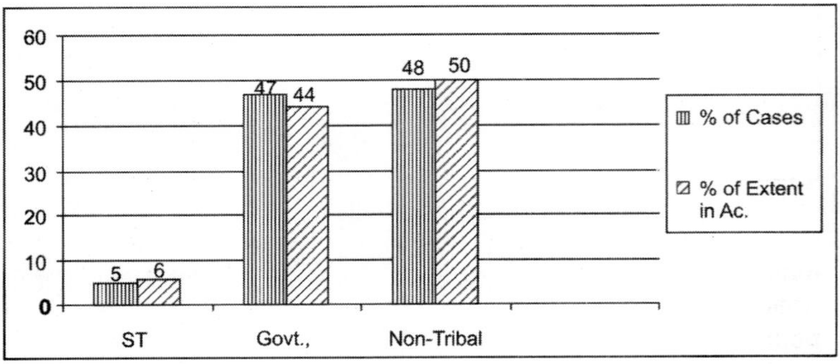

In all, 141 cases were booked covering an extent of 610 acres of land, of which 120 cases, covering land of 531 acres were disposed. Among the disposed cases, tribals could secure orders in 5 per cent of the cases, covering 6 per cent of the disputed land, whereas non-tribals got orders in 48 per cent of the cases, covering 50 per cent of land. The court passed orders in 47 per cent of the cases, covering 44 per cent of land.

Sample Village 3: Mallavaram Mamillu

The total households in the sample village Mallavaram Mamillu number 82, covering a population of 308 persons. Of this, the tribal population comprises 219 persons and non-tribals constitute the remaining 89 persons as per the 2001 Census. The study covers the interviews of a total of 38 representatives of all tribal households to elicit their perceptions on various dimensions of land alienation.

The tribal background of respondents shows that the major tribes inhabiting the village include the Kondareddi, Koya Dora and Konda Kammara. The tribal composition of the village demography reflects the distribution of tribal communities in the region as well.

Figure 4.8

Distribution of Tribal Communities

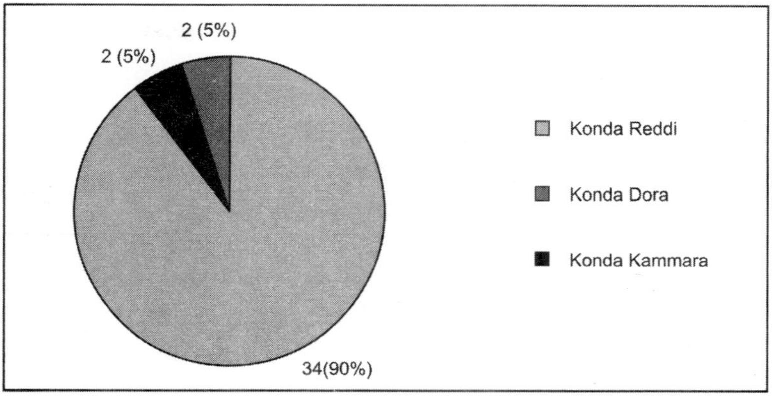

The majority of respondents are males. Only 29 per cent are females. The Konda Reddi women do not venture out from the traditional fabric of the society because of their shyness to outsiders. No political party is involved in any land occupation movement. That might also be the reason for the passive role of tribal women in response to the questions during the field survey. About 97 per cent of the respondents are married and only one remains single.

The age background of the respondents shows that 58 per cent are below 45 years. All age categories above 21 years are represented. Figure 4.9 indicates the age wise distribution of the respondents.

Figure 4.9

Age-wise Distribution of Tribal Respondents

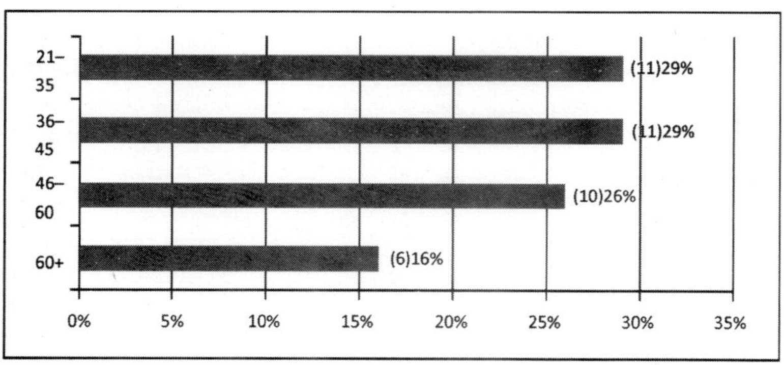

A majority of the households, i.e. about 66 per cent, are illiterate. Interestingly, the literate belonged to all age categories. Eleven are below 45 years, nine above 45 years and five persons are above 60 years.

The age background of sons and daughters of respondents is presented in the Table 4.19.

Table 4.19

Age-wise Distribution of Children of Respondents

Age	*Sons*		*Daughters*		*Total*	
	No.	*%*	*No.*	*%*	*No.*	*%*
Below 5	2	5	1	3	3	4
6–10	5	11	7	18	12	14
11–20	28	62	29	74	57	68
21–35	9	20	2	5	11	13
36–50	1	2	0	0	1	1
Total	45	100	39	100	84	100

Source: Field Data.

The average size of the family is 4. The age profile indicates the following pattern: about 14 per cent of the family members in the sample families are above 21 years old, 82 per cent are between 6–20 years and only 4 per cent are below 5 years.

Table 4.20

Distribution of Children of Respondents by their Education

Education	*Sons*		*Daughters*		*Total*	
	No.	*%*	*No.*	*%*	*No.*	*%*
Illiterate	6	13	0	0	6	7
Up to Std. IV	7	16	6	15	13	16
V–VII	12	27	6	15	18	21
VIII–X	11	24	10	26	21	25
X+	9	20	17	44	26	31
Total	45	100	39	100	84	100

Source: Field Data.

The education pattern of the family members indicates that as many as 7 per cent are totally illiterate, more so in the case of sons than among the daughters. Another 16 per cent have completed up to Standard IV. Only 28 per cent have studied beyond Standard X.

The background of the respondents' children in terms of their marital status is represented in Table 4.21.

Table 4.21

Distribution of Children of Respondents by their Marital Status

Marital Status	*Sons*		*Daughters*		*Total*	
	No.	*%*	*No.*	*%*	*No.*	*%*
Married	2	4	0	0	2	2
Unmarried	43	96	39	100	82	98
Total	45	100	39	100	84	100

The marital status of the family members shows that only 2 per cent are married.

Table 4.22 illustrates the occupation of sons and daughters of the respondents.

Table 4.22

Distribution of Sons/daughters of Respondents by their Activity

Occupation	*Sons*		*Daughters*		*Total*	
	No.	*%*	*No.*	*%*	*No.*	*%*
Cultivation	2	4	0	0	2	2
Agricultural Labour/Casual Labour	10	23	5	12	15	18
Job	5	11	1	3	6	7
Student	26	58	25	64	51	61
Any other	2	5	1	3	3	4
Not Specified	0	0	7	18	7	8
Total	45	100	39	100	84	100

Source: Field Data

The activity profile of the family members reveals that as many as 2 per cent are engaged in cultivation, 18 per cent are in agricultural or casual labour and 61 per cent are engaged in education. The profiling of the family members by their occupation is characteristic of the roles they play according to their age in the tribal communities in the district.

Background of Land Tenure Administration

Mallavaram Mamillu was originally part of Mutta of Dutcharthi. The headquarter of Mutta is Dutcharthi, ten km north of Addateegala Mandal headquarter. Till 1881, this village was part of the Golkonda taluk of Vizagapatam (Visakhapatnam) District. It was originally held on service tenure under the old Golkonda Zamindar's estate and was sold for arrears and bought by the government in 1837. The Muttadars under him thus became direct holders under the government on service tenure. This seriously lowered their status, as they were directly subject to the observation of the Collector's native administration. Several disturbances followed.

At the time of the outbreak of the Rampa rebellion of 1879 in this district, the Golgonda Muttadars had no such grievances against the government as existed in Rampa but they still fretted against the restrictions placed upon their powers. The more daring among them were moved by solicitations from across the border, by a hunger to loot and by a desire to pay off old scores against the police.

The chief was Chekka Venkanna Dora, Muttadar of Dutcharthi, whose grandfather had been the manager of that Mutta. On the death of his master without any children, Chekka Venkanna Dora had obtained a sanad for it, himself. Chekka Venkanna Dora, Muttadar of Dutcharthi, had avoided any overt act of rebellion. But it was the belief of all officers, civil and military, who served in those hills, that he had encouraged Dwarabandala Chandrayya, a tribal leader, on the understanding that his own villages should be spared from plunder. It is beyond doubt that both his villages were not plundered and that he could have, if he liked, crushed the outbreak in Dutcharthi area and prevented the destruction of Addateegala. Therefore, when the rebellion was over, it was decided to remove Chekka Venkanna Dora from his Mutta. His brother was appointed as Muttadar in 1881. At the same time, the six villages which now constitute the Mutta of Anigeru, and which were earlier under the direct control and land administration of the government, were taken from Dutcharthi to reward the loyalty of another influential hill chief. The Muttas of Dutcharthi and

Guditeru, which were thought to be more accessible to the officers of this district, were also transferred from Visakhapatnam to the Godavari Agency in the same year.[1]

Table 4.23

Population of Non-tribals in Village Mallavaram Mamillu from 1961 to 2001

		Mallavarammamillu		
Year	*Total*	*NT*	*ST*	*House Holds*
1961	54	26	28	12
1971	139	81	58	33
1981	211	70	141	51
1991	216	68	148	57
2001	308	89	219	90

Source: District Census Book, Statistical Office, East Godavari District, Kakinada.

HHs: House Holds

The population figures present the presence of non-tribals in Mallavaram Mamillu. In fact, Mallavaram Mamillu, which was earlier known as Mallavarappadu, was an uninhabited village in the year 1951 as per the Census Reports. The population of tribals increased enormously from 58 in 1971 to 141 in the year 1981, due to the migration of tribals from the neighbouring villages as a result of displacement under the Maddigadda reservoir near Addateegala.

The enquiry in the village reveals that the first non-tribal settler's family was 'Palacherla' who belonged to the Kamma upper caste. They migrated from the village Vetlapalem, near Samalkota, 90 km away from Mallavaram Mamillu. The non-tribals of the Palacherla family used to come to the Mutta area of Dutcharthi to participate in the forest timber auctions and later they settled in the village. They developed good terms with the then Muttadar of Dutcharthi and gained access to 200 acres of land in the village and the neighbouring village, Nimmalpalem.

Land Ownership and Possession

Pre-survey Period

The land is classified as Assessed Waste Dry (AWD) prior to the Survey and Settlement period of 1970–1976. The land was surveyed and settled under the Muttas Abolition Conversion into Ryotwari Settlement Regulations 2 of 69. As per the provisions of the Land Transfer Regulations, the non-tribals are not entitled to seek settlement patta over the land classified as government land. In spite of this legal provision, the non-tribals managed to get land surveyed in their favour during the Survey and Settlement period in the post-1970s. Table 4.24 shows the registration of land in the name of tribals and non-tribals in the study village.

In all, 22 tribal families received settled land to the extent of 99.54 acres. However, they had 17.75 acres of land due to submergence under the Maddigadda Reservoir. So the extent of settled land under occupation of tribals is only 81.79 acres, while 4 non-tribal families alone got land to the extent of 44 acres surveyed and settled in their favour. Each non-tribal family holds an average landholding of 11 acres, while tribal families have an average of only 4.54 acres of land. The tribals also lost other common property resources like Poromboke and Assessed Waste Dry (AWD) land of 43.74 acres due to construction of the reservoir.

Table 4.24

Landholdings of Tribals and Non-tribals

Name of the Family	*No. of House-Holds*	*ST/NT*	*Total Land Settled*	*Land Lost Due to Reservoir*			*Unoccupied Land*	
				Tribals (Ac)	*Porom-boke*	*AWD*	*Porom-boke*	*AWD*
Sadala	3	Tribe	7.89					
Chekka	2	Tribe	8.86	2.88				
Nanda	1	Tribe	8.25					
Kosuri	1	Tribe	1.30					
Kondla	1	Tribe	4.88					
Jatla	4	Tribe	16.89	14.87				
Murla	2	Tribe	4.85					
Kavadam	2	Tribe	15.15					
Poloju	1	Tribe	1.66					
Karam	1	Tribe	1.04					
Paidipala	1	Tribe	10.44					

Cont'd...

...Cont'd

Pothuri	1	Tribe	1.84					
Kadabala	1	Tribe	6.65					
Sadhanapalli	1	Tribe	9.84					
Total	22		99.54	17.75				
Palacharla	1	Non-Tribe	38.61					
Hanumanthu	1	N-Tribe	3.59					
Gaddadi	1	N-Tribe	1.70					
Bakuri	1	N-Tribe	0.24					
Total	4		44.14	17.75	31.39	11.85	35.61	23.60

Source: Survey and Settlement Register 1975, MRO Office, Addateegala.

The unoccupied AWD land is of 23.60 acres and Poramboke is of land of 35.61 acres. The total extent of the land is 59.21 acres and is registered as unoccupied. The non-tribal family, Palacherla, was originally in physical possession of 38.61 acres of land. Later, by 1976, they claimed for Settlement Patta of 61.74 hectares of land. Detailed case particulars are given in this chapter in the following paragraphs which will reveal the strategies of the non-tribals to control and hold the land in the study village.

Table 4.25 presents the number of landholdings and the size of landholdings of both the tribals and the non-tribals.

30 tribal families are shown as landholders of 75.50 acres. While 8 non-tribal families have 31.36 acres of landholding. But the total control of non-tribals over the land is not reflected in the land records due to pendency of court cases.

Landholding Pattern

Of the 38 tribal households, 30 households have 189 acres of land as per the field survey. Eight tribal families are landless. The landholding pattern clearly presents the marginalization of tribals from their land. Of the 30 tribal ryots, 22 hold only up to one acre of land, four tribals hold land of one to two acres, two households have two to three acres while only two tribal families hold land between three to five acres. In the case of non-tribals, four families are holding more than 7.50 to 12.50 acres of land, two hold 5 to 7.50 acres of land while three families hold land between one to two acres.

Table 4.25

Possession of Land Held by Tribals and Non-tribals

Name of the Family	*No. of House Holds*	*Caste*	*Tribal*				*Non-Tribal*			
			Government Land		*Ryotwari Land/Ac*	*Forest Land*	*Government Land*		*Ryotwari Land*	*Forest Land*
			With out Patta	*D Patta*			*With out Patta*	*D. Patta*		
Sadala	7	T			16.76					
Pothuri	1	T			1.64					
Murla	5	T			11.52					
Muthyla	1(New)	T			2.00					
Chundru	1(New)	T			2.25					
Kavadam	3	T			9.08					
Nanda	1	T			8.25					
Kosuri	1	T			2.00					
Kadabala	3	T			7.03					
Reddy	1(New)	T			1.70					
Chekka	1	T			1.49					
Paidipala	2	T			5.46					
Mamidi	1(New)	T			1.43					

Cont'd...

...Cont'd

Sadhanaplli	1	T	3.82	
Karam	1	T	1.07	
	30		75.50	
Palacharla	3	NT		22.97
Gudala	1	NT		2.36
Boddu	1	NT		0.20
Bakuri	1	NT		0.24
Padala/ Hanumanthu	1	NT		3.59
Battu	1	NT		2.00
	8			31.36

Source: Record of Rights 2010, MRO Office, Addateegala.

Process of Land Loss

Land Loss Under Maddigadda Reservoir

The Maddigadda Reservoir was constructed during the period 1978–1981. The tribals of Mallavaram Mamillu, Nimmalapalem and Bandakonda villages, in particular, lost 450 acres of patta land and common property resource, Poromboke, to the extent of 84 acres. The Bandakonda village was completely submerged under the reservoir. This irrigation project was aimed to irrigate 4,000 acres of land. But it actually provided water for irrigation to only 2,700 acres of land. Tribals in the study village say that the land being benefited under the reservoir mostly belonged to the non-tribal ryots. The government did not give land compensation to tribal land losers and instead paid ₹ 2,000 per acre of the land lost.

Land Alienation Caused by Voluntary Action of Tribal Muttadar

This case reveals as to how the loopholes in the law and acts of collusion between the tribal Muttadar and non-tribals is a causative factor for the process of land alienation. For the last 53 years the land issue is subsisting between tribals and the non-tribals. Tribals in Mallavaram Mamillu are seeking restoration of alienated land from the possession of the non-tribals.

In 1953, Chekka Lingannadora, a late Muttadar of Dutcharthi, granted lease for 100 acres, locally called 'Buruguloddi' and another 100 acres called 'Mal lavarappadu' in Nimmalapalem village in favour of one non-tribal, Tsalika Ramanna of Vetlapalem, a plains village near Samalkota, on the condition that the land be brought under cultivation. Ramanna relinquished his share in the lease agreement. The said land was further leased out by the then Muttadar to family members of the Palacherla family of Vetlapalem in 1954. This issue of lease came to the notice of the Agent to Government (District Collector) and he cancelled the lease in 1958, holding that the alienation of land is against the conditions of 'sanad' originally granted by the British Government to Muttadar and also against the interests of the tribals. However, the government intervened and set aside the order of the District Collector on appeal moved by a non-tribal landholder in GO Ms No. 1681 dated 17 August 1960 and remanded the matter to the District Collector to determine the social status of the Muttadar.

The District Collector who took up the matter afresh for enquiry, reaffirmed in 1961 that the Muttadar is a tribal and as such land lease granted by him to a non-tribal is null and void. A directive was also issued in 1962 by the Collector for eviction of non-tribals from the land. Further, appeals filed against the said order were dismissed by the government confirming the order of the Collector in GO Ms No. 1997 dated 27 December 1962.

The tribal Muttadar supported the case of the non-tribal in order to continue his possession of the land in the Scheduled Area. The tribal Muttadar openly stated in the enquiry that he was a non-tribal and did not belong to the tribal community. On the appeal moved by the Muttadar, the government set aside the order of the District Collector in GO Ms No. 779 dated 8 August 1967 observing that 'the Muttadar is a non-tribal as such there is no prohibition of land transfer between non-tribals, and land lease is a valid transfer.'

Muttas were abolished in 1969 and the government had brought in Survey and Settlement Regulations 2 of 69. These Regulations permit the non-tribals too, to seek patta over the land in their occupation if they were in continuous possession and enjoyment of land for a period of 8 years prior to the notified date and such occupation would not be in violation of the Land Transfer Regulations 1 of 59 or other laws in the force. The non-tribal lease holders applied for Settlement Pattas for the land, which were disallowed by the Settlement Officer. Then, the unsuccessful non-tribals moved the appeals which were also dismissed by the Director of Survey Settlements for default in their representation in 1977. Meanwhile, the Tahsildar of Yellavaram Taluk assigned 29–79 hectares of land of the total extent of 61.74 hectares to 14 landless tribals. The Director of Survey Settlements allowed the claim for the pattas again on the petition filed by the non-tribals in 1981.

The Tahsildar filed a revision petition before the Commissioner of Survey Settlements and the land records confirmed the order of Director of Settlements in 1985. The High Court of Andhra Pradesh set aside the orders of the Commissioner on the Writ Petition filed by the Advocate General and directed the Director of Settlements to re-examine the case as to whether the Muttadar be treated as a landholder or not, within the meaning of the Estate Abolition Act, and whether he ceased to be a member of the hill tribe by the virtue of being a landholder under the Estate Abolition Act. After an enquiry, the Collector (Director of Settlements) passed an order holding that the lease effected between the tribal Muttadar and the non-tribals was a prohibited transaction and the non-tribal failed to establish their title over the property in 1994. The Commissioner of Settlements also confirmed the order of the Director of Settlements and dismissed the appeal filed by non-tribals in 1997. The non-tribals moved a Writ Petition 35068/97 challenging the orders of the Commissioner of Settlements, and the High Court reversed the order observing that even if the Muttadar is taken to be of a hill tribe, the lease granted by him to the non-tribal is not illegal. A Writ Appeal was filed in 2004 by a local woman contesting the order of a single judge, which is pending. However, the non-tribals continue their possession and enjoyment of land without any interference except in the assigned land which is in possession of the tribals. But they still own 61.74 hectares of land.

Threat of Eviction Faced by Tribals: Forest Case

Kadabala Kannayya, a member of the Konda Reddi Scheduled Tribe of Mallavaram Mamillu, was granted settlement pattas of over 9.49 hectares of land covered by survey numbers 26, 27 and 33 under 2 of 69 Muttas Abolition and Conversion into Ryotwari Settlement Regulations in 1975. They used to raise millets like bajra, jowar, ragi, and maize on the dry land slope. Integrated Tribal Development Agency, Rampachodavaram, also extended support for raising of cashew crop on the land in 1986. The land is adjacent to the reserve forest and Bapanamma stream passes through this stretch. The land is frequently submerged due to floods in the Bapanamma hill stream. The said land was taken on lease from the then Muttadar of Dutcharthi in 1955.

The District Forest Officer, East Godavari District filed an appeal in 1981 challenging the settlement patta granted to the tribals and sought for its cancellation. The contention of the Appellant or the District Forest Officer was that the natural forest growth is found in the landholdings of the tribals and as such no settlement patta should be granted on such land.

After enquiry into the case, the Director of Survey and Settlements, East Godavari District in AP No. 69/81, held that there is no field inspection report stating findings that there is standing forest timber in the patta land, and on the other hand, there is available evidence of tribals that he raised dry crops on the said land. Finally, the Director passed an order in 1992 dismissing the appeal of the District Forest Officer.

Land Encroachment Case

After the death of Kadabala Kannayya, a part of his land was occupied by a neighbouring non-tribal, Padala Vimala Devi. The son of Kadabala Kannayya, namely Venkatswamy, filed a petition before the Special Deputy Collector (Tribal Welfare), Rampachodavaram, under the Land Transfer Regulations 1 of 70 in LTRP No. 9/11 against the said Vimala Devi seeking the restoration of land. After the receipt of notice from the Special Deputy Collector's Court, the non-tribal filed a Writ Petition No. 9126/11 saying that settlement patta was given to her father over 3.64 hectares of land under 2 of 69 Settlement Regulations and she did not encroach upon the land claimed by the tribals. Her further contention was that proceedings under Land Transfer Regulations shall not be initiated as settlement patta was already granted under 2 of 69 Regulations to her father through whom she received the land. The High Court stayed the proceedings before the Special Deputy Collector's Court, Rampachodavaram. The non-tribals are able to use legal institutions at a higher level in their favour as tribals cannot afford to make their plea before it. The High Court did not give any scope to verify through the executive functionaries as to whether or not the non-tribal petitioner had encroached upon the land of tribals. Based on the affidavits of non-tribal parties, the courts passed orders. By virtue of these orders, the non-tribals continue to possess the encroached portion of the land belonging to tribals without any interruption.

Fraudulent Settlement Patta Case

This case goes back to more than 40 years and still the non-tribals successfully continue the litigation. Hanumanthu Satyanarayana, a head of forest workers, under a forest contractor, Kandru Ramachandra Rao, belonging to the Kapu upper caste, came to Dutcharthi Mutta area between 1955 and 1960. Satyanarayana occupied the land which belonged to a Konda Reddi family 'Murla' in Mallavaram Mamillu. Murla Abbai Reddy, a tribal, filed an application before the Special Assistant Agent to Government, Peddapuram, in case No. LTRP 45/75 for the restoration of land of an extent of 3.00 acres covered by S. No. 40 from the possession of the non-tribal Satyanarayana. The Court directed the implementing authorities to put the said land in the possession of the tribal by evicting the non-tribal Satyanarayana. Murla Abbai Reddy further filed an application for a direction to give physical possession of houses situated in the said land to them. That petition was dismissed by the Special Assistant Agent in 1976. Aggrieved by the order, Murla Abbai Reddy, the tribal filed an appeal before the Agent to Government in CMA No. 27/1977. The Agent allowed the appeal made by Murla Abbai Reddy in 1987.

Then, Hanumanthu Satyanarayana filed a WP No. 7899/1987 before the High Court and obtained interim suspension of the order of the Agent to the Government. Finally, the Writ Petition was dismissed by the High Court in 1996 with a direction to avail the alternative remedy, i.e. Revision before the government under the provisions of Land Transfer Regulations 1 of 70. Both the High Court and lawyers pleading on behalf of the non-tribals were well aware that there is an alternative remedy provided under the Land Transfer Regulations 1 of 70, but they continued the proceedings for almost a decade. These are legal tactics being engineered by elite sections to deprive the opportunities to tribals by seeking early justice and weakening them in all aspects. In fact the Land Transfer Regulations 1 of 70 is a complete code of law which provides different mechanisms to the aggrieved persons to redress their legal grievances. Still, the intervention of High Court at the instance of the non-tribals is a causative factor for delayed justice to the tribals.

Then, Satyanarayana filed a Revision Petition before the government on the plea that no stay was granted by the government. He again filed WP 19011 of 1997 before the High Court. The High Court disposed the petition with a direction not to dispossess him from the land, pending the disposal of the Revision Petition. Meanwhile, the Joint Collector cancelled the Settlement Patta issued to Hanumanthu Satyanarayana. Then, the successor of the unsuccessful non-tribal, his daughter, namely Padala Vimala Devi, challenged the said order before High Court in WP No. 9847/2002 . The High Court allowed her petition in 2009.

Again, after more than a decade, the government passed an order in GO Ms No. 212 in 2008, rejecting the Revision Petition filed by the non-tribal on the ground that the settlement patta obtained by him was cancelled by the Joint Collector, East Godavari District. Then Vimala Devi again filed a WP No. 28028 of 2008 challenging the order of Government issued in GO No. 212. The High Court passed an interim direction not to evict her from the land. Tribals have no means to counter the continued litigation of the non-tribals. Therefore, it is very clear that the non-tribals continue their litigation taking undue advantage of the vulnerability and poverty of the tribals. The settlement pattas granted to non-tribals during the survey period created a bottleneck for the tribals to seek restoration of alienated land. The unexplained delay in the courts helps the non-tribals to possess the disputed land for years together.

Implementation of Land Transfer Regulations and Outcome: 1976–2010

The cases were filed before the Special Deputy Collector (Tribal Welfare) initial authority under the Land Transfer Regulations for the eviction of the non-tribals and restoration of the land to the tribals. Since the inception of the court, seven cases covering 144.37 acres of land were filed before the authority, of which the tribals succeeded in 5 cases which covered an extent of 63 acres of land, while the other single case covering 77 acres of land is still pending. But this land is an addition to the other extent of land covered by cases being dealt by either Settlement Courts or High Court of Andhra Pradesh directly.

Claims to Forest Land

Nine tribal families have been in occupation and enjoyment of 25.90 acres of forest land for several years. They filed claims seeking forest land titles under Forest Rights Recognition Act 2006, but their claims were rejected on the ground that the podu land were not classified as 'forests'. The concerned officials did not give copies of the orders facilitating the unsuccessful tribal claimants to prefer appeals under the Forest Rights Act. Thus, the Forest Rights Act has not created any impact on recognition of forest land rights in Mallavaram Mamillu. Neither the Revenue Department granted titles over such land nor did the adjudicating bodies under the Forest Rights Act recognize their forest land occupation. Table 4.26 demonstrates the details of the claimants.

Table 4.26

Outcome of Implementation of Recognition of Forest Rights Act

S. No.	*Name*	*Father's Name*	*Extent (Acres)*	*Status*	*Reason*
1.	Chekka Sanyasi Rao	Ganga raju	0.4	Rejected/	Reasons shown as out of Forest Area
2.	Murla Jogi Raju	Peddabbai	2.5	Rejected/	-
3.	Murla Venkateswarlu	Abbai	3.4	Rejected/	-
4.	Murla Yerramma	Abbai	2.3	Rejected/	-
5.	Paidipala Ammanna	Swamulu	3.1	Rejected/	-
6.	Paidipala Lakshmi	Chinnabbai	1.9	Rejected/	-
7.	Paidipala Thammireddy	Swamulu	2.9	Rejected/	-
8.	Paidipala Venkayamma	Narayana	2.2	Rejected/	-
9.	Sundru Venkayamma	Padabbai	7.2	Rejected/	-
			25.9 Acres		-

Source: ITDA Office, Rampachodavaram.

Sample Village 4: Indukurupeta

In Indukurupeta, a total of 1,052 families had a population of 3,711 persons. Of the total, 423 form the tribal population while the remaining 2,888 is non-tribal population. The study covers the interviews of a total number of 36 representatives of all tribal families from the village Indukurupeta to elicit their perceptions on various dimensions of land alienation. It also consists of one hamlet village, Pothukonda. There are 57 tribal families and 3 non-tribals families in the village. The study does not cover this hamlet village because the non-tribal families in the village are not the landed class.

Social Demography

The major tribes in the village are Konda Reddy, Konda Dora, Koya Dora and Konda Kammara. The distribution of communities in the village is also representative of the tribes in this region as well.

The majority of respondents are females. Only 42 per cent are males. All the respondents are married.

The age background of the respondents shows that 67 per cent are below 45 years. All age categories above 21 years are represented. Figure 4.11 indicates the age-wise distribution of the respondents.

Figure 4.10

Distribution of Tribal Communities (Indukurupeta)

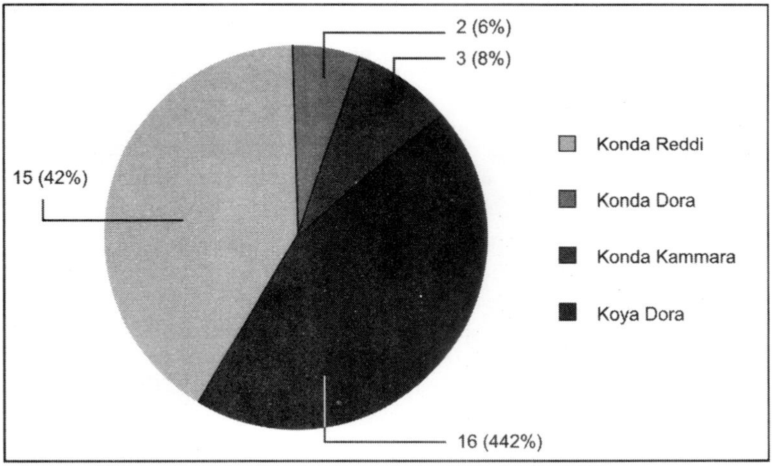

Figure 4.11

Age-wise Distribution of Tribal Respondents

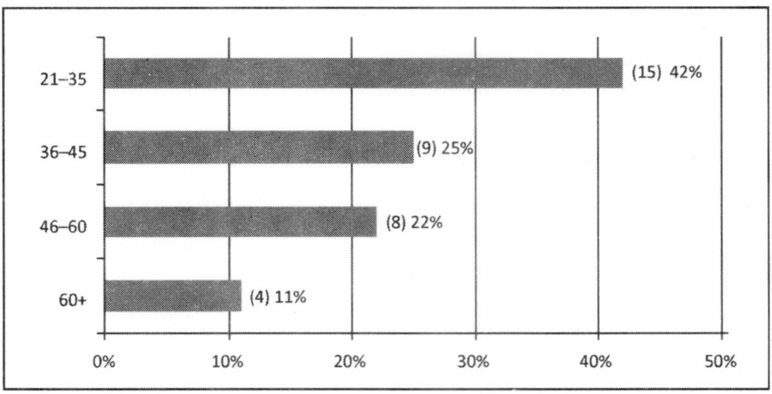

A majority of about 44 per cent of the population is illiterate. Interestingly, the literate persons belong to all age categories: 15 are below 45 years, three are above 45 years and two are above 60 years.

The average size of the family is four. The age profile indicates that about 13 per cent of the members in the sample families are above 21 years old, 83 per cent are between 6–20 years and only 4 per cent are below 5 years. The age background of sons and daughters of respondents is presented in the Table 4.27.

Table 4.27

Distribution of Children of Respondents by their Age

Age	*Sons*		*Daughters*		*Total*	
	No.	*%*	*No.*	*%*	*No.*	*%*
Below 5	1	4	1	4	2	4
6–10	3	11	6	22	9	16
11–20	16	59	20	74	36	67
21–35	7	26	0	0	7	13
36–50	0	0	0	0	0	0
Total	27	100	27	100	54	100

Source: Field data.

The education pattern of the family members indicates that as many as 9 per cent are totally illiterate. There are more non-literates among the sons compared to the daughters. Another 17 per cent have only completed up to Standard IV. Only 35 per cent have studied beyond Standard X. The education of sons and daughters of respondents is presented below in the Table 4.28.

Table 4.28

Distribution of Sons/Daughters of Respondents by their Education

Education	*Sons*		*Daughters*		*Total*	
	No.	*%*	*No.*	*%*	*No.*	*%*
Illiterate	4	15	1	4	5	9
Up to Std. IV	4	15	5	18.5	9	17
V–VII	6	22	5	18.5	11	20
VIII–X	3	11	6	22	9	17
X+	9	33	10	37	19	35
Not Specified	1	4	0	0	1	2
Total	27	100	27	100	54	100

The marital status of the family members shows that only 6 per cent are married. Details of marital status of the members of the respondent households are presented in the Table 4.29.

Table 4.29

Distribution of Sons/Daughters of Respondents by their Marital Status

Marital Status	*Sons*		*Daughters*		*Total*	
	No.	*%*	*No.*	*%*	*No.*	*%*
Married	3	11	0	0	3	6
Unmarried	24	89	27	100	51	94
Total	27	100	27	100	54	100

Source: Field Data.

The activity profile of the family members reveals the characteristic features of their age and roles specific to one's age. As many as 11 per cent are engaged in cultivation, 11 per cent are in agricultural or casual labour and 70 per cent are engaged in studies. The distribution of family members by their activity is characteristic of the roles they play according to their age within the tribal communities in the district.

Table 4.30

Distribution of Sons/Daughters of Respondents by their Activity

Occupation	*Sons*		*Daughters*		*Total*	
	No.	*%*	*No.*	*%*	*No.*	*%*
Cultivation	6	22	0	0	6	11
Agricultural Labour/Casual Labour	4	15	2	7	6	11
Job	1	4	0	0	1	2
Student	14	52	24	89	38	70
Any other	2	7	1	4	3	6
Not Specified	0	0	0	0	0	0
Total	27	100	27	100	54	100

Source : Field Data.

Land Ownership and Possession

The population of non-tribals was 1,640 in 1961 which doubled by the year 2001. The tribal land alienation problem is aggravated due to the heavy influx of the non-tribal population to Indukurupeta. There is no effective mechanism or law in place to check the infiltration of the non-tribal population to Indukurupeta.

Table 4.31

Tribal and Non-Tribal Population (1961–2001)

	Indukurupeta		
Year	*Total*	*NT*	*ST*
1961	1,742	1,640	102
1971	2,353	2,127	226
1981	2,765	2,423	342
1991	3,290	2,917	373
2001	3,711	3,288	423

Source: District Census Book, Statistical Office, East Godavari District, Kakinada.

The land held by the tribals and the non-tribals is given as per the Record of Rights maintained during the year 2010. These records show the name of the cultivator and the extent of land held by them along with the survey number and other particulars. The classification of land is also shown in the records.

Table 4.32 presents the land in possession of the tribal families as per the Record of Rights.

Table 4.32

Land Held by Tribals

Name of the Family	*Caste*	*As per 2010 ROR 1B Landholdings*	*Patta/Extent (Acres)*
Kosu	Tribe	7	20.51
Komaram	Tribe	3	12.10
Pathara	Tribe	2	3.30
Chavalam	Tribe	9	7.40

Cont'd...

...Cont'd

Sarapu	Tribe	3	4.47
Balem	Tribe	1	0.46
Parada	Tribe	3	2.90
Boraga	Tribe	1	0.32
Eeriti	Tribe	2	3.28
Bandam	Tribe	1	0.23
Turram	Tribe	11	12.70
Teegala	Tribe	1	0.82
Karam	Tribe	5	17.37
Kotam	Tribe	2	8.16
Kunjam	Tribe	8	22.23
Madi	Tribe	3	3.51
Madakam	Tribe	8	21.60
Murram	Tribe	2	1.40
Total	18	72	142.76

Source: Record of Rights, I. B. Register 2010, MRO Office, Devipatnam.

Figure 4.12 presents the landholdings of the tribals of different villages and the extent covered. The data reveals the land situation of tribal residents in the Indukurupeta village.

Figure 4.12

Tribal Landholdings in Indukuru, Pothukonda and Indukurupeta Villages

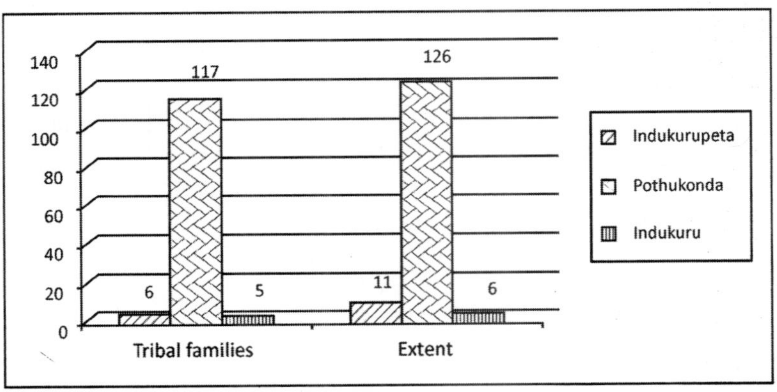

As per the Record of Rights, 72 tribal families have 128 landholdings covering a land extent of 143 acres. But the majority of landholding belongs to the tribals living in the hamlet village of Pothukonda. About 117 tribal families possess 126 acres of land followed by the six tribal families in the Indukurupeta village who possess 11 acres and five tribal families of neighbouring village 'Indukuru'.

Figure 4.13 presents the number of non-tribals and their landholding pattern as per the Record of Rights.

Figure 4.13

Non-tribals and Caste-wise Landholding Pattern as per the Record of Rights

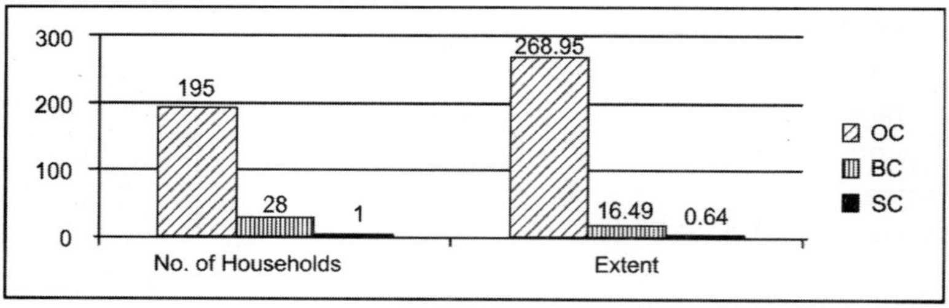

Table 4.33

Castewise and Categorywise Landholdings

Category-wise Landholdings			*Extents in Occupation as per RoR 2010 (Acres)*	*Total (Acres)*
Category	*Caste wise*			
OC 195	Kapu	184	241.04	268.95
	Kamma	9	23.39	
	Bhramin	2	4.52	
BC 28	Khammari	5	1.7	16.49
	Golla	1	0.65	
	Rajaka	4	3.88	
	Bukkala	1	0.34	
	Telukula	9	6.24	
	Yerukula	3	0.45	

Cont'd...

...Cont'd

	Devanga	2	1.26	
	Athirasalu	2	1.04	
	Mohamadian	1	0.93	
SC 1	Mala	1	0.64	0.64
224			286.08	286.08

Source: Record of Rights Register 2010, MRO Office, Devipatnam.

About 286 acres of land is under the occupation of the non-tribals besides 15 acres of common property resources like pond, well, pathway, etc. Of the 224 non-tribal ryots, 194 belonged to the forward communities, 29 belonged to the Backward Class while one family belonged to the Scheduled Caste. Of the 194 forward caste non-tribals, 184 ryots belonged to Kapu caste and held 241 acres of land. This is a noticeable point. Another noticeable factor is that the land in occupation of the non-tribals was classified as Assessed Waste Dry (Government). So, rights on such land vests with the government alone.

Table 4.33 presents castewise and categorywise landholdings as per the Record of Rights 2010 Registers.

The following data presents the enjoyment of land by tribals and non-tribals as per the Record of Rights 2010.

Figure 4.14

Land Possession among Tribals and Non-Tribals

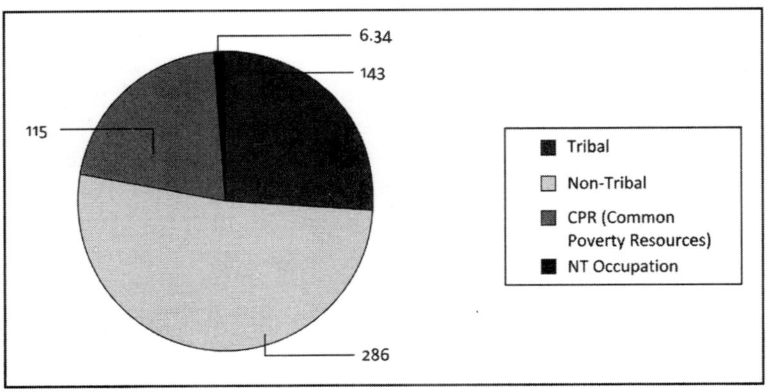

About 115 acres of land in the village is part of common property resources. About 10 non-tribal families occupy 6.34 acres while one tribal family occupies 0.26 acres. The encroachment of the common property resources by a non-tribal is a clear violation of 1 of 70 Regulations, because the right over such land vests only with the government.

Table 4.34 is computed from the same Records of Rights to show the pattern of landholdings held by both the tribals and the non-tribals in Indukurupeta.

Table 4.34

Distribution of Landholdings among Tribal and Non-tribal Households

Category	*No. of Holdings ST (Families)*	*Extent (in Ac)*	*No. of Holdings (NT)*	*Extent (in Ac)*
Large	0	0	0	0
Medium	12	55.28	13	71.54
Semi-medium	13	37.19	29	81.29
Small	10	15.16	49	69.33
Marginal	37	35.13	133	63.84
	72	142.76	224	286

The semi-medium, small and marginal farmers are comparatively more in number in the non-tribal communities than in the tribal communities.

Table 4.35 presents trends of land alienation from the pre-survey settlement period (pre-1970) till 2010 as well as the extent of landholdings of tribals in Indukurupeta village.

It is evident from the 'D Register' (Settlement Patta Register) which presents the increased control of non-tribal over land in the study village in between pre-survey and post-survey period (1970–76), that the non-tribals possess more extent of land than the tribals. As per the 'Fair Adangal', the recorded landholdings of non-tribals prior to the settlement was 98 acres but increased to 222 acres after settlement. There was a remarkable increase of 124 acres of land. It is evident that the non-tribals could obtain settlement pattas over 124 acres more through fraudulent methods.

Table 4.35

Trends of Land Alienation from the Pre Survey Settlement Period (Pre-1970) till 2010

Category	*Land-holdings*	*Pre-Settlement (Fair Adangal–1970)*	*Land Holdings*	*After Settlement (Under 2/70 Reg. Pattas*	*Landholdings*	*2010/as per RoR/ Pre sent Enjoyment*
Non-tribal	186	98	334	222	224	286
Tribal	2	3	60	102	128	143

Figure 4.15 shows the steady increase of land extent in the hold of non-tribals from pre-abolition period of Estate land tenure system till 2010 .

In the light of these changes the total number of non-tribal peasants rose from 186 in the pre-1970s to 224 by 2010. The land controlled by them also increased from 98 acres to 286 acres, which is a remarkable increase of 91 acres. It may be mentioned here that Land Transfers are prohibited completely in favour of non-tribals in the Scheduled Areas. Although the number of landholdings increased, the land controlled by them is stable and safe. Thus, despite the prohibited Land Transfer Regulations which are in force, land alienation has become a continuous phenomenon in Indukurupeta.

Of all the 36 representatives covered by the study in Indukurupeta, 25 are landless including four tribal families still

Figure 4.15

The Steady Increase of Landholdings of Non-Tribals from pre-Abolition Period of Estate Land Tenure System to Till the 2010 Period

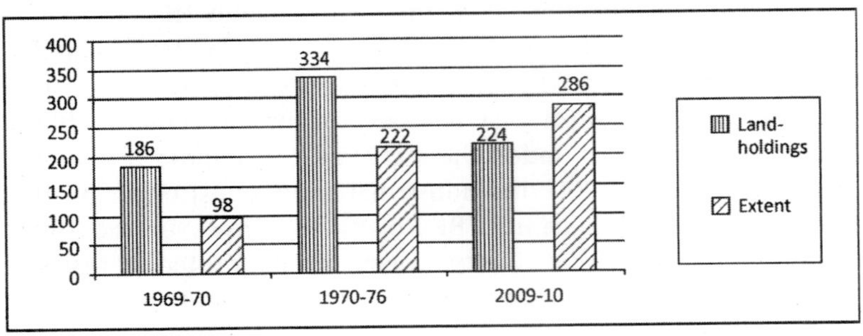

fighting for the restoration of their land from the possession of non-tribals and 11 tribal households have only 28 acres of land. The other land showing ownership of the tribals, all belonged to Pothukonda, a hamlet of Indukurupeta village and the neighbouring village, Indukuru.

Process of Land Loss

Misuse of Permission Clause

The case reveals how the Permission Clause for permitting land transfers between tribals and non-tribals under the Land Transfer Act is misused by the non-tribals to validate their occupation of land in Scheduled Areas. Chavalam Srinivasu Dora, a tribal from Indukurupet village, narrates how they had lost land to non-tribals and regained possession after three generations. His grandfather mortgaged 3 acres of land to a non-tribal, Pathala Ramulu and took a loan. One day, the non-tribal Ramulu took the thumb impression of his grandfather on documents and submitted them to the Rajahmundry Sub Collector's office. The Sub Collector granted permission in SR No. 16/44 to the non-tribal permitting him to purchase the mortgaged land from the tribals. The permission letter shows that the proposed sale arose out of an earlier mortgage transaction which was effected between the tribal and the non-tribal parties. By virtue of the permission letter, the non-tribal Ramulu obtained a registered sale deed from the tribal in 1945 for the land. But the Sub Collector did not question whether any similar permission was obtained for the earlier mortgage transactions held between the tribal and the non-tribal parties. Subsequently, Ramulu also obtained a Settlement Patta for this land during the Survey and Settlement operations held under 2 of 70 Regulations. The Settlement Officer did not question the validity of the mortgage land transaction effected between the tribal and the non-tribal under the Land Transfer Act 1917. The transfer of land between the tribal and the non-tribal is prohibited without previous consent from the Sub Collector or District Collector for such land transfers in the Agency Areas under the Act 1917. The possession and enjoyment of land by the non-tribal was questioned in the proceedings of SDC Court in LTRP No. 486/77. However, the court, without looking into the validity of permission granted by the Sub Collector, declared the possession of land by the non-tribal Ramulu as valid under the Land Transfer Regulations 1 of 59 as amended by 1 of 70 (LTR). However, the occupation of the non-tribal was challenged again before the same authority in a case LTRP No. 332/03 under the LTR. The Special Deputy Collector's Court, after enquiry, held that there is no previous consent from the Special Assistant Agent for the earlier mortgage transactions held between the tribal and the non-tribal. As such, the permission obtained by the non-tribal for lone sale transaction is not valid. But the non-tribal family occupied the land for more than 60 years without any legal right until this order was passed by the Special Deputy Collector's Court.

Land Loss through Mortgage, Sale and Other Transactions

Belam Venkata Ratnam (80 years) belonging to the Konda Kammari tribal community, was a resident of Indukurpeta village. He did carpentry work in the village fifty years ago. He was given *inam* wetland of 2.50 acres and 3.00 acres dry land for his services in the village. He has six children. As he was unable to maintain his family, he mortgaged the land and later sold all the inam land to non-tribals. Narrating one case among others of land alienation, he says that of the 2.50 acres, he sold 0 .50 acres for ₹ 2,000 in 1972 to one non-tribal, Sanampudi Jeevaratnam, in order to repay the sundry debts and meet the family expenditure. The Special Deputy Tahsildar (Tribal Welfare) filed a case before the Agency Divisional Officer (ADO) in ADO LTR 42/2007 against the non-tribal as his occupation of land is in violation of LTR 1 of 70. The court held that as the non-tribal purchased the land from a tribal, Venkatratnam, in 1972, it was illegal. But instead of giving directives to the authorities for restoration of land to Venkataratnam, the court ordered to assign the same to eligible landless tribals in the village. The original tribal owner Venkataratnam was not aware of the proceedings. The Mandal Revenue Officer did not even hand over the land to him even though he too was a landless poor tribal in the village. Now Venkataratnam remained a landless poor tribal. He says the copy of the order has been requested from the Mandal Revenue Office but it is not made accessible to him.

He gave a detailed account of the process of tribal land alienation in the village recalling the past. The village used to be under the Polavaram Estate. This estate was under the proprietary of a non-tribal zamindar of Kocharlakota family. He had sold away the village to the Maharaja of Pithapuram to tide over his financial crisis. The zamindar of Pitapuram preferred to give land to the non-tribals on lease as the tribals were unable to pay the estate tax to him. In some cases, as tribals were unable to pay estate tax to the zamindar, the land originally in possession of the tribals was taken over slowly by the non-tribals. Later, non-tribals with the help of Estate Tax receipts obtained from non-tribal clerks of Estate, had managed to obtain settlement pattas in their favour during the Survey and Settlement operations held during post-70s.

Further, some of the non-tribals took the land on mortgage or lease from the tribals. During the survey operations they created the tax receipts in their favour and obtained settlement pattas fraudulently on tribal land. The Settlement Officers did not conduct any enquiry in the village calling for objections from the tribals. Explaining the process of loss of tribal land Venkataratnam says that

> in olden days a tribal family of Karam Chinnaludora used to cultivate Ac.100 in the village. At present, the family is having land of Ac.10. The remaining land is under the control of non-tribals only. Similarly, the tribal family of Sarapu Ramulu used to cultivate land of Ac.30, but his sons are now not even cultivating one acre of land. In earlier days tribal family members of Panda Thammanna Dora used to cultivate land of Ac. 50 personally. But no land is in the possession of their successors. They long back mortgaged their land to non-tribals and lost their land. Presently, the family members of Panda are working in their own fields as agricultural labourers.

Thus, Indukurupeta presents a classic example of the ever increasing depeasantization of tribal peasants and increasing concentration of land in the hands of the non-tribals.

The non-tribal migration to the village has been more prevalent during the last 50 years. The non-tribals have their eyes on the village land. The non-tribals preferred to bring sons-in-law as 'illotom' by offering land as 'pasupukunkuma' at the time of marriages to their daughters. This social phenomenon further increased the non-tribal settlements in the village and encroachments upon the land belonging to tribals. Majority of the non-tribals belonged to the Kapu community which has strong relations with their caste people in and out of the Agency Areas.

Creation of Fake Tax receipts during Land Settlement

A tribal, Annika Peda Venkateswarlu, filed a case against non-tribal Badireddy Venkata Reddy, in ADO LTR 70/2007, seeking restoration of land to an extent of 2.14 hectares covered by S. No. 156/1 situated in Indukurupeta. The claim of the tribal is that the land originally belonged to his ancestors and later non-tribals came to possess it. The claim of non-tribal is that it is his ancestral property and succeeded to him from Dasari Bulli Tammayya. In support of his claim, he produced a 'Muchilaka' copy issued by the then zamindar and the tax receipts. During the enquiry it was revealed that the land was classified as banjara land (government waste land) as per the Settlement Fair Adangal prepared during the Survey and Settlement of land. For the purpose of making a false claim before the enquiry officer under Land Transfer Regulations, the non-tribal created old Muchilaka (arrangement of land) and tax receipts as if his ancestors and he had been in possession of the land by virtue of the said documents. These documents are proved false by the fact that the land was classified as banjara land (government land) as per the fair Adangal prepared in 1970s by the Survey and Settlement team. However, he says that he was not able to get a copy of the fair Adagal from the office of Taluk at Devipatnam despite several requests. The enquiry officer secured a copy from the office and appreciated the document of fair Adangal during the enquiry to negate the claim of the non-tribals.

Creation of Unregistered Sale Agreements for Land Retainment

The case facts in CMA No. 49/2004 on the file of Additional Agent to the government court, Rampachodavaram reveals that the non-tribals created unregistered sale agreements to escape from the legal clutches under the LTR 1of 70, in order to retain the land in their possession at Indukurupeta. The land in the case is 1.41 acres, covered by RS No. 23/7 and 84/2. The claim of the non-tribal Ombolu Peda Venkanna is that he purchased the land from another non-tribal under two unregistered sale agreements dated 15 November 1969 and 12 November 1969, prior to the commencement of LTR 1 of 70. He got it registered as the sale deeds bearing No. 600/73 and 302/73 on 30 April 1973, and as such the land transfer effected between the non-tribals is valid. During the enquiry, the Court noticed that the alleged unregistered sale agreements show that the alleged vendor gave his thumb impressions, whereas the registered sale deeds show his signature. Further, the year of purchase of the alleged unregistered sale agreement stamp papers was shown as 1961 and 1965, but alleged transactions took place in the year 1969. The court held that the non-tribal created the unregistered sale agreements in 1969 to continue possession and enjoyment of the land, as the LTR 1 of 70 does not prohibit transfer of land between non-tribals prior to its introduction. The court directed that the land be handed over to the eligible landless tribals in the village by evicting the non-tribals.

LTR Court Cases and Outcome

A total of 199 cases were booked since the inception of the court and the land covered under these was 679 acres. Of these cases, 17 cases were disposed in favour of tribals covering a land extent of 96 acres, while the non-tribals were able to secure orders in 102 cases on 338 acres of land. About 51 cases were in favour of the government covering 175 acres and the remaining 29 cases covering 71 acres are pending for disposal.

The data shows that the tribals could get favourable orders only in 10 per cent of the cases covering 16 of the cases, while 60 per cent of the cases were decided in favour of non-tribals, covering 55 per cent of the land. Around 30 cases covering 29 per cent of land in favour of the government were disposed of. Even combining both the government and the tribal cases would constitute only 39 cases covering 45 per cent of the land in respect of the disposed cases.

Figure 4.16

LTR Court Cases and Outcome in Indukurupeta

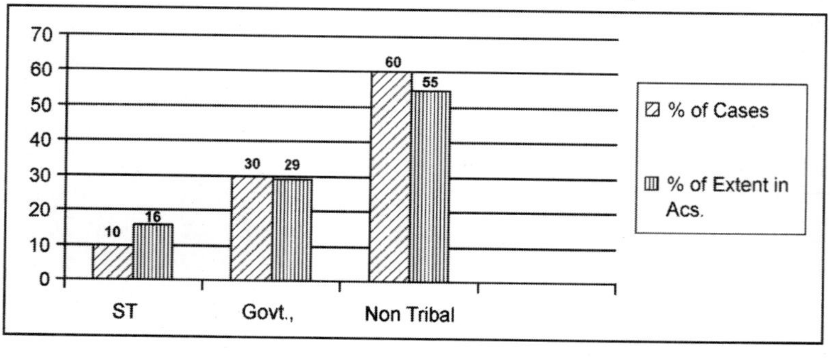

Taxonomy of Tribal Land Rights Deprivation

This sub-chapter traces out a typology of the various processes of tribal land alienation in the study villages and explores the effectiveness of tribal protective Land Transfer Regulations and possible means to improve access of Scheduled Tribes to land. The typology of land alienations arises from the case studies of land cases dealt by the courts and field data obtained.

Table 4.36 presents the variation in the extent of land actually possessed by the tribals and extent of lands shown in the records. The variation gives a distorted picture in understanding the land ownership of the tribals.

The total number of tribal households in all the sample villages is 212. Of them, 117 landholders possess 345 acres of land as per the field data. However, the Record of Rights register shows that 215 landholders possess 406 acres of land in the sample villages. So, there is a variation in land area and the number of landholders. Thus, the land records do not reflect the ground reality of land situation of tribals. This will also become a hurdle in assigning land to the eligible tribal landless in the villages in future.

Table 4.36

Extent of Variation in the Actual Possession of Land Held by Tribals and Land Shown in Records as their Own

Name of the Sample Village	*No. of Tribal Respondents (Total Households)*	*Land-holders*	*Possession of land (Ac)*	*As per 2010 Record of Rights*	*Extent (Ac)*	*No. of Land-less Poor*
Indukurupeta	36	11	28.00	72	143.00	25
Mallavaram Mamillu	38	30	189.00	30	75.00	8
Nellipudi	75	45	93.00	74 (as per survey)	132.00	30
Veerabhadrapuram	63	31	34.80	39	56.00	32
Total	212	117	344.8	215	406	95

Source: Field Data and Record of Rights, MRO Offices, Rampachodavaram Division.

The land issues witnessed in the study villages show land rights deprivation among tribal communities. The deprivation includes benami transfers, forceful occupation by non-tribals, transfer of land by non-tribals to other non-tribals through sale or mortgage transactions, by creating unregistered documents purposefully mentioning the predate of commencement of Land Transfer Regulations 1 of 70 to escape from the clutches of law. According to these Regulations, land transfers affected between the non-tribals after 3 February 1970 are null and void. To avoid this, antedating has become one of the powerful means for non-tribals to enable the courts to sustain their claim. Thus, the manipulated processes of non-tribal peasantry are legalized through court litigations over a period of time.

Irregular procedures were adopted by the Survey and Settlement officers while conducting survey and settlement operations and granting pattas over the land situated in the Scheduled Areas in favour of the non-tribals. The Settlement Officers granted pattas to the non-tribals without conducting an enquiry as to how the non-tribal claimants had secured the land and from whom. There are two conditions to be fulfilled to allow the claim of non-tribals for granting of patta. One of the requirements is the 8 years continuous period of land possession prior to the notified date of 14 July 1970. Secondly, such occupation or possession shall not be in violation of Land Transfer Regulations. Taking this lacuna in the legal provisions, the non-tribal claimants secured pattas by creating fake tax receipts, 'Muchalaka' documents, 'Krishika' or '*veesa badi*' pattas from the offices of land tenures of Mutta and Estates in order to show that they had been in possession of land for the prescribed eight years prior to the notified date of Settlement Regulations. The case studies prove that the Settlement Officers, in connivance with non-tribals, conveniently ignored the other equally important condition to be fulfilled is that 'the land in occupation shall not be in violation of Land Transfer Regulations. This is the major reason for variation in land in the possession of non-tribals between the pre- and post-Survey and Settlement period.

The state itself is responsible for facilitating land alienation among the tribals by involving the Muttadarani of Rampa Mutta. Similarly, the Muttadar of Dutcharthi himself claimed to be a non-tribal in order to lease out the land to non-tribals with the support of the state machinery. The rejection of forest rights claims in the name of revenue forest shows the land rights deprivation among tribals. The implementation of tribal protective land laws has been severely hampered by the reluctance of the land administration and weak political will. The interventions of the Court at the instance of the non-tribal litigants facilitate mainly the non-tribals to retain the land in their occupation for years. Although the non-tribals do not have a statutory right to hold the land which is classified as 'government', the continued act of encroachment of government land remains unchallenged by the implementing authorities of the Land Transfer Regulations, which is the another causative factor for reducing the survival space of land dependent tribals.

Land Administration: An Overview

The study in the four study villages shows few commonalities in the process of tribal land alienation. The systematic and dubious methods adopted by the non-tribals in obtaining settlement pattas during the survey and settlement process is the same as in the land tenure study villages of Estate and Mukhasa. The land administration was under the control of private non-tribal landlords in these two study villages. This lent a support to the non-tribals to create tax receipts and other land documents to prove their occupation of the land which is not factual during the survey and settlement period after abolition of Estates and Mukhasa. The delay in abolition of Mukhasa is another contributing factor for increasing land alienation in the Mukhasa village of Nellipudi. The non-tribal migrants did not face any difficulty in getting land on lease from the non-tribal proprietors in Mukhasa and Estate land tenure villages. The process of extracting land revenues in these land tenure villages helped the non-tribal peasants rather than the original inhabitant tribals and in fact, went contrary to their interests.

The other study village, Mallavaram Mamillu, presents a challenging aspect that the tribal protective legal measures did not help the tribals to retain their land ownership, although the land administration was under the control of a tribal Muttadar. The grant of a 'sanad' to a tribal Muttadar can be considered as a legal protection to the tribal land in the Mutta villages under the Andhra Pradesh Agency Land Transfer Act 1917 to some extent, as this Act prohibits transfer of land from a tribal to a non-tribal without permission from the Agent to the Government or the Prescribed Officer. However, the study in the Mutta village, Mallavaram

Mamillu, presents that a non-tribal gained access to the land by scuttling the legal process in collusion with the tribal Muttadar. The tribal Muttadar claimed himself to be a non-tribal to avoid legal wrangles in support of the non-tribal land interests.

The study in the government village Veerabhadrapuram, shows a completely different picture. The land survey process, initiated in the early 19th century, itself facilitated the non-tribals to get the land surveyed in their name without any restrictions of law. The common feature of the policy governing the land administration in all the study villages is the generation of revenue. The policy helped the economically stronger non-tribal sections rather than the tribals to get land on lease either from the proprietors of land tenures or as settlement from the government. Transferring the land held by such non-tribals further to other non-tribals has rendered the problem of land alienation critical and created legal hurdles to claim back the alienated tribal land for the original tribal land transferors. Another common feature in all the study villages is the importance given to documentary evidence rather than the oral testimonies, by both the administrative and legal structures in the validation of land titles.

Political Dimensions

There is no political intervention from the mainstream parties in support of the tribal land issue. However, the land occupation movement of Maoists in the areas of the study village, Veerabhadrapuram, created a positive impact to some extent in increasing access to land ownership among tribals.

The interventions of other splinter left groups as CPI (ML) New Democracy and CPI (ML) Liberation have presence in Nellipudi, but it appears that the parties did not take a strong decision to oppose the land occupation by the non-tribals for two reasons. The parties took a strong stand against the non-tribal Mukhasadar, demanding abolition of Mukhasas and liberating his control over the land. However, the parties did not take a strong political decision opposing non-tribal occupations. Perhaps, it is not a priority for them. The left political parties work ideologically on the frame of class struggle. Here they refer the class rich and poor sections. But in the context of Scheduled Areas, the constitutionally recognized class is Scheduled Tribe and Non-Scheduled Tribe for the purpose of implementation of Land Transfer Regulations 1 of 70. This law is an outcome of the Fifth Schedule to the Constitution of India. Similarly, the majority of the population belonged to the Scheduled Caste which constituted 43 per cent of the total population in the study village. The land occupation of the Scheduled Caste and other Backward Caste in the study village were not treated as a hindrance to the class ideological interests by the left parties.

The presence of left parties in the other study village, Mallavaram Mamillu, is conspicuously absent in support of the tribal land cause. The dispute between the tribals and the non-tribals in respect of land ownership has become a subject matter only for the scrutiny of the courts.

Indukurupeta village presents a contrasting picture in its land relations and other social aspects. A majority of the landholders belonged to the upper caste, Kapu whose domination is very much registered in and around the village. The leadership of the National Congress Party is under the hold of Kapu non-tribal landlords. One of the Kapu non-tribal landlord, Mutyala Rayudu, represented the Legislative Council in the State, and hailed from a tribal village Gondi, in the same mandal, Devipatnam. Although the CPI (ML) New democracy has a stronghold in some tribal pockets in the Mandal, they were able to mobilize its cadre for expropriation process of non-tribal landholdings. Thus, the domination of the non-tribal peasantry and their control over the land has remained unchallenged in the village.

One needs to look into whether the literacy among the tribals of the younger generation has created any impact in increasing land access. It is noticed that the formally educated tribal literates have stayed away from the tribal land struggles or the attempts being made by their parents for regaining alienated land. The common feature in all the study villages is that it is the 'illiterates' who are mainly involved in the land struggles or articulation of their land concerns. The legal awareness among the tribals in all the study villages is poor and the mainstream education curriculum does not teach them about the constitutional land right protection extended to the tribals. The curriculum in schools or colleges in tribal areas is not related to the tribal areas or tribal communities specifically, and land governance literacy which is a key factor in the retrieval of alienated land or securing access to land justice for tribal communities in the Scheduled Areas, is poor. Thus, the literacy levels in the study villages did not show any specific impact in the field of land concerns of the tribals. Secondly, the tribals did not possess a proper understanding or sufficient exposure to the procedural aspects of the administrative and legal justice systems.

Thus, all the above observations may help to identify major trends in the tribal land alienation.

Figure 4.17 delineates some of the processes through which the tribals have lost their land in the study villages, as well as villages covered by the case studies in the report as a whole.

Content Analysis of Judgements given Under Land Transfer Regulations 1 of 70

The outcome of the legal proceedings initiated against the non-tribal land occupants in all the sample villages is consolidated in Table 4.37 to assess the impact of Land Transfer Regulations 1 of 70. This legislation is in essence and substance, meant for restoration of alienated land which originally belonged to tribals and now in the possession of non-tribals, back to tribals.

Out of the 341 cases disposed, covering an extent of 1,539 acres of the disputed land, non-tribals were able to obtain favourable orders in 55 per cent of the cases, which covered 55 per cent of the land. While in the case of tribals, only 12 per cent of the cases were met in their favour, covering an extent of 17 per cent of the land. In the cases of the government, *suo moto* cases were 33 per cent, covering an extent of 28 per cent of land. Even assuming for the purpose of argument that the land covered by the cases went in favour of the government, and will be available for distribution among the tribals, even then the tribals would get 45 per cent of the disputed land. Thus, we can infer that the legal machinery and the existing legal provisions are unable to mete out justice to the tribals.

Content Analysis of Judgments

Further, content analysis of judgments given by the Special Deputy Collector's Court in favour of non-tribals demonstrates that the non-tribals could acquire legitimacy for their landholdings in the Scheduled Areas through legal processes. A detailed study of the

Figure 4.17

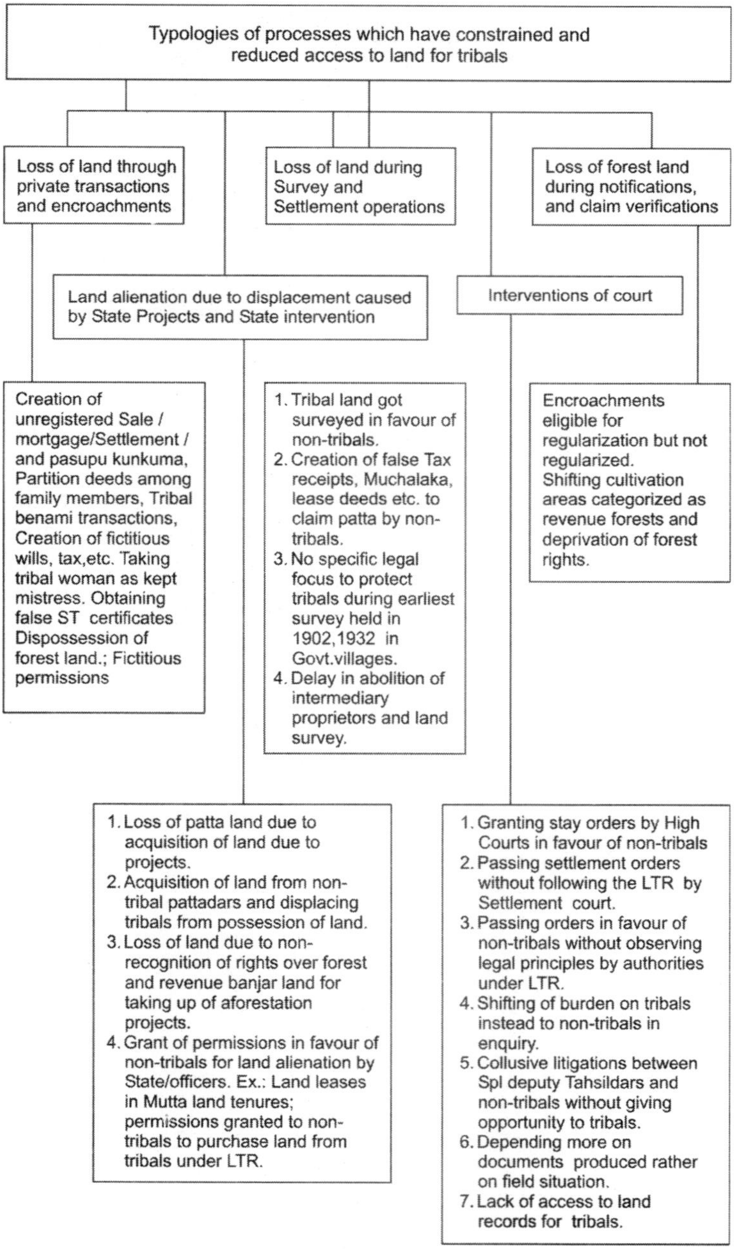
Typologies of processes which have constrained and reduced access to land for tribals
Loss of land through private transactions and encroachments
Loss of land during Survey and Settlement operations
Loss of forest land during notifications, and claim verifications
Land alienation due to displacement caused by State Projects and State intervention
Interventions of court
Creation of unregistered Sale / mortgage/Settlement / and pasupu kunkuma, Partition deeds among family members, Tribal benami transactions, Creation of fictitious wills, tax,etc. Taking tribal woman as kept mistress. Obtaining false ST certificates Dispossession of forest land.; Fictitious permissions
1. Tribal land got surveyed in favour of non-tribals.
2. Creation of false Tax receipts, Muchalaka, lease deeds etc. to claim patta by non-tribals.
3. No specific legal focus to protect tribals during earliest survey held in 1902,1932 in Govt.villages.
4. Delay in abolition of intermediary proprietors and land survey.
Encroachments eligible for regularization but not regularized.
Shifting cultivation areas categorized as revenue forests and deprivation of forest rights.
1. Loss of patta land due to acquisition of land due to projects.
2. Acquisition of land from non-tribal pattadars and displacing tribals from possession of land.
3. Loss of land due to non-recognition of rights over forest and revenue banjar land for taking up of aforestation projects.
4. Grant of permissions in favour of non-tribals for land alienation by State/officers. Ex.: Land leases in Mutta land tenures; permissions granted to non-tribals to purchase land from tribals under LTR.
1. Granting stay orders by High Courts in favour of non-tribals
2. Passing settlement orders without following the LTR by Settlement court.
3. Passing orders in favour of non-tribals without observing legal principles by authorities under LTR.
4. Shifting of burden on tribals instead to non-tribals in enquiry.
5. Collusive litigations between Spl deputy Tahsildars and non-tribals without giving opportunity to tribals.
6. Depending more on documents produced rather on field situation.
7. Lack of access to land records for tribals.

Table 4.37

Outcome of Legal Proceedings (1976–2010)

Mandal	*Village*	*Land Tenure*	*Total cases*		*In Favour of ST*		*In Favour of NTs*		*In Favour of Govt*		*Pending*	
			Booked	*Ext (Ac)*	*No. of Cases*	*Ext (Ac)*	*No. of Cases*	*Ext (Ac)*	*No. of Cases*	*Ext (Ac)*	*Booked*	*Ext (Ac)*
Gangavaram	Nellipudi	Mukhasa	141	610.26	6	31.19	58	266.31	56	233.30	21	79.46
Addateegala	Veerabhadrapuram	Government,	38	276.75	1	8.00	24	224.04	6	16.60	7	28.11
Addateegala	Mallavaram Mamillu	Mutta	7	144.37	5	63.25	1	4.10	0	0	1	77.02
Devipatnam	Indukuru peta	Estate	199	679.46	17	95.83	102	337.61	51	175.38	29	70.64
			402	1,807.42	42	270.98	186	842.93	113	425.28	61	268.23

Source: Data computed from the LTR Case Registers, SDC office, Rampachodavaram.

judgments reveals the arguments advanced by non-tribals to secure orders from the court and conclusions made by the courts in the adjudication process, which affected the intended land justice to tribals under the Land Transfer Regulations.

A half or 50 per cent of the cases decided in favour of non-tribals numbered to be at least 30, were taken up for analysing the orders in order to know the reasons being given by the court to pass orders in favour of the non-tribals and its legal validity in the light of provisions under the provisions of Land Transfer Regulations and the legal precedents of the higher courts.

Nellipudi Village: Out of 58 cases, 30 cases were examined.

Table 4.38

Reasons Shown for Giving Orders in Favour of Non-tribals-Nellipudi

S. No.	*Rationale/Reasons Shown*	*No. of Cases*	*Extent in Acs.*
1.	The petitioners are not tribals, as such there is no application of LTR to the case.	1	10.00
2.	Unregistered sale agreements, ante-dated, as such do not attract the provisions of LTR 1 of 70.	6	27.95
3.	Partition deeds held among non-tribals, no deprivation of tribal land rights.	3	15.32
4.	Lands are inams as per records, occupations by non-tribal not hit by LTR.	2	4.67
5.	Registered mortgage deeds executed between non-tribals prior to the date of commencement of LTR; so valid.	2	7.86
6.	Registered sale deeds between non-tribals prior to LTR 1 of 70; so valid.	5	12.77
7.	Transactions between tribals, no violation of LTR (but in actuality it is a tribal benami).	1	19.00
8.	Settlement deeds and Pasupu kunkuma transactions among the family members, not hit by LTR.	5	10.27

Cont'd...

...Cont'd

9.	Humanitarian grounds, the non-tribal is a landless poor.	1	1.88
10.	Admittedly Transaction held after 1 Of 70 Reg. But father-In-Law transferred land To daughter-In-Law, considered as valid.	2	4.50
11.	Mortgage deed executed by tribal but prior to Act 1 of 1917 came into force.	1	4.86
12.	Application of Principle of Res judicata, case dropped.	1	2.05
	Total	30	121.13

Veerabhadrapuram : Out of 24 cases, 18 cases were examined.

Table 4.39

Reasons Shown for Giving Orders in Favour of Non-tribals - Veerabhadvapuvam

S. No.	*Rationale/Reasons Shown*	*No. of Cases*	*Extent in Acs.*
1.	Registered sale deeds effected prior to commencement of 1 of 70 Regulations, held among non-tribals.	5	62.68
2.	Registration of landholdings in the name of non-tribal in the Resurvey Register in 1932.	7	79.38
3.	Unregistered sale agreements effected prior to 1 of 70 Regulations, considered as valid.	2	7.50
4.	Registered sale agreement effected prior to 1 of 70 Regulations.	1	4.20
5.	Assignment patta granted on government land in favour of non-tribal, considered as valid.	1	2.83
6.	Ryotwari Pattadar Pass book and title deeds issued under Record of Rights Act, considered as valid without taking up a scrutiny under LTR provisions.	1	4.00
7.	Paper Land Lease transactions on paper being shown in favour of tribals (Benami), considered as valid, without verifying the field situation.	1	7.75
	Total	18	168.34

Indukurupeta: Of the 102 cases decided in favour of the non-tribals, 67 cases were examined.

Table 4.40

Reasons Shown for Giving Orders in Favour of Non-tribals-Indukurupeta

S. No.	*Rationale/Reasons Shown*	*No. of Cases*	*Extent in Acs.*
1.	Non-tribals filed Settlement Patta granted by Settlement Officer under 2 of 70 Ryotwari Settlement Regulations. No enquiry was held on the genesis of land titles acquired by non-tribals and from whom. Note: However, the court issued order in favour of non-tribals without looking into the proceedings of the Settlement Officer, which is contrary to the procedure of Settlement Regulations as well as Land Transfer Regulations 1 of 70. For instance, 8 years possession was required, prior to 2 of 70 Regulations to grant the patta. This provision was not followed in the proceedings No. LTRP 168/83 case. Settlement Officer granted patta based on Mutchala, tax receipts, Encumbrance Certificates, given by the Estate proprietors. Only based on such patta, claims under LTR were allowed by the SDC court.	36	70.60
2.	Cases filed against non-tribals were dropped observing that cases attracted the principle of Res judicata.	1	1.75
3.	Registered sale transactions held between non-tribals prior to the commencement of 1 of 70 Regulations. Note: No verification of classification of land and the genesis of title over the land was held. The rejected orders of Settlement Officer for grant of patta were also taken into consideration to allow the land claims in favour of non-tribals.	9	18.36
4.	Non-tribals appeared before the court did not make claim for the land mentioned in the notice, The court allowed the oral submissions of non-tribals and dropped the case.	7	21.10
5.	Decree passed by Civil suit was taken into consideration and allowed the claim of non-tribals, followed by Settlement patta. (LTRP 311/80-)	1	17.35
6.	Based on amarakam accounts maintained by zamindars, considered as valid without conducting enquiry into earlier land transfers held on the disputed land.	1	4.17

Cont'd...

...Cont'd

7.	Court allowed the claim of non-tribals based on the recitals mentioned in the sale papers that instead of Konda Kammara (ST) as kammarlu.	1	7.32
8.	Unregistered Sale Agreements effected between Non-Tribals prior to the Commencement of LTR 1 of 70, were considered as valid and proper, although the post-regd. Sale Transactions are null and void. Based on the recitals mentioned in the prohibited land transfer papers that sale agreement was made prior to the commencement of 1 of 70 Regulations.	5	6.71
9.	Oral testimony of non-tribal claimants stating that land was given to their daughters as 'Pasupu kunkuma', also considered as valid. Note: Pasupu kunkuma is nothing but a gift which is prohibited under LTR.	2	15.40
10.	The oral statements of non-tribals submitting that the land covered by present enquiry are distinct to the land in their occupations, considered as a ground to allow their claims, without any further enquiry into the ground situation. In fact, 3 cases are classified as Banjara land/Govt waste land as per fair adangals.	4	19.09
	Total	67	181.85

1. The cases filed by the Special Deputy Tahsildars on the behalf of tribals failed to provide adequate record or evidence before the Court in support of their cases against non-tribal occupants. In almost all cases, the enquiry was held based on the records produced by the non-tribals. There are no recorded instances to suggest that appeals were filed by the unsuccessful Special Deputy Tahsildars in a regular course of time in higher courts in order to reverse the orders issued in favour of non-tribals.
2. It is also notable that the orders passed by the Special Deputy Collector shows a baseless common observation in all the cases that 'no tribal was in possession of land in question at any time.' The case records reveal that this observation is not based on any enquiry, either at the field level or based on the material available. In some cases, the non-tribals even produced Encumbrance Certificates (ECs) to show that no tribal was involved in any of the transactions. In fact, the Encumbrance Certificates show the details of registered land

transactions only but not the unregistered ones at the Sub Registrar's office. But the Court relied on these certificates without conducting an enquiry order to know if any unregistered land transactions were effected between the tribal and the non-tribal parties at any point of time.

3. The incorporation of names in Re Settlement Registers (RSR) are considered as Settlement Pattas and the claim of the non-tribals was allowed on this ground by the court, particularly in the government village of Veerabhadrapuram.
4. In some cases, a factual mistake was shown as a strong ground to allow the claim in favour of the non-tribal parties. The petitions filed by tribals for the restoration of land from the non-tribal were dismissed by the court on the ground that the land particulars were not adequate. This decision was made by the court instead of directing the concerned staff to conduct a field verification.
5. In some cases it is mentioned in the orders that the 'non-tribal respondent appeared before the court and did not claim the land', covered by the notice issued by the enquiry officer. Based on oral testimony of non-tribal parties, cases are shown as dropped without any physical verification of land at the field level.
6. In most cases, the orders were passed by the court observing that transactions were held among the non-tribals, as such the transfers were not affected by the provisions of Land Transfer Regulations 1 of 59 as amended by 1 of 70. It is true that the Regulations 1 of 70 prohibits transfer of land between the non-tribals only after 3 February 1970. The Land Transfer Regulations were not given retrospective effect in order to cover the earlier transactions effected between the non-tribal parties in respect of land situated in the Scheduled Areas. The study reveals that the court passed orders without conducting proper enquiry into the past land transactions, if any were held between the tribal and the non-tribals. The court relied upon the one or two land transfer deeds produced by the non-tribal parties in the proceedings without looking into the genesis of the title from the date of commencement of the Andhra Pradesh Agency Area Land Transfer Act, 1917. The court failed to see as to how the original non-tribal seller gained access to land situated in the Scheduled Areas and

whether the non-tribal claimants have been in continuous possession and enjoyment of the land in question prior to the enforcement of the prohibited Land Transfer Laws. In fact, under the law, the burden is on the non-tribals to prove that their title and possession over land situated in the Scheduled Areas is not contrary to the provisions of Land Transfer Regulations. However, the orders passed in the study cases reveal that the court passed orders observing that 'tribals failed to prove their case showing that they were in the possession of the land at any point of time after the commencement of Land Transfer Regulations and land was transferred from them to the non-tribals.'

7. The other reason shown in the cases is the application of the principle of Res judicata to the facts of the cases. The High Court held that the mere fact that on an earlier occasion, a petition filed under the Regulations was dismissed does not confer any right on the non-tribal so long as void transactions subsist, and the principle of Res judicata has no application.[2] The other settled legal principle is that the non-tribal parties in the land disputes cannot plead on this principle that the Constitution of India is not adhered to and the orders are obtained earlier. The High Court of Andhra Pradesh held that the principle of Res judicata will not apply if the proceedings were initiated by a third party or by the same party on the basis of any further new evidenciary material.[3] Further, the High Court of Andhra Pradesh observes that if the parties are different and the emerging facts are new and distinct from the earlier proceedings the principle of Res judicata has no application. However, the study of content of the orders reveals that the Court allowed the claim of non-tribals applying the principle of Res judicata contrary to the legal precedents. Thus, the erroneous application of the principle of law in tribal land cases to assist the non-tribals in legitimizing their illegal land occupations in the Scheduled Areas was applied.

8. The manifestations of court litigations by the non-tribals are also shown in the evidence by orders made in several cases. The courts approved the land claims of the non-tribals merely on appreciation of the unregistered sale agreements produced by the non-tribal parties in order to avoid the legal clutches of 1 of 70 Regulations. The court relied on such self-served

unregistered sale papers which are purposefully prepared to show that the land transactions were held prior to the commencement of prohibited Land Transfer Regulations. In some cases the non-tribals purposefully got listed in the post-1970 registered sale transactions in such a way to show that already an agreement was in force prior to the commencement of 1 of 70 Land Transfer Regulations. Based on such self-served declarations, the courts allowed the claim of non-tribals on the land. As per the proviso of section 17 of the Indian Evidence Act, the legal validity of such unregistered documents is very limited and useful for the purpose of corroboration. Only thus, the very purpose of 1 of 70 is defeated for it gives credence to such unregistered land papers.

9. The other grounds shown in the orders are that the non-tribal land occupants are settlement patta holders and as such their possession of land cannot be disturbed. However, the Andhra Pradesh Scheduled Area Land Transfer Regulations are to invalidate any transfer of land situated in the Agency Tracts in favour of the non-tribal. In order to actualize that intention, the Regulation had set up the Special Deputy Collector's (TW) Court. Ryotwari Settlement Regulations 2 of 70 or Ryotwari Settlement Regulations 2 of 69 or other similar Settlement Regulations were enacted to provide the Ryotwari Settlement Patta of certain land in the Scheduled Areas of Andhra Pradesh. These Regulations also enact that a non-tribal will not be entitled to a Ryotwari patta if his possession or occupation of the land is void or illegal under the Land Transfer Regulations. The High Court of Andhra Pradesh held that Land Transfer Regulations 1 of 70 prevails over the provisions of Ryotwari Settlement Regulations and no ryotwari patta can be granted in violation of the provisions of LTR and such patta would not bind the authorities under Land Transfer Regulations.[4] Thus, the court passed orders in favour of non-tribals based on the settlement patta. It is to be considered as an improper enquiry into tribal land disputes.

10. Further, an appropriate way to read these two Regulations would be to allow both of them to operate, while giving primary importance to the operation of Land Transfer Regulations. Where the Regulations 1 of 59 as amended by 1 of 70 decides that possession and occupation by the non-tribal is

void, then that would prevail against any Ryotwari Patta that might have been granted under Ryotwari Settlement Regulations. However, the court in the proceedings initiated against the non-tribals, observed that the non-tribal can retain possession of land situated in the Scheduled Areas as he was granted Settlement Patta, without conducting an enquiry about how he gained access to such land before getting the Settlement Patta. Therefore, the enquiry officer narrowed the scope of the enquiry under the Land Transfer Regulations and simply passed orders in favour of the non-tribals based on such Settlement Pattas. Thus, an inference can be drawn that while the Settlement Regulations brought an end to the feudal system of land tenure administration, on the other hand it opened the floodgates of Scheduled Areas for the non-tribals to claim legal right over the tribal land. During the Survey and Settlement operations under these regulations, several irregularities were freely committed by the non-tribals in these operations, in collusion with the lower survey and settlement officials. In the Settlement Regulations 2/69 and 2/70, it had been stipulated that the non-tribals had to prove eight years of continuous possession prior to 1969 and 1970 and absence of any prohibited transfer as per Land Transfer Regulations, to be eligible for the grant of the patta. However, these were openly flouted by the non-tribals.

11. The rejected settlement orders for grant of patta to the non-tribals, passed by the Settlement Officers under Ryotwari Settlement Regulations were also considered as valid legal entitlement by the court in the studied cases. The observations made by the Settlement Officers in the cases are as 'the land classified as inams and non-tribals are in occupation, however they are not entitled pattas' under the Regulations of 2 of 70.
12. The court even allowed claims based on the documents like Muchalaka, tax receipts issued by the clerks of Estates, conditional pattas granted by the Zamindar, land entrustment documents as Amarakam accounts, etc. It appears that the non-tribals have easy access to these documents from the abolished Estate clerks, etc. The courts, without summoning the documents from the proper custodian of documents, in order to know the genuineness of the documents produced by non-tribal parties, approved the photocopies produced by the non-tribals.

13. Although the non-tribals are not legally entitled to hold government land in the Scheduled Areas, the court allowed the claim of the non-tribals based on assigned land under D'Form pattas in favour of the non-tribals. The High Court of Andhra Pradesh clearly held that the assignment pattas granted to non-tribals are null and void.[5]
14. Although the social status claim of the parties is not under the jurisdiction of enquiry court under Land Transfer Regulations, the enquiry officer took into cognizance, the recitals in the sale documents, in order to disallow the claim of the tribals. For instance, in a case decided in favour of non-tribals, 'Kammarlu' instead of 'Konda Kammara', a notified Scheduled Tribe, is mentioned in the land transfer documents relating to tribals. The non-tribal took undue advantage of the mistake and pleaded before the court that the vendors are non-tribal Kammarlu and that there is no prohibited land transfer involved. The court appreciated the contention of the non-tribals without seeking proper verification from the concerned Revenue or Tribal Welfare Departments so as to know whether the land transferor is a Scheduled Tribe Konda Kammara or not.
15. The courts allowed the land transactions of 'pasupu kunkuma' (gift being given to daughters by parents at the time of marriage) observing that the transactions held are within the family members of non-tribal parties only, and there is no violation of law. In fact, pasupu kunkuma is nothing but a 'gift' as per the decision of the full bench of Andhra Pradesh High Court, reported in AIR 2002. The term 'transfer' in Section 3 of the provisions of Land Transfer Regulations 1 of 59 includes the term 'gift' transaction as well. Thus *pasupu kunkuma* transactions effected between non-tribal parties are contrary to the provisions of Land Transfer Regulations 1 of 59 and they are null and void.
16. The Court also allowed the claims of the non-tribals based on fictitious tribal benami transactions without conducting any verification at the field level.

Therefore, the content analysis of the judgements clearly reveals that the courts are not geared up to reverse the exploitive land relations and other dubious means through which the non-tribals have secured land in the Scheduled Areas of East

Godavari District of Andhra Pradesh. In fact, the illegal occupation by non-tribals has gained legitimacy through the intervention of the legal system. The court orders passed in such cases in favour of non-tribals buttress this argument. Particularly, the lower level enquiry courts do not follow the legal precedents set out by the higher Courts in the administration of land justice. Thus, the present conflict resolution mechanism is not fit to serve the constitutional intention of rendering land justice to tribals who have lost control over their land in the Scheduled Areas. The analysis of the orders clearly shows that the current laws are inadequate to deal with the tribal land problem. There is a need to plug the loopholes in the law.

Notes

1. *A.P. District Gazetteers* (1976) East Godavari District, Govt. of A.P., Central Press, Hyderabad.
2. Ch. Satyanarayana vs. Agent to the Government & District Collector, Visakhapatnam, WP 6065/1979, High Court of Andhra Pradesh, Hyderabad.
3. 2003 (6) ALD (NOC) 68, Hyderabad.
4. Gadde Nagabhushanamma vs. Govt. of A.P., 1999 (5) ALD 430, Hyderabad.
5. P. Gangamma vs. Vasudha Misra, District Collector, West Godavari, 1998 (2) ALD 35, Hyderabad.

CHAPTER 5

Conclusion

It is evident from the study that the extent of land alienation prevalent in the Scheduled Areas of the East Godavari District is a cause for public concern. The process of land alienation has not stopped even after the promulgation of tribal protective land laws. Tribals have lost their land due to plural attacks, including the exploitative mechanism compounded by forcible acts of the non-tribal settlers and the interventions of the state in dispossession of their land. The Forest Department intervention is another manifestation of resource displacement of tribals. The tribal land alienation issue is further complicated by the mainstream political parties due to their tilt towards the non-tribal vote bank policies. The special protection extended for tribal rights through various legislations, form part of the welfare measures of the State, with the support of main opposition parties without converting it into a reality. The study also discloses the enormity of the yawning gap between formulating the laws and their proper enforcement. As a result of land alienation, the tribals have lost livelihood opportunities and their cultural linkage with the natural resources. Perhaps, the tribal belt has to experience more and more incursions of the non-tribals, industrial interests in future and lose its character specified under Fifth Schedule of the Constitution if there is no restriction to such ingressions. The magnitude of the problem is of national importance and needs to be tackled and solved through Parliamentary intervention and effective enforcement of the laws.

To answer one of the major questions posed in the beginning, this study provides strong evidence to support the hypothesis that denial of the land rights of the tribals is essentially due to the introduction of an alien land administration which marginalized tribes in subsequent legal proceedings. At the root of the problem in the study villages, lies the fact that there is an inherent lacuna in the state policy that tends to be biased against tribals and which, in turn, perpetuates land alienation.

The process of land alienation traces back to the management of land administration by the proprietors of different land tenures in the Agency Tracts. The process of decision-making at the land tenure institutions for the fiscal revenue purpose during pre- and post-independent era has become a death note on the survival of tribals, as the policy invited non-tribals to gain access to land, affecting the local tribals' land use and tenurial relationships. The policy adopted by the rulers encouraged the non-tribals to immigrate in large numbers and settle down in the Scheduled Areas. The British Government permitted zamindars and the Mukhasadars to take hold of the land administration which led to the slipping of land from the hold of the tribes to the non-tribals. The tribal chieftains of Muttas adopted diverse methods to transfer land to non-tribals after which the tribals were deprived of their land.

The study reveals that large chunks of land were transferred from the non-tribal proprietors of Mukhasas, zamindars and non-tribal claimant Muttadars. The tribal Muttadar of Dutcharthi claimed to be a non-tribal to get land transferred in Mutta area to non-tribals and in order to escape the Land Transfer Act 1917. There are no measures to check the influx of non-tribals because the non-tribal land tenure administrators declared an open policy to hand over the land to either tribals or non-tribals on lease by grant of conditional pattas called 'Krishika patta' in Mukhasa villages and 'Veesa badi patta' in Estate villages to raise the land revenue. The British land survey policy which intended to generate revenue, triggered the idea of land survey for determination of landholders, unmindful of tribal interests in government villages. That is the reason for alienation of land in favour of non-tribals which started during the survey periods 1902 onwards. Tribals, who have no idea of legitimacy of the survey records and determination of boundaries except earmarking traditional boundaries of hills and trees, lost control over the resources. The internal migration among the tribal communities further weakened the levels of their articulation in land alienation matters. The original tribal inhabitants moved to other places and the new tribals entrants of the village are not in a position to question the occupations of the non-tribals in the villages.

The laissez faire policy of the state has also worked against the interests of the tribals. The initial Act framed in 1917 restricted the transfer of land between tribals and non-tribals without obtaining consent from the Agent or the prescribed officer. But there is no special machinery set up to check the illegal transfers or making a special provision applying to non-tribal proprietors of land tenures like Mutta, Estate, Mahals, etc. The law was made but no specific provision was made to protect the interests of tribals by imposing restrictions on land registrations in favour of non-tribals during the surveys carried in 1902 and 1932 in government (ryotwari) villages. This is a major lacuna in the land policy governing the tribal land alienation issues. Even in the Land Transfer Regulations made in 1959, no rules were made till 1969 for its operationalization. There was no change in the evidence law to give credence to the oral evidence of tribals whose value system was based on verbal rather than on written form in administrative or court enquiries. Similarly, the Land Transfer Regulations 1 of 70 was restricted to prospective land transfers between non-tribals without covering the past land transactions. This gives a lot of scope to non-tribals to retain the land in their hold, and litigation never ends. The legal presumption clause under the Land Transfer Regulations 1 of 70, which advocates that the land situated in the Scheduled Areas once belonged to tribals unless the contrary is proved, remained a presumptive statement, rather than a useful legal provision in the context of the legal framework. As a result, the law has acted as a mediating agency in a significant manner in favour of the non-tribals in change of land ownership and use.

The registration of land leases by the proprietors and state in favour of non-tribals in a complementing manner tended to sit side by side with the state's rights to impose restrictions by law. The open policy of the state to invite non-tribals to tribal areas by offering land, negated the rights of the tribals. It sits within the contrary context of a tribal society's definition of land ownership and relationship. Institutional and legal frameworks are the product of particular sets of needs that are dictated by a dominant political society of non-tribals through the processes of government and public administration, which negated the customary right of tribals over land. Further, the institutional framework gives more credence to the written records rather than to oral testimony and traditional land tenure systems. In fact, no provision under law was made to record or cover concealed land transactions held between tribals and non-tribals.

Like other tribal people around the Scheduled Areas, the tribals in the study district have experienced displacement and loss of land and natural resources on which their cultural identities depend. They have also experienced the fundamental dynamics of power and inequality, in accessing land justice. The most fundamental inequality in the Scheduled Area is between the non-tribal elites who are able to access administrative and legal structures of the state and the vast majority of the tribals who cannot do so.

The class division of tribals and non-tribals is best capitalized to consolidate vote banks by the political parties by promising the implementation of tribal protective Land Transfer Regulations on one hand and diluting the same through other interventions in support of land occupation of non-tribals in the Agency Tracts. Creating Scheduled Tribes Protection Cell in the framework of political parties and facilitating the tribal individuals to head the same, is a strategic intervention of the parties to capture the tribal vote banks. It is important to note, however, that the success of individuals in gaining access to the administrative or political or constitutional advisory bodies does not benefit the tribals at large. On the contrary, it runs counter to the interests of the tribals. The record of the Tribal Advisory Council meetings, also proves their nominal role in protecting the interest of tribals.

The political dimension in tribal land alienation issue is highly political with parties taking sides to favour the non-tribal population in Agency Areas. This is further evident from the proceedings of the Tribal Advisory Council and the attempts made to repeal the Tribal Protective Land Transfer Regulations 1 of 70 to lure the non-tribal voters in the month of April 1988. However, the attempts were negated by the tribals and their supportive groups way back in 1988. Similar proceedings were held in July 1999 to facilitate the non-tribals to construct houses in the Scheduled Areas by issuing possession certificates.

Another such move was made by the political parties during the period 1969–1970. The enactment of Land Transfer Regulations 1 of 70 has been parallelled by the introduction of Survey and

Settlement Regulations 1 of 69, 2 of 69 and 2 of 70 after abolition of intermediary land tenure proprietorship, to scuttle the tribal protective laws in a systematic attempt by the state. As described by Gunnar Myrdal in famous *Asian Drama*, (*Asian Drama*, 1969 pp. 66 and 277), the role of the state in the case of the land alienation problem, was that of a 'soft state', which is dominated by powerful non-tribal interests that exploit the power of the State or Administrative mechanisms to serve their own interests, rather than the interests of the tribals. Policies decided upon are often not enforced, if they are enacted at all, and in that the authorities, even while framing the policies, are reluctant to place obligations on people on the forefront.

In fact, the abolition of intermediary proprietors of land tenures is proclaimed to end the feudalistic and capitalistic mode of control over the resources. However, the state intervention further reproduced a legitimate non-tribal landholding class in tribal areas.

The provision of settlement of land to the non-tribal ryots, if they have been in their occupation for a period of 8 years prior to the notified date under various Settlement Regulations is a 'proactive' provision. Even the ineligible non-tribal encroachers secured regularization of land occupation under these Settlement Regulations, which are otherwise illegal under the Land Transfer Regulations 1 of 70. No enquiry was made under these Land Transfer Regulations purposefully by the Settlement Officers before granting pattas in favour of non-tribals. Moreover, in matters of land settlement, even the legal process provides ample scope for manipulation and corruption. Due to this process of land alienation in many cases, the tribals have themselves turned into bonded labourers or underpaid agrarian labourers on their own land.

The tribal protective legislations and bringing the Scheduled Tracts into Fifth Scheduled Areas under the Constitution of India, is carved out from the 'Segregated isolationistic' approach which had its roots in the Government of India Act, 1870, which intended to specify tracts as 'Scheduled Tracts'. However, with the intervention of the Planning Commission of India another diametrically opposite approach of the isolation, the 'policy of assimilation' of tribal culture and population in the mainstream of national life has been applicable. This policy change is helpful to maintain the landed interest of the non-tribals in the Scheduled Areas to hold land. Because of this policy, a strong non-tribal class has emerged in the

Scheduled Areas. This class is a by-product of both state policies of the pre- and post-Independent era. The non-tribal entrepreneurship in the Scheduled Areas is considered to be a vehicle for tribal development. But in no time, the selfish motive of non-tribals ransacked the native title of tribal land and pushed tribals to the margins. Further, the selfish propensities of the non-tribal class have started controlling the political and administrative structures in the state in order to sustain their interests in tribal areas.

The Land Transfer Regulations 1 of 70 is an outcome of the Srikakulam Naxalite Movement. Similarly, the constitution of the Koneru Land Committees is also a follow up of agenda of land reforms put forward by Maoists before the government of Andhra Pradesh in 2005. However, the role of the Left parties is conspicuously absent in follow up of implementation of protective Land Transfer Regulations through the administrative or legal set up. This helps the non-tribals to show their legitimacy over the land in their hold, secured through legal interventions.

The Land Transfer Regulations prohibits transfer of all immovable property in Scheduled Areas of the state unless the recipient is a tribal or a co-operative society whose members are all tribals. In other words, even a transfer from a non-tribal to another non-tribal is prohibited. A presumption is laid down in section 3(1)(b) of the Land Transfer Regulation that until the contrary is proved, it will be presumed that any immovable property in the possession of a non-tribal in the Scheduled Area has been obtained by transfer from a tribal. Thus, the burden of proving lawful ownership of any immovable property in the possession of a non-tribal is on the non-tribal. If he fails, the land is to be taken over by the government and distributed to eligible tribals.

The legal presumption in the law and further objective of the provision has had a trace in the argument of the report of the Schedule Areas and Schedule Tribes Commission (Dhebar Commission), in 1961. The Dhebar Commission recommended that 'all surrenders (of tribal land) must be only to the State, which should hold the surrendered land as trustee for the tribals'. Once it is understood that the state is not the owner but a trustee under legal duty to protect the natural resources, the state sovereign would be precluded from taking the possession of the land without the owner's consent, the consent being a free and informed one. The customary rights of tribals are often not recognized and thus those who depended on such resources were not considered eligible for compensation.

The Supreme Court had occasion to explain the rationale and legislative purpose of the Land Transfer Regulations in *P. Rami Reddy* vs. *State of Andhra Pradesh* (AIR 1988 SC 1626). It was held that as land in tribal areas passed into the hands of the non-tribals from the tribals, the law cannot remain content with merely freezing such transfers but should aim at restoring as much as possible land to the tribals.

The Fifth Schedule to the Constitution of India, gives the executive extraordinary powers for peace and good governance of the Scheduled Areas. Para 5 (2) of the Schedule speaks of the power to regulate or prohibit or restrict the transfer of land and the allotment of land in the Scheduled Areas. The Supreme Court in *Samata* vs. *State of Andhra Pradesh* (AIR 1997 SC 3297), has interpreted this provision as a prohibition on transfer of land into the hands of non-tribals as per with provisions of the Land Transfer Regulations. It has been held that the provisions of the Fifth Schedule and those of the Land Transfer Regulations must be read together and harmoniously construed in order to preserve tribal autonomy, their culture and bring about economic empowerment to ensure social, economic and political justice for preservation of peace and good governance in the Scheduled Areas.

The weak enforcing machinery, non-transparency and lack of accountability in the process of administration in land justice through Special Courts, stand as evidence for the continual infringement of tribal protective land laws by the powerful sections of the non-tribal population, in collusion with the state institutions. The Special Deputy Tahsildars, who are filing cases on behalf of tribals under the Land Transfer Regulations, against the illegal non-tribal occupants of land, never filed appeals if they did not succeed in the court litigation at the lower court level. The neglect of the state machinery clearly shows their unwillingness to evict non-tribals by pursuing further legal recourse at the higher judicial level. Dereliction is seen even on part of the enforcing machinery in not implementing orders issued by the authorities in favour of the tribals under the Regulations.

The legal framework and machinery confronted with perpetuation of non-tribal exodus and growing land alienation has failed to inspire confidence among the tribal communities that they can get back their alienated land through the legal process. The legal system in place is inappropriate for fair play of justice.

> The competition between tribals and non-tribals in accessing land justice in the context of Land Transfer Regulations 1 of 70 is characterized as 'a race between a handicapped one-legged person and an able bodied two legged person' by the Supreme Court of India.[1]

Non-tribals in all the study villages were able to secure favourable orders in 55 per cent of the cases, covering 55 per cent of the disposed cases, which show that the present legal system and the law is an inadequate tool to deal with the tribal land alienation problem.

Thus, failure on the part of the government to freeze the land alienation situation or restore tribal land is evidence of encouraging unlawful encroachment of land by non-tribals in the Scheduled Areas and is, therefore, injurious to the lawful rights of the tribals. In fact, the object of the Fifth Schedule to the Constitution is to preserve the land in the Scheduled Areas to the tribals. It prohibits the government from allotting land held by tribals to the non-tribals. It prohibits infiltration of the non-tribals into the Scheduled Areas and prevents the exploitation of tribals by the non-tribals in any form.

This has resulted in tribal communities to take up struggle with the support of frontal groups of CPI (ML) left parties, to take possession of land from non-tribals. The state process of legitimization of land occupation of non-tribal settlers completely marginalized the idea of tribals getting back their alienated land from the non-tribals.

In the light of the above, a land information infrastructure needs to support informed decision-making, not only within the government, but also in the community and for individuals. The task for planners can be particularly challenging as the existing legal framework does not support the tribals in getting back alienated land in the Scheduled Areas. Tribal land rights protection requires a rethinking on the part of the government about governance structures to bring about an equitable balance of rights and responsibilities between non-tribals and the tribal community as well as the state, in usage of land and their relationship with land. The inclusiveness of tribals in the decision-making process in land disputes should be an essential element to inspire confidence in the administration of justice in land matters. The protective clauses for tribal rights are undermined by the blatant unwillingness of the state machinery which is a reflection of their ideology to bring about tribal development by bringing tribals into the mainstream, without reversing the historical injustice done to tribals in tribal land matters.

The plural land tenure administration and alien legal framework to determine land ownership has excluded the customary rights of tribal communities and impinged upon their capabilities and entitlements. The land tenure institutions and parallel legislations to protect tribal land rights regime have expanded the choices to non-tribal outsiders to gain access to land through appropriately formulated 'rules of the game', to meet their goals and objectives. This has resulted in the marginalization of tribals with regard to their land and natural resources.

The tribal land alienation conflicts are not clearly explainable along Marxist or capitalist lines. In other words, the land conflicts are not merely between the capitalists and the workers. These land conflicts can run along different and less predictable lines and can range from local to regional or state level, involving a wide diversity of government institutions and identities. The weak administrative structures of the land governance is a complemental factor to exploitive and forcible manifestations of the non-tribals. If tribals are dispossessed forcibly, it is difficult to identify the exploitive element. The tribal land alienation problem is, therefore, a function of plural elements at play at the ground level. It is for this reason that the meaning of word 'transfer' under Regulations 1 of 70 was further expanded by the High Court, holding that dispossession from land by non-tribals also attracts the word 'transfer'.

The present study, based on a few case studies and sample villages, reflects the status of legal entitlements of tribals. This study is basically the mapping of the processes of tribal land alienation and tribal legal entitlements. The impact of other business interests, state interventions and other forces in loss of tribal land is not covered at the state level. The neo-economic policies and its reflection on the land alienation is an important factor which can be taken up for further research. At present, very few studies emphasize on tribal land alienation in the state. Therefore, there is a need for further research on this subject

Recommendations

Legislative Changes

1. Retrospective effect is to be given to all Land Transfer Laws from 1917 onwards in Andhra area and from 1359 Fasli (1949 AD) onwards in Telangana area.
2. Enforcement officers must be empowered to exercise *suo moto* powers under Land Transfer Regulations (LTR) in filing LTR cases without any period of limitation or constraints in the name of reasonable period. This legal change is required to avoid the often used Res judicata principle in court cases.
3. There must be a special provision to record concealed land transactions held between tribals and non-tribals as well as among the non-tribals in land records.
4. The penal provision for violation of Land Transfer Regulations should be extended to the officers who disregard the orders issued by Courts or Government in implementation of Land Transfer Regulations.
5. The oral evidence in tribal land cases should be given an overriding importance over any contrary documentary evidence produced by non-tribal parties.
6. To ensure the resumption of alienated land, a tribunal with members of tribal community representative, tribal rights activists and government officials should be set up at the Integrated Tribal Development Agency level and at the lower level, Gram Sabha should be given power to adjudicate land disputes. The decision at the Integrated Tribal Development Agency level should be made final and the interference of the High Court should be permitted only in the case of clear violations and without staying operation of the orders passed by the Tribunal.
7. The provisions enabling to file appeals against the orders passed by the authorities, under both the Land Transfer Regulations and the Ryotwari Settlement Regulations should be amended to enable the tribal parties to question the irregularity or illegality of the orders given in favour of the non-tribals earlier.
8. The jurisdiction of civil courts in entertaining the civil suits in nature of injunction or declaration title over the land situated in the Scheduled Areas at the instance of the non-tribals, should be barred.

Land Administration for Effective Implementation of Land Transfer Regulations

1. Separate machinery should be set up for restoration of alienated tribal land and filing of appeals against unfavourable orders.
2. Updating land records by physical verification and incorporating the names of actual cultivators in the revenue records is necessary. These records, in addition to the court orders, must be accessible to tribals at the Gram Panchayat level.
3. The government land must be made accessible to tribals and illegal non-tribal encroachers should be evicted.
4. At the State level, a committee must be set up with the representatives of the government, civil society organizations and experts on tribal land issues to monitor the implementation of Land Transfer Regulations and give timely directions from time to time to the enforcing authorities.
5. At the Integrated Tribal Development Agency level, similar committees must be set up.
6. The Special Deputy Collectors in the Scheduled Areas must be given postings after a compulsory intensive training on Land Transfer Regulations and other relevant laws. Frequent sensitization programmes on tribal land rights need to be organized for both Special Deputy Collectors and other enforcing machinery.
7. The Integrated Tribal Development Agencies must be empowered to control the influx or infiltration of the non-tribal population by taking steps in the light of Land Transfer Regulation provisions, and with coordination of all licensing departments should be assigned to check the establishment of shops, enterprises and constructions for housing or for any other commercial purpose.
8. Police interference on behalf of the non-tribals and against the interest of tribals should be restrained and erring officials should be punished.

Note

1. *P. Rami Reddy & others vs. State of A.P. & another,* 1988 (22) Reports (SC) 364.

Appendices

Appendix 1

The Agency Tracts Interest and Land Transfer Act, 1917 (Act No. 1 of 1917)

(14th August 1917)

An Act to regulate, the rate of interest and the transfer of land in the Ganjam, Visakhapatnam and Godavari Agency Tracts.

Preamble: Whereas it is expedient to limit the rate of interest and to check transfers of land in the Agency Tracts of Ganjam, Visakhapatnam, and Godavari Districts;

It is hereby enacted as follows:

1. **Short Title:**
   This Act may be called the Agency Tracts Interest and Land Transfer Act, 1917.
2. **Definition:**
   In this Act unless there is anything repugnant in the subject or context :
   a. 'Agency tracts' means the scheduled districts as defined in Acts XIV and XV of 1847 and included within the districts of Ganjam, Visakhapatnam and Godavari.
   b. 'Agent' means 'Agent to the Governor' in the districts of Ganjam and Visakhapatnam and 'Government Agent' in the district of Godavari.
   c. 'Hill tribe' means any body or class of persons resident in the Agency tracts (not being a landholder as defined in

[the Andhra Pradesh (Andhra Area) Estates Land Act, 1908 (Act 1 of 1908) that may form time to time be notified as such for the purposes of the Act by the State Government].

d. 'Immovable Property' does not include standing timber, growing crops or grass.

e. 'Prescribed' means prescribed by rules made under this Act.

f. 'Transfer' means mortgage with or without possession, lease, gift, exchange or any other dealing with property not being a testamentary disposition and includes a charge or any contract relating to immovable property.

3. Maximum interest that may be allowed as against a member of hill tribe:

In any suit instituted after the commencement of this Act, notwithstanding any agreement to the contrary:

a. Interest on any debt or liability shall not as against a member of a hill tribe allowed or decreed at a higher rate than twenty-four percentum per annum nor shall any compound interest or any collateral advantage be allowed as against him;

b. The total interest allowed or decreed on any debt or liability as against a member of a hill tribe shall not exceed the principle amount.

4. Transfer of immovable property by a member of a hill tribe:

a. Notwithstanding any rule of law or enactment to the contrary, any transfer of immovable property situated within the Agency Tracts by a member of a hill tribe shall be absolutely null and void unless made in favour of another member of a hill tribe, or with the previous consent in writing of the Agent or of any other prescribed officer.

b. Where a transfer of property is made in contravention of sub-section (1), the Agent or any other prescribed officer may, on application by any one interested, decree Ejectment against any person in possession of the property claiming under the transfer and may restore it to the transferor or his heirs.

c. Subject to such conditions as may be prescribed an appeal against a decree or order under sub-section (2) if made by the Agent shall lie to the State Government and if made by any other officer shall lie to the Assistant Agent or to the Agent as may be prescribed.

5. Suits against a member of a hill tribe to be instituted in the Agency Courts:

Notwithstanding the provisions of any law to the contrary, every suit against a member of a hill tribe instituted after the commencement of this Act shall be instituted only in the Courts of the Agency tracts.

6. Attachment of immovable property:

In execution of a money-decree against a member of a hill tribe, no immovable property owned by him within the Agency tracts shall be liable to be attached and sold except as and if prescribed.

7. Farming of rules:

a. The State Government may from time to time make rules to carry out the purposes of the Act.

b. All rules made under this section shall be published in the (Official Gazette) and, on such publication, shall have the same effects if enacted in this Act.

8. Savings:

a. This Act shall not affect transfer made or debts or liabilities incurred before the coming into force of this Act.

b. Nothing in this Act shall affect a landholder's right to proceed against the ryot in accordance with the provisions of the [Andhra Pradesh (Andhra Area) Estates Land Act, 1908 (Act 1 of 1908)] or the first charge declared by Section 5 of that Act, or the provisions of the said Act regarding relinquishment of a holding by a ryot.

Appendix 2

The Andhra Pradesh Scheduled Areas Land Transfer Regulation, 1959 (Regulation No. 1 of 1959)

(4th March, 1959)

A Regulation to regulate the transfer of land in the Scheduled Areas of the East Godavari, West Godavari, Visakhapatnam, Srikakulam (Adilabad, Warangal, Khammam and Mhaboobnagar) districts of Andhra Pradesh.

Be it enacted in the Tenth Year of the Republic of India as follows:

1. **Short title and commencement:**
   a. This Regulation may be called the Andhra Pradesh Scheduled Areas Land Transfer Regulation, 1959.
   b. It shall come into force at once.
2. **Definitions:**
   In this Regulation, unless the context otherwise requires:
   a. 'Agency tracts' means the Areas in the districts of East Godavari, West Godavari, Visakhapatnam, Srikakulam, (Adilabad, Warangal, Khammam and Mhaboobnagar) declared from time to time as Scheduled Areas by the President under sub-paragraph (1) of paragraph 6 of the Fifth Schedule to the Constitution;
   b. 'Agent' means the person designated by the State Government as an 'Agent to the Government' in the districts of East Godavari, West Godavari, Visakhapatnam, Srikakulam, Adilabad, Warangal, Khammam and Mhaboobnagar as the case may be;
   c. 'Agency Divisional Officer' means the person designated by the State Government as 'Agency Divisional Officer' for the purpose of this Regulation;
   d. 'Immovable property' includes standing crops, timber and trees, but does not include growing grass.
   e. 'Prescribed' means prescribed in rules made under this regulation;

f. 'Scheduled Tribe' means any tribe or tribal community or part of or group within any tribe or tribal community and specified as such in relation to the State of Andhra Pradesh by Public notification by the President under clause (1) of Article 342 of the Constitution'.

Clause (f) is substituted as per the Andhra Pradesh Scheduled Areas Land Transfer (Amendment) Regulation, 1978*.

g. 'Transfer' means mortgage with or without possession lease, sale, gift, exchange or any other dealing with immovable property, not being a testamentary disposition and includes a charge on such property or a contract relating to such property in respect of such mortgage, lease, sale, gift, exchange or other dealing.

3. Transfer of immovable property by a member of a Schedule Tribe:

(1) a. Notwithstanding anything in any enactment, rule or law in force in the Agency tracts any transfer of immovable property situated in the Agency tracts by a person. Whether or not such person is a member of a Scheduled Tribe, shall be absolutely null and void, unless such transfer is made in favour of person, who is a member of a Scheduled Tribe or a society registered or deemed to be registered under the Andhra Pradesh Co-operative Societies Act, 1964 (Act 7 of 1964) which composed solely of members of the Scheduled Tribes.

b. Until the contrary is proved, any immovable property situated in the Agency tracts and in the possession of a person who is not a member of Scheduled Tribe, shall be presumed to have been acquired by person or his predecessor in possession through a transfer or his predecessor in possession through a transfer made to him by a member of a Scheduled Tribe.

c. Where a person intending to sell his land is not able to effect such sale, by reason of the fact that no member of a Scheduled Tribe is willing to purchase the land or is willing to purchase the land on the terms offered by such person, then such person may apply to the Agent, the

Agency Divisional Officer or any other prescribed officer for the acquisition of such land by the State Government, and the Agent. Agency Divisional Officer or the prescribed officer, as the case may by order, take over such land on payment of compensation in accordance with the principles specified in Section 10 of the Andhra Pradesh Ceiling on Agricultural Holdings Act, 1961 (Act X of 1961), and such land shall there upon vest in the State government free from all encumbrances and shall be disposed of in favour of members of the Scheduled Tribes or a society registered or deemed to be registered under the Andhra Pradesh Co-operative Societies Act, 1964 (Act 7 of 1964) composed solely of members of the Scheduled Tribes or in such other manner and subject to such conditions as maybe prescribed];

1a. Where a Transfer of immovable property is made in contravention of sub-section (1), the Agent, the Agency Divisional Officer or any other prescribed Officer may, on application by any one interested, or on information given in writing by a public servant, or suo motu decree ejectment against any person in possession of the property claiming under the transfer, after due notice to him in the manner prescribed and may restore it to the transfer or his heirs.

b. If the Transferor or his heirs are not willing to take back the property or where their whereabouts are no known, the Agent, the Agency Divisional Officer or prescribed officer, as the case may be, may order the assignment or sale of the property to any other member of a Scheduled Tribe (or a society registered or deemed to be registered under any law relating to Co-operative Societies for the time being inforce in the State) composed solely of members of the Scheduled Tribes, or otherwise dispose of it, as if it was a property at the disposal of State Government.

2 a. Subject to such conditions as may be prescribed, an appeal against any decree or order under sub-section (2), shall lie within such times as may be prescribed:

(i) if the decree or order was passed by the Agent, to the State Government;

(ii) if the decree or order was passed by the Agency Divisional Officer, to the Agent; and

(iii) if the decree or order was passed by any other officer, to the Agency Divisional Officer or Agent, as my be prescribed.

b. The appellate authority may entertain an appeal on sufficient cause being shown after the expiry of the time limit prescribed therefore.

(4 For the purpose of this section, the expression 'transfer' includes a sale in execution of decree and also a transfer made by a member of a Scheduled Tribe in favour of any other member of a Scheduled Tribe benami for the benefit of a person who is not a member of a Scheduled Tribe; but does not include a partition or a devolution by succession.)

3A. Special provision in respect of mortgages without possession:

Notwithstanding anything contained in this Regulation or in any enactment, rule or law inforce in the Agency Tracts,

1. any person, whether or not such person is member of a Schedule Tribe, may, subject to the provisions of Clause (2) mortgage without possession, any immovable property situated in the Agency tracts, to any Co-operative Society including a land mortgage bank, or to any (XXX) bank or other financial institution approved by the State Government;

Explanation

For the purpose of this clause, 'a bank' means a banking company as detained in Clause (c) of Section 5 of Banking Regulation Act, 1949 and includes the State Bank of India constituted under the State Bank of India Act, 1955, a subsidiary bank as defined in the State Bank of India (Subsidiary Banks) Act, 1959, a corresponding a new bank as specified in the First Schedule to the Banking Companies (Acquisition and Transfer of Undertakings) Act, 1970, the Agricultural Refinance and Development Corporation established under the Agricultural Refinance and development Corporation Act, 1963, a Regional Rural Bank established under the Regional rural Banks Act, 1976, and any other banking institution notified by the Central Government under Section 51 of the Banking Regulation Act, 1949;

2 In respect of every mortgage which was executed at any time either before or after the date of commencement of the Andhra Pradesh Scheduled Areas Land Transfer (Amendment) Regulation, 1971, in the event of the immovable property so mortgaged or any part thereof being brought to sale in default of payment of the mortgage money or the interest thereof or for any other purpose, the said property shall be sold only to a member of a scheduled Tribe or society registered or deemed to be registered under the Andhra Pradesh Co-operative Societies Act, 1954(Act 7 of 1954) which is composed solely of members of the Scheduled Tribes.

Explanation:

For the purpose of Section 3-B and this section a Cooperative Society having as its members all or any of the following, namely:

a. the individual members of the Scheduled Tribes;
b. one or more Co-operative societies which does not have among its members any person who is not a member of a Scheduled Tribe;
c. the Government shall be deemed to be a society registered or deemed to be registered under the Andhra Pradesh Co-operative Societies Act, 1964 (Act 7 of 1964) which is composed solely of members of the Scheduled Tribes.

3B. Restriction on registration of documents:

Notwithstanding anything contained in the, Registration Act, 1908, no document relating to transfer of immovable property situated in the agency tracts shall be registered by any person situated in the agency tracts shall be registered by any registering officer appointed under the said Act, unless the person presenting the document furnished a declaration by the transferee in the prescribed form which shall be subject to verification in the prescribed manner that the transferee is a member of a Scheduled Tribe or a society registered or deemed to be registered under the Andhra Pradesh Co-operative Societies Act, 1964 which is composed solely of members of the Scheduled Tribes'.

4. Suits against a member of a Scheduled Tribe to be instituted in the Agency Courts:

Notwithstanding anything contained in any enactment, rule or law inforce in the Agency tracts, every suit against a member of a Scheduled Tribe instituted after the commencement of this Regulation shall be instituted only in the Court having jurisdiction over the Agency tracts.

5. Attachment and sale of immovable property:

No immovable property situated in the Agency tracts and owned by a member of a Scheduled Tribe shall be able to be attached and sold in execution of a money decree against such member, except to the extent and the manner prescribed.

6. Revision:

The State Government may revise any decree of order passed by the Agent, the Agency Divisional Officer or any other prescribed officer under this Regulation;

Provided that this power shall be exercised only after due notice to the parties affected by the decree of order and after giving them a reasonable opportunity of being heard.

6-A. Penalty:

1. Any person who, on or after the commencement of the Andhra Pradesh Scheduled Areas Land Transfer (Amended) Regulation, 1978.
   a. Acquires any immovable property in convention of the provisions of this Regulation; or
   b. Continues in possession of such property after a decree for ejectment is passed;

   Shall on conviction be punished with rigorous imprisonment for a term which may extend to one year or with fine which may extend to two thousand rupees or with both.
2. When a Court imposes a sentence of fine or a sentence of which fine forms a part, the Court may, when passing a judgement, order any part of the fine recovered to be paid to the member of a Scheduled Tribe who is a transferer, as compensation.

7. Provisions of Limitation Act to apply to proceedings under this Regulation:

The provisions of the Indian Limitation Act, 1908 (Central Act IX of 1908), shall, in so far as they are not inconsistent with the provisions of this Regulation or the rules made there under, apply to proceedings under this Regulation.

8. Power to make rules:

1. The State Government may, from time to make rules to carry out the purposes of this Regulation.
2. All rules made under this section shall be published in the Andhra Pradesh Gazette and on such publication shall have the same effect as if enacted in this Regulation.

9. Repeal:

The Agency Tract Interest and Land Transfer Act, 1917 (Madras Act of 1 of 1917) is hereby repealed to the extent to which any of the provisions contained therein correspond or are repugnant, to any of the provisions contained in this Regulation.

10. Savings:

1. The provisions contained in this Regulation shall not affect:
   a. any transfer made or sale effected in execution of a decree of before the commencement of the Agency Tracts Interest and Land Transfer Act, 1917(Madras Act 1 of 1917); or
   b. any transfer made or sale effected in execution of a decree after the commencement of the said Act and before the commencement of this Regulation, if such transfer or sale was valid under the provisions of the said Act.
2. Nothing in this Regulation shall affect a land-holder's right to proceed against a ryot in accordance with the provisions of the Andhra Pradesh (Andhra area) Estates Land Act, 1908 (Act 1 of 1908) or the first charge declared by section 5 of the Act or the provisions of that Act regarding relinquishment of the holding by a ryot or the provisions of the Central Provincial Tenancy Act, 1898 (Central Act IX of 1898);

   Provided that no relinquishment of a holding by a ryot who is a member of a Scheduled Tribe shall be valid unless the previous sanction of the State Government, or subject to the rules made in this behalf the previous consent in writing of the Agent or the prescribed Officer, has been obtained thereto.

References

A.V. Thakkar Committee (1947) Report of the Excluded and Partially Excluded Areas Sub-committee, August 18.

Adarsha Adivasi Mahila Samithi & others Vs. Agent to the Govt., Khammam & others, 2003 (5) ALD 284.

All India Reporter (AIR) March 1985, Supreme Court (SC) AIR Publication, Nagpur, pp. 389–404.

Ambagudia, Jagannath (2010) 'Tribal Rights, Dispossession and the State in Orissa', *Economic and Political Weekly*, Vol. XLV, No. 33, August 14.

Amrendra Prapat Singh (Appellant) Vs. Tej Bahadur Prajapati & others, AIR 2004, Supreme Court, p. 3782.

Andhra Pradesh District Gazetteers (1976) East Godavari District, Govt. of Andhra Pradesh, Central Press, Hyderabad.

Andhra Pradesh Girijan Welfare Students and Youth Union Vs. State of A.P. W.P. No. 1755/90, dated 5 December 1984.

Arnold, David (1982) 'Rebellious Hillmen: The Gudem-Rampa Risings 1839–1924', in Ranajit Guha (ed.), *Subaltern Studies I*, Oxford University Press, Delhi.

— (1986a) Agent Godavari, to Chief Sec. 29 July 1884, G.O. 2618, Jdl. 27 September 1909, Godavari Statistical Appendix, pp. 413–14 cited in 'Rebellious Hillmen: The Gudem-Rampa Risings 1839–1924', in Ranajit Guha (ed.), *Subaltern Studies III*, Oxford University Press, Delhi.

— (1986b) Committee of Circuit's Report, 1787, p. 4 cited in Ranajit Guha (ed.), *Subaltern Studies III*, Oxford University Press, Delhi.

— (1986c) 'Rebellious Hillmen: The Gudem-Rampa Risings 1839–1924', in Ranajit Guha (ed.), *Subaltern Studies III*, Oxford University Press, Delhi.

Ashok Vs. Baba Rao & another, 2002 (6) ALT 296.

Ashokvardhan, C. (2006) *Tribal Land Rights in India*, Centre for Rural Studies, Lal Bahadur Shastri National Academy of Administration, Mussoorie.

Balagopal, K. (1989) 'Pitting the Tribals against the Non-tribal Poor', *Economic and Political Weekly*, 27 May, p. 1151.

— (2004) 'Foreword', in *Land Rights of Adivasis* by P. Trinadha Rao, Laya Publications, Visakhapatnam.

— (2007) 'Land Unrest in Andhra Pradesh III: Illegal Acquisition in Tribal Areas', *Economic and Political Weekly*, 6 October, p. 4031.

Banerjee, Abhijit and Iyer, Lakshmi (2008) 'Colonial Land Tenure, Electoral Competition and Public Goods in India', Working Paper, January (www.hbs.edu/research/pdf/08-062).

Baviskar, A. (1994) 'The Fate of the Forest: Conservation and Tribal Rights', *Economic and Political Weekly*, 17 September.

— (2006) 'The Politics of Being "Indigenous"', in Bengt G. Karlsson and Tanka B. Subba (eds), *Indigeneity in India*, Kegan Paul, London.

Bengwayan, Michael A. (2003) *Intellectual and Cultural Property Rights of Indigenous and Tribal Peoples in Asia*, Minority Rights Group International, London.

Beteille, Andre (1974) *Studies in Agrarian Social Structure*, Oxford University Press, Oxford.

Bhowmik, K.L. (2004) *Tribal India: A Profile in Indian Ethnology* cited in Supreme Court Case 2004 (3 SCC 429; 2004 SCC CRI 818).

Bhushan, Bharath M. (2011) *Land Rights of Women in Andhra Pradesh: A Status Paper* (mimeograph), Rural Development Institute, Hyderabad.

Bijoy, C.R. (2006) 'Adivasi Rights and Struggles of Autonomy: A Review of the Indian Experience', in K. Krishnan (ed.), *Adivasi Groups in 2000* (mimeo).

Bijoy, C.R. and Raman, K.R. (2003) 'The Real Story: Adivasi Movements to Recover Land', *Economic and Political Weekly*, Vol. 38, No. 20, May 17–23.

Brennan, F. (1995) 'Parliamentary Responses to the Mabo Decision', in M.A. Stephenson (ed.), *Mabo: The Native Title Legislation: A Legislative Response to the High Court Decision*, Queensland University Press, St Lucia, pp. 1–25.

Brockett, C.D. (1990) *Land, Power and Poverty: Agrarian Transformation and Political Conflict in Central America*, Unwin Hyman, Boston, pp. 23–26.

CESS (2007) Report on Human Development, Begampet, Hyderabad.

Ch. Satyanarayana Vs. Agent to the Govt. & Dist. Collector, Visakhapatnam, W.P. 6065/1979 (un-reported).

Colletti, Lucio (1975) *Early Writings: Karl Marx*, Penguin Books, London, p. 20.

D.V.L.N. Murthy Committee (2005) Report on Tribal Land Issues, Ministry of Rural Development, Government of Andhra Pradesh, Hyderabad.

D'Souza, Nafisa Goga (1991) 'Land Holding Systems in Tribal Areas', *Social Action*, Vol. 41, No. 1, January-March, ISI, New Delhi, pp. 345–50.

Deogaonkar, S.G. (1994) *Tribal Administration and Development*, Concept Publishing Company, New Delhi.

Deputy Collector Vs. Venkata Ramanaiah & another, AIR 1996 (SC) 224.

Desai, M., Rudolph, S.M. and Rudra, Ashok (eds) (1984) *Agrarian Power and Agricultural Productivity in South Asia*, Oxford University Press, Delhi.

Deva, Satya (1981) 'Alienation and Administration in Developing Countries', *Mainstream*, July.

Dhanagare, D.M. (1988) 'Subaltern Consciousness and Populism: Two Approaches in the Study of Social Movements in India', *Social Scientist*, Vol. 16, No. 11, November, p. 20.

Dietrich, G. (2000) 'Dams and People: Adivasi Land Rights', *Economic and Political Weekly*, Vol. 35, No. 38, September 16–22.

Draft National Policy on Tribals (2004) Ministry of Tribal Affairs, Government of India, New Delhi.

Dubey, S.N. and Murdia, Ratan (eds) (1979) *Land Alienation and Restoration in Tribal Communities in India*, Himalaya Publishing House, Bombay, p. 140.

Ellickson, R. (1993) 'Property in Land', *Yale Law Journal*, Vol. 103, No. 6, pp. 1344–62, JSTOR, Lexis.

Elwin, Varrier (1963) *A New Deal for Tribal India*, Ministry of Home Affairs, New Delhi, p. 49.

Fernandes, Walter (1996) 'Land Reforms, Ownership Pattern and Alienation of Tribal Livelihood', *Social Action*, Vol. 46, October-December, p. 428.

Francis, W. (1907) *Madras District Gazetteers: Vizagapatnam*, Vol. I, Government Press, Madras, pp. 318–19.

Furer-Haimendorf, C. von (1945) 'Aboriginal Rebellions in the Deccan', *Man in India*, Vol. 25 cited by Rao, P. Kamal Manohar and Rao, D.L. Prasad (1982) *Tribal Movements in Andhra Pradesh*, Ajanta Publishers, Delhi, pp. 353–72.

— (1985) *Tribes of India: The Struggle for Survival*, Oxford University Press, New Delhi.

G. Nageswararao @ China Nageswararao Vs. Government of A.P. & others, 2007 (6) ALD 621.

Gadde Nagabushanamma Vs. Govt. of A.P. & others 1999 (5) ALD 430.

Ghurye, G.S. (1963) *The Scheduled Tribes*, Popular Press, Bombay, pp. 70–97.

Godavari District Gazetteer (1907) Government Press, Madras, p. 101.

Gopinath Reddy, M., Anil Kumar, K., Trinadha Rao, P. and Springate-Baginski, Oliver (2010) *Obstructed Access to Forest Justice: An Institutional Analysis of the Implementation of Rights*, Andhra Pradesh Forested Landscapes, CESS, Hyderabad.

Government of India (1960–61) *Report of the Scheduled Areas of Scheduled Tribes Commission*, Vol. I, Govt. of India Press, Rastrapati Bhavan, New Delhi, p. 1.

Gupta, Smita (1991) 'Tribal Land Alienation in Kanke Anchal', *The Administrator*, Vol. 36, No. 2, p. 873.

Hemingway, F.R. (1915) *Madras District Gazetteers: Godavari*, Government Press, Madras, p. 67.

Heredia, Rudolf C. (2000) 'Tribal History, Living Word or Dead Letter', *Economic and Political Weekly*, April 29.

Hooja, Meenakshi (2004) *Policies and Strategies for Tribal Development: Focus on the Central Tribal Belt*, Rawat Publications, Jaipur.

ILO (1994) *Indigenous and Tribal Peoples and the ILO*, Geneva.

J.M. Girglani Commission (2005) Committee Report of Ministry of Rural Development, Government of Andhra Pradesh Press, Hyderabad.

Jayaprakash Rao, P. (1985) 'The Struggle for Land: Tribal Revolts in Two Villages', in K. Murali Manohar, P. Ramaiah and C. Sivaramakrishna Rao (eds), *Political Economy of Tribal Development*, Indian Institute of Public Administration, Warangal.

Jha, J.C. (1989) 'The Changing Land System of the Tribals of Chota Nagpur, 1771–1831', in Tarasankar Banerjee (ed.), *Changing Land Systems and Tribals in Eastern India in the Modern Period*, Subarnarekha, Calcutta.

K. Mahalaxmi & another Vs. Government of Andhra Pradesh & others, 2000 (5) ALD 588.

Kakarla Nageswara Rao & other Vs. Govt. of A.P. rep by its secretary (Tribal Welfare) Dept. Hyderabad 1995 (3) ALT 164.

Kandula Brahmaiah Vs. The Deputy Collector (Tribal Welfare) Rampachodavaram, E.G. Dist. W.P. 2169/1981 dated 10 December 1986 (un-reported).

Karuppaiyan, E. (1990) 'Alienation of Tribal Land in Tamil Nadu', *Economic and Political Weekly*, June 2, p. 1185.

— (2000) 'Alienation of Tribal Land in Tamil Nadu', *Economic and Political Weekly*, September 9, pp. 3333–34.

Kola Mahalaxmi Vs. Agent to the Government, Khammam & others, 1999 (6) ALD 718.

Koppula Saramma Vs. Govt. of A.P. Social Welfare Dept. & others, 2001 (3) ALT 501.

Kulkarni, Sharad (1985) 'Maharashtra: Adivasi, Law and Social Justice', *Economic and Political Weekly*, Vol. XX, No. 28, pp. 1171–74.

Kumar, Arun (2006) 'From Landlessness to Ownership: The Tribal Struggle for Property Rights', in Govinda Chandra Rath (ed.), *Tribal Development in India*, Sage Publications, New Delhi.

Kumar, Dharma (ed.) (1982) *The Cambridge Economic History of India*, Vol. 2, Chapters I and II, Cambridge University Press, Cambridge.

Kumar, S. (2001) 'Adivasis of South Orissa: Enduring Poverty', *Economic and Political Weekly*, Vol. 36, No. 43 (October 27-November 2).

Land Records Register (1986) Sub Collector's Office, Rampachodavaram, E.G.
District.

Linga Murthy, N. and Sivaramakrishna Rao, C. (1985) 'Debt-Bondage in Tribal Areas: An Empirical Observation', in K. Murali Manohar, P. Ramaiah and C. Sivaramakrishna Rao (eds), *Political Economy of Tribal Development*, Indian Institute of Public Administration, Warangal.

M. Suresh Bhargava & another Vs. State of A.P. & others, 1989 (2) ALT 516.

Mahipal (2000) 'Panchayats in Fifth Scheduled Areas', *Economic and Political Weekly*, May 6.

Malayappan, R.S. (Reprinted 1984) Report of the Special Development Officer, Govt. of A.P., Hyderabad, p. 8.

Manohar, K. Murali (ed.) (1985) *Political Economy of Tribal Development*, Indian Institute of Public Administration, Warangal, pp. 63–94.

Manohar, K. Murali and Rao, B. Janardhan (1985) 'Land Alienation in Tribal Areas', in Murali Manohar, P. Ramaiah and C. Sivakrishna Rao (eds), *Political Economy of Tribal India*, IIPA, Warangal, pp. 63–94.

— (1992) 'Tribal Agricultural Labour: An Enquiry into the Depeasantisation Process', in Buddhadev Chaudhari (ed.), *Tribal Transformation in India*, Vol. I, Inter-India Publications, New Delhi.

Matlhy,T.J. (1918) *Ganjam Manual*, Madras, p. 139.

Meszaros, Istvan (2006) *Marx's Theory of Alienation*, Aakar Books, New Delhi.

Minutes of the Andhra Pradesh Tribes Advisory Council 37th Meeting held on 5 February 1977 in Hyderabad.

Minutes of the APTAC Meeting held on 17 November 1995 in Hyderabad.

Minutes of the APTAC Meeting held on 14 February 1994 at 11.00 am at Telugu Samkshema Bhavanam, Andhra Pradesh, Hyderabad.

Minutes of TAC 102nd Meeting held on 18 March 2010 in Hyderabad.

Minutes of APTAC 46th Meeting held on 30 April 1982 in Hyderabad.

Minutes of the APTAC 52nd Meeting held on 28 November 1986 in Hyderabad.

Minutes of the APTAC Meeting held on 23 December 1988 in Hyderabad.

Minutes of the APTAC Meeting held on 26 June 1999 in Hyderabad.

Minutes of the APTAC Meeting held on 12 April 2000 in Hyderabad.

Minutes of the Meeting of the TAC held on 24 May 2000 in Hyderabad.

Mohan Lal, Morley (1988) *Poverty Alleviation: The Indian Experience*, Himalaya Publishing House, Delhi, p. 386.

Mohapatro, Prafullo Chandro (1987) *Dynamics of Tribal and Non-Tribal Interactions in Economic Development of Tribal India*, Ashish Publishing House, New Delhi.

N. Durga Rao & another Vs. Special Deputy Collector (TW) Kota Ramachandrapuram W.G. Dist. & others, 2003 (6) ALD (NOC) 68.

Nath, N. and Behera, D.K. (2006) 'The So-called Development, Displacement and Dispossession: An Analysis on Land and Forest Rights of the Project Affected People', in R.M. Sarkar (ed.), *Land and Forest Rights of the Tribals Today*, Serials Publications, Delhi.

Nathan, D. and Kekar, G. (2004) 'Civilizational Change: Markets and Privatization among Indigenous Peoples', in D. Nathan, G. Kekar and P. Walter (eds), *Globalization and Indigenous Peoples in Asia: Changing the Local-Global Interface*, Sage Publications, Delhi.

National Commission Report on Backward Areas Development (1981) Ministry of Social Welfare Department, Government of India, June, p. 50.

Note on Land Problems in Agency Areas of West Godavari (1997) Government of Andhra Pradesh, Social Welfare Department, Hyderabad.

Omvedt, Gail (2005) 'Capitalism and Globalisation, Dalits and Adivasis', *Economic and Political Weekly*, Vol. 40, No. 47, November 19.

P. Gangamma Vs. Vasudha Misra & another 1998 (2) ALD 35.

P. Rami Reddy & others Vs. State of A.P. & another 1988 (22) Reports (SC) 364.

Parliament Digest-Budget Session (2004) NCAS Publications, Pune, p. 53.

Parthasarathy, G. (1979) *Peasant Movements and Changing Agrarian Structure in A.P.*, Department of Cooperation and Applied Economics, Andhra University, Visakhapatnam (mimeo).

Patnaik, S.C. and Patel, S. (1982) 'Impact of Modernisation on Tribals: Economic Dualism and Path of Change (A Case Study of Malkangiri Sub-division in Koraput District)', paper presented at the Seminar on 'Prospectus of Economic Development of Tribals of Koraput District' held in October (Miemo), pp. 2–14.

Peters, P. (1998) 'The Erosion of Commons and the Emergence of Property: Problems for Social Analysis', in R.C. Hunt and A. Gilman (eds), *Property in Economic Context*, Lanham, Mavy land, University Press of America, Oxford, pp. 356–61.

Pinto, Ambrose (1988) 'Fillip to Land Transfers Land Acquisition Bill', *Economic and Political Weekly*, December 5.

Planning Commission Report (2006) Government of India, New Delhi.

Prof. Vidyarthi Committee (1972) Report of the Task Force on Development of Tribal Areas, April 5.

Radhakrishna, R. and Ray, Shovan (2006) *Handbook of Poverty in India: Perspectives, Policies, and Programmes*, Oxford University Press, New Delhi.

Raghavaiah, V. (1971) *Tribal Revolts*, Andhra Pradesh Adimjati Sevak Sangha, Nellore.

— (1979) 'Unrest in Andhra Pradesh', in A.R. Desai (ed.), *Peasant Struggles in India*, Oxford University Press, Bombay, p. 176.

Ramanathan, U. (1999) 'Public Purpose: Points for Discussion', in W. Fernandes (ed.), *The Land Acquisition (Amendment) Bill 1998*, Indian Social Institute, New Delhi, pp. 19–24.

— (2002) 'Common Land and Common Property Resources in Land Reforms in India', in Praveen K. Jha (ed.) *Issues of Enquiry in Rural Madhya Pradesh*, Vol. 7, Sage Publications, New Delhi, p. 204.

Ramnath, Madhu (2008) 'Surviving the Forest Rights Act: Between Scylla and Charybdis', *Economic and Political Weekly*, Vol. 43, Issue 9, March 1.

Rao, B. Janardhan (1987) *Land Alienation in Tribal Areas of Andhra Pradesh*, Kakatiya University, Warangal.

Rao, M.S.A. (1983) 'Non-tribal Colonisation and Tribal Deprivation in Andhra', *Social Action*, Vol. 33, July-September, ISI, New Delhi.

— (2000) *Adivasis in India: Characterization of Transition and Development*, Adhyayana Publications, Warangal.

Ranga Rao, Koneru (2006) *The Land Committee Report 2006*, GoAP, Hyderabad, p. 57.

Ray, N. (1972) 'Introductory Address', in K.S. Singh (ed.), *Tribal Situation in India*, IIAS, Shimla.

Reddy, N. Subba (1988) 'Depriving Tribals of Land: Andhra Move to Amend Land Transfer Laws', *Economic and Political Weekly*, Vol. XXIII, No. 29, July 16, pp. 1458–61.

— (1989) 'Sword of Damocles Over Tribal People of Andhra Pradesh', *Economic and Political Weekly*, July 1, pp. 1442–43.

— (2006) 'Development through Dismemberment of the Weak: Threat of Polavaram Project', *Economic and Political Weekly*, April 15, pp. 1430–31.

Reddy, T. Prabhakar (1989) 'Tribal Land Alienation in Andhra Pradesh', *Economic and Political Weekly*, Vol. 24, No. 28, p. 1573.

Report of Commissioner for SC and ST, Fifth Report (1982–83), Ministry of Tribal Affairs, GoI, Delhi.

Report of the Expert Group on Development Issues to Deal with the Causes of Discontent, Unrest and Extremism (2008) Planning Commission, Government of India, New Delhi.

Report of the Ministry of Rural Development Department of Land Resources (2000) Government of India, Delhi.

Report of the Steering Committee on Empowering the Scheduled Tribes, Planning Commission (2001) Report 91, New Delhi.

Report of the Study Team on Social Welfare and Welfare of Backward Classes (1959) Ministry of Social Welfare, Government of India, Vol. I.

Report of the Tribal Welfare Department (1995) Land Reforms and Land Transfers, Government of Andhra Pradesh, Hyderabad.

Report on Godavari Valley, Girijana Ryotanga Porata Charita, CPI (ML) 1977.

Review of action taken on the minutes of the meetings of the APTAC (1979–80) in Hyderabad.

Roy Burman, B.K. (1982) 'Transfer and Alienation of Tribal Land', in B. Chaudhury (ed.), *Tribal Development in India*, Inter-India Publications, New Delhi, p. 77.

— (1986) *Communal Land System of the Tribals and Problems of Institutional Finance in Manipur and Tripura*, Council for Social Development, Delhi.

Roy Burman, J.J. (2009) 'Adivasi: A Contentious Term to Denote Tribes as Indigenous Peoples of India', *Mainstream*, Vol. XLVII, No. 32, July 25.

Rupavath, Ramdas (2009) *Tribal Land Alienation and Political Movements: Socio-Economic Patters from South India*, Cambridge Scholars, UK, pp. 126–27.

Samata Appellants Vs. State of Andhra Pradesh & others with Ms. Hyderabad Abrasives & Minerals(P) Ltd. (Appellant) & State of Andhra Pradesh & other, Respondents, AIR 1997 Supreme Court 3297.

Sarapu Chinna Pothuraju Dora Vs. District Collector, East Godavari District, 2002 (1) ALT 699.

Sardesai, G.S. (1948) *New History of the Marathas*, Vol. II, Phoenix Publications, Bombay, p. 355.

Sastry, M.S.K. (2011) *Agency Laws in Andhra Pradesh*, ALT Publications, Hyderabad.

Sastry, V.N.V.K. (1989) *Between Gonds Rebellion*, Udyama Publications, Hyderabad.

Satyanarayana, K. (1975) *A Study of History and Culture of the Andhras*, People's Publishing House, New Delhi, p. 44.

Saxena, K.B. (1991) 'Tribal Land Alienation and Need for Policy Intervention', *The Administrator*, Vol. 34, pp. 89–98.

— (2006) 'Alternative Economic Survey, India 2005–06: Disempowering Masses, Development as Destitution', pp. 263–74.

Scott, James C. (1976) *The Moral Economy of the Peasant Rebellion and Subsistence in Southeast Asia*, Yale University Press, New Haven.

Senapati, N. and Sahu, N.K. (1966) *Orissa District Gazetteers, Koraput*, Odisha Government Press, Cuttack, pp. 70–71.

Shah, G. (1990) *Social Movements in India: A Review of Literature*, Sage Publications, New Delhi.

Sharan, Ramesh (2005) 'Alienation and Restoration of Tribal Land in Jharkhand: Current Issues and Possible Strategies', *Economic and Political Weekly*, October 8.

Sharma, T.R. (1979) 'Karl Marx: From Alienation to Exploitation', *Indian Journal of Political Science*, Vol. 40, No. 3, September.

Singh, Nandita (1997) 'Emerging Problems of Ownership and Exploitation of Communal Land in Tribal Society', *Man in India*, Vol. 77, pp. 233–34.

Sivaramakrishana Rao, C. and Bobbili, A. (1985) 'Tribal Movements in Andhra Pradesh: A Short History', in K. Murali Manohar, P. Ramaiah and C. Sivaramakrishna Rao (eds), *Political Economy of Tribal Development*, Indian Institute of Public Administration, Warangal.

Special Deputy Collector (TW), Rampachodavaram, E.G. Dist. & others Vs. Datla Venkapathi Raju & others, 2003 (1) ALD 386 (D.B.).

Sullivan to Chief Sec. 9 September 1879, ibid.; Joint Magistrate, Chodavaram, to District Magistrate, 18 March 1879, MJP, No. 313, 25 March 1879.

Sundar, Nandini (ed.) (2009) *Legal Grounds*, Oxford University Press, New Delhi.

Sundaram, K. and Tendulkar, Suresh (2003) 'Poverty among Social and Economic Groups in India in 1990s', *Economic and Political Weekly*, December 13.

Swaminadhan, D. (2004) Tribal Welfare and Development: Draft Policy, Ministry of Tribal Affairs, Govt. of India.

The Economist, 'A Specter Haunting India', 17 August 2006 (http://www.economist.com/world/asia/displaystory.cfm?story_id=7799247).

Thurston, E. and Rangachari, K. (1909) *Castes and Tribes of Southern India*, Vol. III and IV, Cosmo Publications, Delhi, p. 355 and pp. 64–65.

Trinadha Rao, P. (2004) *Tribal Development in Question*, Laya Publications, Visakhapatnam.

— (2006) 'Nature of Opposition to the Polavaram Project', *Economic and Political Weekly*, April 15, pp. 1437–39.

— (2007) *Persisting Alienation of Tribal Land*, A.P. Social Watch Report, Hyderabad.

Trivedi, H. (1993) *Tribal Land Systems: Land Reform Measures and Development of Tribals*, Concept Publications, New Delhi.

Uma Maheshwari, R. (2007) 'Polavaram Rehabilitation via Forced Consensus', *Economic and Political Weekly*, June 23.

UNDP, Human Development Report (2004) *Cultural Liberty in Today's Diverse World*, Oxford University Press, New York.

Upadhyay, S. and Upadhyay, V. (2002) *Handbook on Environmental Law, Volume I: Forest Laws, Wildlife Laws and the Environment*, LexisNexis Butterworths, New Delhi.

Vemana Somalamma & another (Appl), Veera Sunkar Deo & another (Pet) Vs. Deputy Collector (TW), Rampachodavaram, E.G. Dist, 1993 (1) ALT 409 (F.B.).

Vidyarthi, L.P. (1963) *The Maler: The Nature-Man-Spirit Complex in Hill Tribe of Bihar*, Bookland Pvt. Ltd., Calcutta.

Viegas, Philip (1991) *Encroached and Enslaved*, Indian Social Institute, Delhi, p. 32.

Vuppuluri Veera Venkata Raju & others Vs. Special Deputy Tahsildar, Tribal Welfare, Gangavaram (V&M), E.G. District & others 2007 (6) ALD 292.

Vyas, N.N. (1975) 'Tribal Land Alienation: Recent Changes and New Dimensions', *Tribe*, Vol. 9, No. 3, p. 8.

Xaxa, Virginius (1999) 'Tribes as Indigenous People of India', *Economic and Political Weekly*, Vol. XXXIV, No. 51, December 18, pp. 3589–95.

Yunus, S.A. (1977) *Orissa Chapter in Land Alienation and Restoration in Tribal Communities in India*, by Dubey, S.N. and Murdia, Himalaya Publishing House, Bombay.

Index